# INEQUALITY IN THE WORKPLACE

# INEQUALITY IN THE WORKPLACE

Labor Market Reform in Japan and Korea

**Jiyeoun Song**

**CORNELL UNIVERSITY PRESS**   **ITHACA AND LONDON**

First published 2014 by Cornell University Press
Printed in the United States of America

Library of Congress Cataloging-in-Publication Data

Song, Jiyeoun, 1975– author.
    Inequality in the workplace : labor market reform in Japan and Korea / Jiyeoun Song.
        pages cm
    Includes bibliographical references and index.
    ISBN 978-0-8014-5215-4 (cloth : alk. paper)
  1. Labor market–Japan.  2. Labor market–Korea (South)
3. Manpower policy–Japan.  4. Manpower policy–Korea (South)  I. Title.
    HD5827.A6S655    2014
    331.120952—dc23        2013035320

Cornell University Press strives to use environmentally responsible suppliers and materials to the fullest extent possible in the publishing of its books. Such materials include vegetable-based, low-VOC inks and acid-free papers that are recycled, totally chlorine-free, or partly composed of nonwood fibers. For further information, visit our website at www.cornellpress.cornell.edu.

Cloth printing        10 9 8 7 6 5 4 3 2 1

*To my parents, Deungil Song and Soonnam Hwang*

# Contents

List of Tables and Figures    ix

Acknowledgments    xi

Acronyms, Abbreviations, and Terms    xv

Introduction    1

**1.** Japanese and Korean Labor Markets and Social Protections in Comparative Perspective    19

**2.** The Politics of Labor Market Reform in Hard Times    46

**3.** The Institutional Origins of the Labor Market and Social Protections in Japan and Korea    67

**4.** Japan: Liberalization for Outsiders, Protection for Insiders    84

**5.** Korea: Liberalization for All, Except for Chaebŏl Workers    119

Conclusion    162

Notes    179

References    201

Index    223

# Tables

**I.1** Variations in labor market reform 5

**1.1** Employment protection regimes for regular workers
in Japan and Korea, summary scores by three main areas 25

**1.2** Major legislative changes in the Japanese and Korean
labor markets, 1986–2011 27

**1.3** Wage-setting institutions 35

**1.4** Union organization rates and collective
bargaining coverage 38

**1.5** Public spending on labor market programs and
social protections 40

**1.6** Non-statutory social welfare spending by
private sectors (% of GDP) 42

**1.7** Coverage of social welfare programs in
Japan and Korea, 2005 43

**2.1** Theory of labor market reform, inequality, and dualism 54

**4.1** Percentage of Japanese firms implementing early
retirement program 95

**4.2** Japan's labor market and social protection reform
since the mid-1980s 99

**5.1** Korea's labor market and social protection
reform since the late 1980s 131

# Figures

**I.1** Economic growth rates in Japan and Korea
(real GDP growth rates) 12

**1.1** Employment protection regimes for regular workers 22

**1.2** Employment protection regimes for temporary workers 23

**1.3** Proportion of the non-regular workforce in
Japan and Korea 30

**1.4** Changes in the workforce in the Japanese and
Korean labor markets 32

**1.5** Gaps in enterprise tenure by firm size in
Japan and Korea, 1981–2007                                      33

**1.6** Wage differentials across firm size in Japan and
Korea, 1981–2007                                                37

**1.7** Seniority-based wage curve in the Japanese and
Korean labor markets                                            39

**2.1** Proportion of the regular workforce in Japan and Korea      58

**2.2** OECD EPL Index for regular employment and
average enterprise tenure years                                 59

**2.3** Average enterprise tenure years in the Japanese and
Korean labor markets, 1981–2007                                 60

**2.4** Average enterprise tenure years for Japanese and
Korean male workers by age group                                62

**3.1** Number of labor disputes in Japan, 1970–2003               71

**3.2** Labor ministers in Korea, 1961–2007                        76

**4.1** Share of stable shareholdings and cross shareholdings
in the Japanese stock market, 1987–2003                         86

**5.1** Numbers of labor disputes and workdays lost
in Korea, 1986–2007                                             124

**5.2** Unit labor cost in Japan and Korea manufacturing,
1970–2009                                                       125

# Acknowledgments

This book could not have been completed without the support of numerous individuals and institutions. I am deeply indebted to several scholars in the Department of Government at Harvard University, Torben Iversen, Susan J. Pharr, Jorge I. Domínguez, and Margarita Estévez-Abe, all of whom have provided intellectual guidance and moral support over the years. Torben provided me great intellectual stimulation and critical advice for this project from the beginning, and he never lost confidence in me even when I was questioning myself. His constructive comments and challenging questions on earlier drafts pushed me to sharpen my analytical framework, tighten empirical presentation, and develop more generalizable arguments. Susan offered invaluable feedback and encouragement on the project. Her sharp questions led me to consider the big picture and to develop more succinct but powerful claims. Her insights and knowledge of Asian politics, particularly Japanese politics, contributed to solid foundations. Jorge was extremely generous in reading numerous manuscript versions and giving me incisive comments. Jorge's office door was always open, from day one, when I arrived at Harvard in the summer of 2001. His strategic advice and unwavering support kept me strong. Margarita (now at Syracuse University) was also very generous in sharing her time when I needed to discuss ideas and arguments. Margarita's in-depth knowledge and understanding of labor markets, social protections, and Japanese politics helped me to shape the project. She also offered me a rewarding opportunity to work as a teaching fellow for her classes, which was the start of my career as a teacher. I owe all of these advisors a great debt of gratitude. I hope to follow in their footsteps to become a great scholar, good teacher, and generous mentor in the future.

I am also very grateful to Professor Byung-Kook Kim, my undergraduate advisor at Korea University, who guided me to this great profession. He has always been supportive of my work and helped to open many doors for me. Professors Andrew D. Gordon and Mary C. Brinton at Harvard University helped me to enhance my knowledge and understanding of Japanese industrial relations and the labor market. I owe special thanks to Steph Haggard, Henry Laurence, and Kathy Thelen, who generously participated in an author's conference organized and funded by the Program on US-Japan Relations at Harvard University. They read an early manuscript and gave me invaluable comments and suggestions. Steph was extremely helpful at various stages and invited me to the Workshop on Social Policy and Labor Markets in Korea at the School of International Relations and Pacific Studies, University of California, San Diego, to present my work and receive feedback from other workshop participants. I appreciate his time and help.

I also have many friends and colleagues to thank. At Harvard, I was fortunate to have a wonderful group of friends. I thank Daniel Aldrich, Lucy Barnes, Shameem Black, Amy Catalinac, Magnus Feldmann, Daniel Ho, Rieko Kage, Andy Kennedy, Wendy Pearlman, Alison Post, Yongwook Ryu, Gergana Yankova-Dimova, and Jong-Sung You for their advice, help, and comradeship. I am also grateful to participants in the Comparative Politics Workshop, the Political Economy Workshop, and the Contemporary Japanese Politics Study Group for valuable feedback. I am very glad to have the chance to express my thanks to my Korean friends at Harvard with whom I went through good and bad times: Sei Jeong Chin, Youngjeen Cho, Hunsang Chun, Jeomsik Hwang, Soo-yeon Jeong, Hakyung Jung, Jee Young Kim, Sang-Hyun Kim, Suhan Kim, Ji-eun Lee, Eunmi Mun, Seongmun Nam, Wonmok Shim, Jiwuh Song, Joo-Hyun Song, Hayan Yoon, and Hyung-Kon Yum. I owe special thanks to Geunwook Lee for his advice, help, and friendship over the years. Geunwook has preceded me in every step, from graduate study to job searches and publication, and he has always been a source of advice. Finally, I thank my good old friends from college who have shared with me the joys and sufferings of writing, searching for jobs, and settling into the profession as political scientists: Jin Seok Bae, Jai Kwan Jung, Engsoo Kim, Joo-Youn Jung, Heonjoo Jung, Woochang Kang, Suhyun Lee, and Hyunji Lee. In particular, Jung Kim has generously provided me with practical and strategic advice and shared his wisdom with me whenever I faced challenges. My friends outside of academia treated me to delicious food and drinks, and helped me keep a sense of humor. Most of all, they taught me that there is a life beyond graduate school.

The Department of International and Area Studies and the Department of Political Science at the University of Oklahoma, where I have been a member of the faculty since 2009, provided a wonderful environment in which to concentrate on revisions. The very final stage of revision was completed in the Graduate School of International Studies at Sogang University. I appreciate institutional support from Sogang University. I also thank Lesley Goodman for her editorial help in preparing the manuscript. She helped me make this book far more readable.

Many institutions have provided me with financial and research support for this project. First of all, I thank the Korean Foundation for Advanced Study for funding my study at Harvard during the period of 2001–2006. At Harvard I benefited from generous financial and research support from the Edwin O. Reischaeur Institute of Japanese Studies, the Department of Government, and the Graduate

School of Arts and Sciences. In particular, the Reischauer Institute provided me with crucial financial support for language training, summer research trips, and field research, as well as office space during my graduate study. This book would have taken additional years to complete if I had not received a postdoctoral fellowship from the Program on US-Japan Relations at Harvard University. The program provided a congenial and wonderful work environment during the period of 2008–2009 and generously organized and funded an author's conference. I owe special thanks to Shinju Fujihira, an associate director of the program, for his advice and friendship over the years. My work was also supported by an Academy of Korean Studies Grant funded by the Korean Government (MOE) (AKS-2007-CB-2001). Lastly, I am grateful for the financial support of the International Programs Center and the College of Arts and Sciences at the University of Oklahoma for allowing me a break from teaching responsibilities to focus on revising my manuscript during the summers of 2010, 2011, and 2012.

For my field research in Japan and Korea, I am deeply indebted to many bureaucrats, politicians, union leaders, business leaders, policy experts, and academic scholars, who generously shared their insights and knowledge about labor market and social protections. Without their help, this project would not have moved forward. In Japan, I received generous research support from the Institute of Social Science at the University of Tokyo. I am indebted to Professor Junji Nakagawa for his advice and guidance, who has been my mentor since the summer of 2004. I thank Professors Nobuhiro Hiwatari, Keisuke Nakamura, Michio Nitta, Greg Noble, and Mari Osawa, who helped me at various stages of my research. I am also very grateful to Professors Yasuhito Asami, Ikuo Kume, Mari Miura, and Steven Reed, who assisted my field research in Japan. In Korea, I received excellent institutional support from the East Asia Institute (EAI) during my field research and several follow-up summer research trips. The EAI has provided a congenial and intellectual work environment over the years.

I express my special thanks to two anonymous reviewers who provided extremely constructive comments and insightful suggestions to improve my manuscript. I feel very fortunate to have had such wonderful reviewers. Roger Haydon of Cornell University Press supplied guidance and strong support for my project throughout the publication stages. I appreciate Roger's help immensely.

Portions of chapters 3, 4, and 5 have previously been published in *Asian Survey* 50 (6): 1011–1031 (©2010 by The Regents of the University of California); *Governance* 25 (3): 415–438 (©2012 Wiley Periodicals, Inc.); *Journal of East Asian Studies* 12 (2): 161–191 (©2012 by the East Asia Institute); and *Adapt, Fragment, Transform,* edited by Byung-Kook Kim, Eun Mee Kim, and Jean C. Oi, 235–278 (Washington, D.C.: Brookings Institution Press, 2012). I thank the editors and publishers for their permission to reproduce portions of these publications in this book.

Last, but not least, I want to express my deepest thanks to my family. My siblings, Eunjung, Dongjoon, and Hyundong, have been the source of happiness, smiles, and strength for me. Even though we have been physically thousands of miles apart, they have made me feel that I am always with them. My brother-in-law, Minsoo Kim, always treated me to fun meals, and my sister-in-law, Junghwa Do, sent me sweets and teas. It was my parents who enabled me to complete the decade-long journey of graduate study and book publication. Without their love and support, I could not have gotten this far. My parents raised me to appreciate the value of learning, to do my best at whatever I decide to do, and to be a better person. Although my parents cannot read my book written in English from cover to cover, I know that they are proud to place a copy of the book with their daughter's name on the front cover on the best spot of the bookshelf in the living room. I dedicate this book to my mother, Soonnam Hwang, and my father, Deungil Song, with love, gratitude, and respect.

## A Note on Conventions

Japanese and Korean names are written according to East Asian conventions (family name followed by the given name), except in cases where authors have identified themselves with given names first (e.g., English-language publications). Macrons have been omitted for commonly used place names (e.g., Tokyo). All translations are by the author unless otherwise indicated.

## Japan

| | |
|---|---|
| Denki Rengō | Japanese Electrical Electronic and Information Union |
| DPJ | Democratic Party of Japan |
| Jidōsha Sōren | Confederation of Japan Automobile Workers' Unions |
| JSP | Japan Socialist Party |
| Keidanren | Japanese Federation of Economic Organizations |
| *keiretsu* | Loose grouping of large business conglomerates |
| Keizai Dōyūkai | Japanese Association of Economic Executives |
| LDP | Liberal Democratic Party of Japan |
| MOL | Ministry of Labor |
| MOHLW | Ministry of Health, Labor and Welfare |
| Nikkeiren | Japanese Federation of Employers' Association |
| Nippon-Keidanren | Japanese Business Federation |
| Rengō | Japanese Trade Union Confederation |
| *shuntō* | Spring offensive |
| Sōhyō | General Council of Trade Unions of Japan |

## Korea

| | |
|---|---|
| chaebŏl | Family-owned and -managed large business conglomerates |
| EPB | Economic Planning Board |
| DJP | Democratic Justice Party |
| DLP | Democratic Liberal Party |
| FKI | Federation of Korean Industries |
| FKTU | Federation of Korean Trade Unions |
| GNP | Grand National Party |
| HCI | Heavy and Chemical Industrialization |
| KCIA | Korean Central Intelligence Agency |
| KCTU | Korean Confederation of Trade Unions |
| KEF | Korean Employers' Federation |
| MTI | Ministry of Trade and Industry |
| MOL | Ministry of Labor |
| NCNP | National Congress for New Politics |

| NCTU | National Congress of Trade Unions |
| NDRP | New Democratic Republican Party |
| PCIRR | Presidential Commission on Industrial Relations Reform |
| PDP | Peace Democratic Party |
| RCRLL | Research Committee on the Revision of the Labor Law |
| *samkŭm* | Three prohibitions on workers' basic rights |
| *samje* | Three systems for labor market flexibility |
| UDP | Unified Democratic Party |
| ULD | United Liberal Democrats |

## General

| CMEs | Coordinated market economies |
| IMF | International Monetary Fund |
| LMEs | Liberal market economies |
| OECD | Organisation for Economic Co-operation and Development |
| PR | Proportional representation |
| SMD | Single-member district |
| SMEs | Small- and medium-sized enterprises |
| VOC | Varieties of capitalism |

# INEQUALITY IN THE WORKPLACE

# INTRODUCTION

*Haken no Hinkaku* (*Haken's Dignity*), a popular Japanese TV drama that aired in 2007, portrayed the work life of female dispatched workers (or *haken shain*). Dispatched workers are a new sort of worker in Japan, hired on short-term employment contracts and through private employment agencies. As the TV drama illustrated, an increasing proportion of the female clerical workforce in the Japanese labor market has been staffed by non-regular workers, such as dispatched workers, but the hiring of non-regular workers is not a phenomenon unique to the clerical sector. Most *obasan* (middle-aged females) working in retail chain stores, like Daiei supermarkets, are part-timers, and cleaners and security staff at office buildings are fixed-term contract workers. Even highly competitive Japanese manufacturing companies, such as Canon and Toyota, have expanded the hiring of various types of non-regular workers (e.g., part-time, temporary, and contract workers) at their production sites, taking advantage of the low costs of hiring and firing these workers during economic downturns.

These recent changes in the Japanese labor market do not fit well with the traditional model of its labor market, characterized by permanent employment practices, seniority-based wages, and enterprise unions. In the face of the bursting of the asset bubble and the subsequent protracted recession over the past two decades, Japan promoted a series of labor market reforms in order to resuscitate its sluggish economy, allowing employers more options in labor adjustment. Yet its labor market reform was different from the neoliberal or the laissez-faire reforms of the United Kingdom and the United States, represented by easy hiring and firing practices in response to the fluctuations of the business cycle.

1

Japan focused on the liberalization of the labor market for non-regular workers (e.g., part-time, temporary, and contract workers) while maintaining a relatively high level of protection for regular workers (e.g., full-time permanent workers). After two decades of reform, it confronted an increasing proportion of under-paid and under-protected non-regular workers and a rapid rise in labor market inequality and dualism along the dimensions of employment status (e.g., regular workers versus non-regular workers) and firm size (e.g., large firms versus small- and medium-sized enterprises).[1]

Faced with severe challenges for its political economy over the past two decades, Korea is not an exception to such dramatic changes in the labor market. Here regular workers hired in large family-owned and -managed business conglomerates (i.e., chaebŏl) regarded as "too big to fail" were guaranteed to receive job security, high wages, and generous welfare benefits. After the 1997 Asian financial crisis, however, such labor management practices turned out to be a vestige of the good old days. In particular, job security, implicitly promised to male regular workers in large Korean business conglomerates, was no longer applicable for these workers, let alone for workers in small- and medium-sized enterprises (SMEs) and non-regular workers who had always had to bear the costs of labor adjustments during economic hard times. Korea's labor market reform granted a right to employers to lay off regular workers for managerial reasons and to expand the hiring of non-regular workers. In the midst of the Asian financial crisis, a few large chaebŏl firms (e.g., Hyundai Motor Company) in severe financial distress attempted to shed surplus regular workers, but they rarely succeeded, facing a series of labor strikes led by powerful chaebŏl unions at the firm level. A small segment of regular workers (mostly chaebŏl workers) with the protection of strong enterprise unions were capable of overriding the implementation of labor market reform in the workplace and even further reinforcing the privileges of internal labor markets. These workers thus shielded themselves from the pressure to change in the labor market, leaving the others underpaid and unprotected. Korea's comprehensive labor market reform, which was designed to increase labor market flexibility for all workers, has ironically accelerated an economic disparity between insiders and outsiders.[2]

Labor market reform swept over not only Japan and Korea, but also western Europe, the other side of the world, which has also confronted severe economic distress, such as sluggish economic growth, rising unemployment, and increasing welfare costs, over the past few decades. In the United Kingdom, labor market reform meant a wide range of policy changes that would undermine the political and organizational power of militant labor unions and increase labor market flexibility during economic downturns. Throughout the 1980s, the Conservative government focused on busting industrial strikes, exemplified by the 1984 miners' strike, by limiting the capacity of labor unions to recruit new members and maintain organizational solidarity as well as by raising the costs for unions to go on strike. In addition, it weakened the level of employment protection for workers, decentralized wage bargaining, and retrenched welfare programs (especially unemployment benefits), which transformed the institutional characteristics of the British labor market and industrial relations into those of the neoliberal model (Blanchflower and Freeman 1993, 2–6; Coe and Snower 1997, 6–8; Henry and Karanassou 1996, 150–152; Mayhew 1991, 2–3).

In the face of skyrocketing unemployment rates in the early 1990s, the Swedish conservative government advanced a series of labor market reforms to urge rapid economic turnaround, including the relaxation of employment protection for temporary workers. Yet, contrary to its British counterpart, it neither weakened the level of employment protection for regular workers (or insiders) nor challenged the political and organizational capacity of labor unions. Rather, it implemented various active labor market policies, such as retraining programs for those affected by labor market reform, as well as restructured unemployment insurance programs (e.g., the reduction of replacement rates and the shortening of the duration of unemployment benefits) in order to incentivize the unemployed to return quickly to the labor market (Björklund 2000; Calmfors, Forslund, and Hemström 2002, 6–15; Clasen and Clegg 2003, 2). By doing so, Sweden attempted to facilitate rapid industrial restructuring in times of economic crisis, while simultaneously reducing workers' resistance to reform and preventing the sharp rise in labor market inequality and dualism (Iversen and Soskice 2009; Iversen and Stephens 2008).

Germany's reform path was different from its British and Swedish counterparts. Its policy makers adopted a two-pronged labor market reform strategy in response to economic distress during the 1990s and 2000s. While Germany retained a high level of employment protection, decent working conditions, and generous social welfare benefits for insiders (e.g., full-time permanent workers), it prioritized reform for outsiders (e.g., part-time or temporary workers) in order to increase labor market flexibility (Palier and Thelen 2010). The 2003 Mini-Job Reform, which exempted part-time workers with low earnings from social security contribution payments, was designed to create more jobs and work incentives, with the goal of reducing labor costs and lowering long-term unemployment rates in the German labor market (Caliendo and Wrohlich 2010; Steiner and Wrohlich 2005). These reform measures contributed to the rapid expansion of low-paid part-time and temporary jobs (mostly for female and young workers), but they have widened an economic disparity between insiders and outsiders over the subsequent decade (Leschke, Schmid, and Griga 2006; Palier and Thelen 2010).

In response to the global and national crises, advanced industrialized countries undertook labor market reform, characterized by deregulation and liberalization of the labor market for greater flexibility, in order to resuscitate economic growth, create more jobs, and offer firms more leeway in labor adjustments.[3] Despite similar pressure to change in the labor market, not all countries adopted the neoliberal model of the labor market, typified by easy hiring and firing practices. Some countries, like the United Kingdom and the United States, were able to shed a surplus of the workforce by laying off workers as well as to save labor costs by cutting wages and retrenching social welfare benefits. Others, like continental European countries, prioritized the liberalization of the labor market for outsiders with the persistence of protection for insiders, which led to the rise in labor market inequality and dualism. If the downsizing of insiders was inevitable, continental European countries adopted early retirement programs for these workers that would transfer the costs of labor adjustments to the state social welfare program. Others, such as the Scandinavian countries, promoted labor market reform for outsiders, but at the same time they expanded social protections for those affected by reform in order to facilitate the rapid return of the unemployed into the labor market and prevent the increase in labor market inequality and dualism (Iversen and Soskice 2009; Iversen and Stephens 2008; Levy 1999; Levy, Miura, and Park 2006; Mares 2003, 213–248; Schoppa 2006, 71–72). Why did countries respond in different ways to similar pressures for labor market reform? Why did some confront a sharp increase in labor market inequality and dualism in the process of labor market reform, but not others? Why did some countries develop compensating policies for those affected by reform, but not others?

This book is about the politics of labor market reform. It examines the ways in which countries deal with the pressure of labor market reform in response to global and national crises. Table I.1 presents four different types of labor market reform, depending on the pattern of reform and the degree of increasing labor market inequality and dualism. As the first dimension of labor market reform, "pattern of labor market reform" refers to the content and scope of reform. Despite labor market reform as an imperative for a rapid economic turnaround in times of crisis, countries diverge in the extent to which they change rules and regulations governing the labor market with respect to the primary target of reform (e.g., insiders, outsiders, or both) and the direction of reform (e.g., protection or liberalization). This study focuses on two different patterns of reform along the lines of the insider-outsider differences (e.g., employment status, firm size, gender, and/or age group): selective labor market reform for outsiders with the persistence of protection for insiders versus comprehensive labor market reform for all workers.

**TABLE I.1**   Variations in labor market reform

| | | PATTERN OF LABOR MARKET REFORM | |
|---|---|---|---|
| | | REFORM FOR OUTSIDERS | REFORM FOR ALL WORKERS |
| Degree of increasing labor market inequality and dualism | High | a. Selective reform for outsiders with the persistence of protection for insiders<br>b. High labor market inequality and dualistic labor market<br>(e.g., Japan, Germany) | a. Comprehensive reform for insiders as well as outsiders<br>b. High labor market inequality and dualistic labor market<br>(e.g., Korea) |
| | Low | a. Selective reform for outsiders with the persistence of protection for insiders<br>b. Low degree of labor market inequality and dualism<br>(e.g., Sweden) | a. Comprehensive reform for insiders as well as outsiders<br>b. Low degree of labor market inequality and dualism |

As the second dimension of labor market reform, the degree of increasing labor market inequality and dualism indicates the effects of labor market reform on the workforce in terms of job security, wages, and social protections. It is inevitable that labor market reform tends to create reform losers (either dispersed or concentrated ones) who will bear the costs of labor adjustments in the process of reform, yet countries adopt different political approaches to them. Despite similar trajectories of labor market reform for greater flexibility, some countries have experienced a drastically widening economic gap in the labor market, whereas others have been successful in keeping a high level of economic equality by employing various compensation policies for reform losers.

The interaction of these two dimensions of labor market reform—the pattern of reform and the degree of increasing labor market inequality and dualism—shapes the varying reform outcomes. Although the four types of labor market reform presented in Table I.1 do not exhaust all variations in the politics of reform, they specify the important analytical dimension of labor market reform. This book emphasizes the explanatory role of the existing institutional arrangements of the labor market by demonstrating how labor market institutions set the boundaries within which reform occurs and shape the political and economic calculations of key reform actors. In this book, I focus on Japan and Korea since they are not well known in the literature and provide very interesting and important non-European evidence of the ways that states have responded to changing labor market conditions in the face of global and national economic crises.

# The Argument in Brief

The variations in the politics of labor market reform under similar pressures to change raise important empirical and theoretical questions. This book points out that the institutional arrangements of the labor market shape the diverging political paths of reform. In particular, it argues that the institutional features of the employment protection system—the institutionalization and coverage of employment protection—account for the patterns of reform (e.g., reform for outsiders versus reform for all workers), and the institutional configurations of industrial relations explain the sharp rise in labor market inequality and dualism by shaping a type of compensation mechanism in the process of labor market reform.

In times of economic crisis, policy makers undertake labor market reform in order to bring forth rapid economic turnarounds, yet reform is constrained by the existing institutional structure of the labor market that shapes the incentives and strategies of key actors in decision making and policy implementation. As illustrated in the politics of welfare retrenchment in advanced industrialized countries (Pierson 1996 and 2001), constituencies created by the expansion of welfare programs are more likely to block any policy changes that would retrench their welfare benefits, which restricts a range of options available and feasible for policy makers in the process of welfare reform politics. Like the politics of welfare retrenchment, the politics of labor market reform, focusing on the liberalization of the labor market, confront the opposition of the workforce that has been under the coverage of employment protection.

In a system where a majority of the workforce is covered by the institutionalized practices of employment protection, it is more likely that insiders, employers, and policy makers form a political coalition for selective labor market reform for outsiders with the persistence of protection for insiders. Unsurprisingly, insiders always prioritize the maintenance of a high level of protection, at least for themselves, under pressure to change in the labor market. Some employers, if not all, may prefer to retain a high level of protection for insiders even during economic downturns, while looking for labor adjustments for outsiders, since they would like to benefit from production strategies and labor management practices developed on the basis of institutionalized protection for insiders.[4] In addition, they may believe that comprehensive labor market reform for all workers is not a feasible option, expecting strong opposition from a large number of privileged insiders as well as policy makers worried about the political costs of reform for insiders. In particular, policy makers are more likely to opt for transferring the costs of labor market reform to outsiders, most of whom are already excluded from the privileges of the internal labor market, in order to minimize the possibility of political backlash from insiders at election time.

By contrast, where the less institutionalized practices of employment protection are only relevant for a small proportion of the workforce, while leaving a majority of the workforce unprotected, employers and policy makers are more likely to promote comprehensive labor market reform for all workers. The majority of employers are less likely to make commitments to job security even for insiders, since they do not expect high returns from investing in and maintaining production strategies and labor management practices on the basis of protection for insiders during economic hard times. In addition, given a small segment of the workforce under employment protection, policy makers are more likely to adopt far-reaching labor market reform, while promising better reform outcomes for the general public through rapid economic turnaround. Meanwhile, insiders are less likely to have any political allies in forming a political coalition in support of protection for insiders, which makes job security for insiders far more vulnerable to the forces for change.

Of course, it is possible that reform for outsiders may affect insiders even if insiders are nominally protected. If reform for outsiders allows employers to replace insiders by easily hiring workers from a liberalized outsider pool for cheaper firing and labor costs, such reform measures would have significant effects on employment and working conditions for insiders. As will be described in the following chapters, to some extent, privileged insiders have accepted (or have been forced to accept) various labor adjustment mechanisms (e.g., performance-based wages, wage restraints, and the flexible allocation of work hours) in the context of the liberalizing pressure of the labor market for outsiders. Nevertheless, reform for outsiders seems to have more indirect and long-term consequences on insiders, as opposed to direct and immediate effects on them, since it has contributed to the resilience of internal labor markets by reinforcing insider privileges at the workplace and widening the economic disparity between insiders and outsiders.

While the institutional features of the employment protection system shape the patterns of reform (e.g., reform for outsiders versus reform for all workers), the configurations of industrial relations affect the degree of increasing labor market inequality and dualism along the lines of employment status and firm size, by facilitating or obstructing the expansion of social protections, as a compensation mechanism in the politics of reform. In particular, social protections play a crucial role in the process of proposing and implementing labor market reform since they are more likely to mediate the problems of labor market reform (e.g., job insecurity and labor market inequality and dualism) and to minimize political opposition to the reform. Under the conditions of centralized industrial relations based on encompassing business associations and labor federations, employers and workers are more likely to adopt "solidaristic" approaches to the workers who bear the costs of labor adjustments during economic downturns by pressuring policy makers to advance social protection programs over the entire economy. Such social protections mediate the consequences of insider-friendly adjustments on the labor market and thus result in the prevention (or at least alleviation) of the rapid rise in labor market inequality and dualism. By contrast, under the conditions of decentralized industrial relations, employers and organized insiders focus narrowly on economic interests at the firm and workplace level. Thus, neither employers nor organized insiders, based on large enterprise unions, are likely to support the development of social protections for those affected by labor market reform, leading to the widening insider-outsider differences.

In sum, this book argues that the two variables of employment protection systems and industrial relations determine the diverging pathways of labor market reform. The institutional features of employment protection shape the pattern of reform—selective reform for outsiders versus comprehensive reform for all workers—by constraining an available range of reform options, especially for employers and policy makers, and the configurations of industrial relations affect the consequences of reform on the workforce by exacerbating or alleviating insider-outsider differences in reform implementation through a mechanism of compensation (or the lack thereof). The lack of compensating policies for those affected by labor market reform accelerates labor market inequality and dualism.

While taking into account the path-dependent trajectories of labor market institutions, this study suggests that the institutional changes and development of the labor market should be understood in a more dynamic way since not all labor adjustments can be explained by the mechanism of positive feedback.[5] Although Japan has retained a high level of protection for insiders, it has also adopted new types of labor adjustments and employment practices in order to increase flexibility for these workers (e.g., the decentralization of wage bargaining, the introduction of performance-based wage systems, and the rapid expansion of the hiring of the non-regular workforce), departing from the traditional Japanese model of the labor market. In other words, the self-reinforcing mechanism of institutional change does not sufficiently explain why some labor market institutions have experienced far more substantial changes than others.

In addition, the variables of employment protection systems and industrial relations cannot completely explain all empirical details in the politics of labor market reform. In particular, Japan and Korea experienced not only economic distress but also important political challenges, such as democratization in Korea and the collapse of the political system in Japan dominated by the Liberal Democratic Party (LDP), which might affect the process and outcome of labor market reform. Thus, I will use a process-tracing method to elaborate the ways in which the institutional features of the labor market interact with other political and economic variables in the politics of reform. Nevertheless, I suggest that two variables of the labor market, employment protection systems and industrial relations, explain the essence of the politics of labor market reform over the past two decades.

## Prior Approaches to the Politics of Labor Market Reform

The existing literature on the politics of labor market reform focuses on political and economic variables. The first strand of the literature points out that the political partisanship of the government is a crucial factor in accounting for the politics of labor market reform (Bradley et al. 2003; Garret 1998b; Huber, Ragin, and Stephens 1993; Huber and Stephens 2001; Korpi 2006). These scholars argue that a leftist government is more likely to protect the interests of labor by limiting the scope of labor market reform, while a conservative government is more likely to undertake far-reaching labor market reform in favor of the interests of business. Another group of scholars in support of the political partisanship theory emphasizes the linkage between political party and a specific group of labor (especially insiders), as opposed to the assumption of labor as a homogeneous entity (Iversen and Soskice 2009; Iversen and Stephens 2008; Palier and Thelen 2010; Rueda 2007). Rueda (2007) claims that the rise in labor market inequality and dualism between insiders and outsiders can be attributed to the social democratic party's political strategy of prioritizing the interests of insiders, its core electoral constituencies. Meanwhile, others argue that the social democratic party prevents economic disparity between insiders and outsiders by expanding social protection programs for outsiders, most of whom have been more seriously affected by the series of labor market reforms (Iversen and Soskice 2009; Iversen and Stephens 2008).

Another wave of scholars claim that political institutions, such as neo-corporatist institutions or electoral systems, are determining factors in the politics of labor market reform. The neo-corporatist institution approach points out that a neo-corporatist political institution—composed of business, labor, and government—ensures the political representation of societal interest groups (especially organized labor) in policy making and defends the interests of labor in the process of labor market reform (Martin and Thelen 2007; Visser and

Hemerijck 1997). Meanwhile, the electoral system approach argues that different electoral rules shape the different political incentives and strategies of politicians and political parties and thus lead to specific patterns of policy change (Iversen and Soskice 2006; Martin and Swank 2008). According to the electoral system approach, the proportional representation (PR) system, based on the principle of consensus, is more likely to facilitate incremental reform and safeguard the interests of workers, as opposed to the single-member district (SMD), or the majoritarian electoral system, which is centered on the logic of winner take all.

While these two approaches (the political partisanship and the political institution approaches) emphasize the explanatory role of political variables in labor market reform, other scholars argue that economic crisis accounts for the varying reform outcomes by illustrating that the exigencies of crisis facilitate more drastic and immediate labor market reform than otherwise (Drazen and Grilli 1993; Fajertag and Pochet 2000; Gourevitch 1986; Kruger 1993; Przeworski 1991; Williamson and Haggard 1994). They assume that more severe economic crisis leads to more comprehensive labor market reform. In fact, national and global economic crises triggered a series of labor market reforms in advanced industrialized countries over the past few decades with the explicit policy goal of resuscitating sluggish economies.

Each of these theoretical approaches provides insights into labor market reform, but they fall short of explaining variation in reform politics revealed by empirical evidence from the cases of Japan and Korea and accounting for more general patterns of labor market reform across advanced industrialized countries. Although the British Conservative government initiated far-reaching labor market reform during the 1980s, Japan's conservative LDP government preserved protection for insiders despite the decade-long economic recession, while extensively liberalizing the labor market for outsiders. Regarding the political institution approach, although continental European and Scandinavian countries alike developed the PR electoral system, they experienced diverging political pathways of labor market reform. Most continental European countries reinforced labor market inequality and dualism between insiders and outsiders, whereas the Scandinavian countries maintained a relatively high level of equality. If economic crisis determines labor market reform, it remains puzzling why Greece, Italy, and Spain, all of which experienced severe pressure from the financial crisis of 2011–2012, have not opted for the laissez-faire style of reform, characterized by easy hiring and firing practices, which is widely employed in countries such as the United Kingdom and the United States.

This book argues that the institutional arrangements of the labor market—employment protection systems and industrial relations—have the most explanatory power with respect to variation in the politics of labor market reform across advanced industrialized countries. The majority of the empirical materials used in the book were collected during fifteen months of field research in Japan and Korea between June 2005 and August 2006 and additional follow-up research trips to the two countries during the summers of 2007, 2010, and 2012. To test my theoretical framework, I relied upon government documents, policy reports by government and quasi-governmental research institutes, parliamentary debates, the position papers of business associations and labor federations, and more than sixty interviews with policy makers, union leaders, business leaders, and policy experts in the two countries. Based on data from this research, this book develops an analytical framework centered on the institutional arrangements of the labor market to explain the diverging pattern of reform and the different degree of labor market inequality and dualism.

## Why Japan and Korea?

This book focuses on Japan and Korea, two important capitalist economies in East Asia and under-explored cases within the existing literature on the politics of labor market reform, which is primarily based on empirical findings drawn from the cases of western Europe and North America. Japan and Korea differed in their trajectories of political development (e.g., Japan has been a democratic country in the postwar period, and Korea remained under the rule of authoritarianism until 1987), their levels of economic development (e.g., as of 2009, Japan's GDP per capita was estimated to be $39,738, and Korea's GDP per capita was estimated to be $17,078, without taking into account purchasing power parity), and the size of their economies (e.g., Japan had the third largest economy, measured by GDP, as of 2011, and Korea the fifteenth largest economy as of 2009).[6]

Yet they shared several important features of political economy that make a comparative study of these two countries very relevant.[7] The developmental state framework, first articulated in Chalmers Johnson's work on Japan's postwar economic growth, *MITI and the Japanese Miracle*, identifies Japan and Korea as state-led developmental models (or *dirigiste* states) (Amsden 1989; Evans 1995; Johnson 1982 and 1999; Wade 1990; Woo 1991; Woo-Cumings 1999).[8] With analytical focus on the institutional configurations of the national political economy, ranging from the financial system and corporate governance to the labor market, comparative political economists label Japan's and Korea's economic systems as "stakeholder capitalism," "coordinated market economies," or "non-liberal economies," which are distinct from the "shareholder capitalism," "liberal market economies," or "liberal economies" of the United Kingdom and the United States

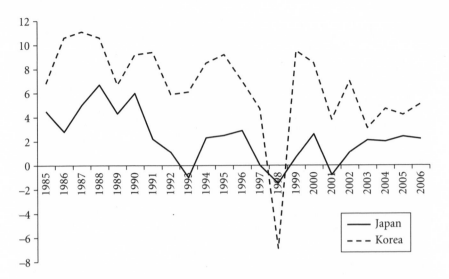

**FIGURE I.1**  Economic growth rates in Japan and Korea (real GDP growth rates) *Source:* Japanese Prime Minister's Office and Statistics Office at the Japanese Ministry of Internal Affairs and Communications, http://www.kantei.go.jp/ foreign/index-e.html and http://www.stat.go.jp, accessed July 10, 2011; Bank of Korea, Economic Statistics System and Korean National Statistical Office, http://ecos.bok.or.kr and http://kostat.go.kr, accessed July 10, 2011.

(Albert 1993; Berger and Dore 1996; Crouch and Streeck 1997; Hall and Soskice 2001; Soskice 1999; Streeck and Yamamura 2001; Tiberghien 2007).

Japan and Korea are also well-known examples of successful economic development with equitable income distribution (J-I. You 1998; World Bank 1993). Even after the slowdown in high-speed growth after the first oil crisis, Japan continued to record sustainable growth rates before the collapse of the bubble economy, with average annual rates of 9.3 percent between 1956 and 1973 and 4.1 percent between 1975 and 1991 (Gao 2001, 1). Similarly, since the early 1970s, Korea has demonstrated rapid economic growth at an average annual growth rate of 7.8 percent between 1971 and 1997 (Wade 1990; Woo 1991).[9] Unlike other economic developmental models (e.g., those in Latin America), the model of the East Asian miracle maintained a low level of income inequality by allowing all workers to benefit from rapid growth. Japan was ranked sixth place in income equality among sixty-six countries (measured by income quintile), and Korea was ranked twentieth (J-I. You 1998, 40).

This model of success came under intense pressure from institutional changes in the face of political and economic challenges during the 1990s and 2000s (Amyx 2004; Grimes 2002; B-K. Kim 2003; Samuel Kim 2000; Tiberghien 2007).

As shown in figure I.1, Japan confronted sluggish economic growth after the burst of the asset bubble in 1991, with an average growth rate of 1 percent in this period, and Korea experienced a severe economic downturn during the 1997 Asian financial crisis. To make matters even worse, Japan and Korea were not able to avoid a sharp increase in inequality, even though the levels of inequality in the two countries were still not as high as those in the Anglo-Saxon countries (Förster and Mira d'Ercole 2005; Jones 2008 and 2009; Ohtake 2008; Tachibanaki 2005; Tiberghien 2011; Yun 2009). The Gini coefficient—an indicator of the level of income inequality—increased from 0.304 to 0.321 in Japan and from 0.266 to 0.312 in Korea between the mid-1980s and the mid-2000s.[10] The ratio of 90 percent earning to 10 percent earning (ninth to first earning deciles) also presented a similar pattern of rising income inequality, an increase from 3.00 to 3.11 between 1996 and 2006 in Japan and from 4.04 to 4.56 between 2000 and 2006 in Korea (OECD 2008, 358). Over the past two decades, Japan and Korea alike experienced a rapid rise in inequality.

Under these adverse economic conditions, Japan and Korea, known for rigid labor markets, promoted a series of labor market reforms intended to create greater flexibility in employment contracts and working conditions and hours in the hopes of a rapid economic turnaround. What makes these two cases a more interesting comparison is that Japan and Korea not only adopted different labor market reform approaches, despite the similar institutional settings of their political economies, but they also experienced convergence in the sharp rise in labor market inequality and dualism. In Japan, the conservative LDP-led government liberalized the rules and regulations governing employment contracts and working conditions for non-regular workers (or outsiders) in order to enable employers to adjust flexibly to economic distress and changing business environments. Nevertheless, it retained a high level of employment protection for regular workers (or insiders), even when faced with the protracted economic recession during the 1990s and 2000s. By contrast, Korea, under the rule of center-left governments with pro-labor presidents, prioritized comprehensive labor market liberalization for greater flexibility, especially targeting regular workers in the chaebŏl sector, while simultaneously improving not only workers' basic rights and but also protections for non-regular workers.

Interestingly, notwithstanding their different patterns of labor market reform, both Japan and Korea confronted a widening economic gap between insiders and outsiders, like many continental European countries (Barbieri and Scherer 2009; Japan Institute for Labor Policy and Training 2010; Korea Development Institute 2006; Palier and Thelen 2010; Polavieja 2003; Thelen and Busemeyer 2008; Yun 2009). In Japan, the portion of the workforce constituted by regular workers, identified as full-time permanent workers with indefinite employment contracts, declined from 83.4 percent to 66.5 percent between 1986 and 2007.[11] Meanwhile, Korea experienced a fluctuation during the same period, with regular workers making up 47.9 percent of the workforce (as of 2000) and 58.9 percent of the workforce (as of 1993).[12] As of 2007, regular workers constituted 54 percent of the overall workforce in the Korean labor market. In both countries, a shrinking portion of the regular workforce continued to benefit from the privileges of job security, high wages, and generous social protections, whereas an increasing number of the non-regular workforce had to shoulder the costs of labor adjustments during economic downturns.[13] Why did Japan and Korea adopt diverging reform paths in the face of economic crisis? Despite these differences in reform strategy, why did these two countries reinforce labor market inequality and the segmentation of the dualistic labor market between insiders and outsiders? Why did Korea fail to alleviate the problems of labor market inequality and dualism, even though its reform focused on narrowing economic disparity between insiders and outsiders?

Japan and Korea are an ideal set of comparative case studies with which to answer these questions about labor market reform by controlling several key variables that might affect outcome variables. As elaborated above, both countries adopted state-led developmental strategies to stimulate economic growth, established large firm-centered economic structures—Japan's *keiretsu* and Korea's chaebŏl—and developed a set of interdependent market institutions based on strategic coordination in their national political economies (e.g., stable inter-firm relations, debt-financing systems, and specific skills training systems) (Hall and Soskice 2001; Johnson 1982; B-K. Kim 2002; E. M. Kim 1997; Soskice 1999; Woo 1991).[14] These similarities would lead one to predict that Japan and Korea would follow similar political trajectories of labor market reform under similar challenges to their national political economies. Yet Japan and Korea experienced convergence as well as divergence in the politics of labor market reform.

Japan's institutionalized practices of employment protection, covering a large proportion of the workforce, resulted in the liberalization of the labor market for outsiders with the persistence of protection for insiders.[15] In the process of insider-friendly labor market reform, Japan's decentralized industrial relations, based on large enterprise unions, further deepened labor market inequality and dualism by enlarging gaps between insiders (e.g., regular workers in large firms) and outsiders (e.g., peripheral non-regular workers) since employers and insiders under decentralized industrial relations are less likely to develop social protections for outsiders affected by labor market reform.

Meanwhile, Korea's situation resulted in comprehensive labor market reform for all workers under the less institutionalized practices of employment protection covering a small proportion of the workforce. Despite far-reaching labor market reform at the national level, its decentralized industrial relations, based on large chaebŏl unions, shielded well-organized insiders in large chaebŏl firms from the pressure of reform, since the power of large chaebŏl unions over-rode the intentions of policy makers in Korea's labor market reform.[16] Chaebŏl unions and organized insiders exerted their political and organizational power in collective bargaining in order to ensure the privileges of internal labor markets at the firm level. In addition, insiders and large chaebŏl employers are more likely to adopt a "segmentalist" approach to those affected by a series of labor market reforms (mostly workers in SMEs and non-regular workers) since they were indifferent to the expansion of social protections beyond the boundaries of the workplace and firm. The institutional constraints of decentralized institutional relations based on large chaebŏl firms and unions prevented the development of comprehensive social protections for reform losers as a mechanism of compensation. These political pathways led the Korean labor market to a high degree of inequality and dualism in the process of implementing comprehensive labor market reform.

One potential problem of case selection is the effects on policy makers of learning reform outcomes of other countries, which might contaminate the method of comparison, since one country may attempt to follow the other's reform as a model of success or to avoid the problems that the other country has already confronted in the process and outcome of labor market reform. Considering that Korea's policy makers (including elected politicians as well as bureaucrats) tend to emulate a broad array of Japan's socioeconomic policies, it is not surprising that they look at Japan's labor market reform first as a reference.[17] For instance, Korea's Worker Dispatch Law in 1998 was drafted on the basis of Japan's Worker Dispatch Law, which had been legislated in 1986.[18] Alternatively, some might argue that Korea adopted comprehensive labor market reform for all workers because its policy makers learned from the limitations of Japan's selective labor market reform for outsiders during recovery from the protracted economic recession.

Despite the difficult problem of case selection derived from the effects of learning about one country's experience on the reform of another, a comparative study of Japan and Korea is still legitimate and valuable. As elaborated in the literature of policy diffusion, most countries (not only Japan and Korea, but also other advanced industrialized countries as well as developing ones) have learned from one another in the process of policy making, especially those that experienced similar problems much earlier or coped successfully with similar problems (Simmons, Dobbin, and Garret 2008; Simmons and Elkins 2004). Since Japan embarked on a series of labor market reforms much sooner than Korea did in response to similar pressures to change, the former has offered a range of reform options for the latter to consider, given the many similarities in their national political economies. Nevertheless, Korean policy makers have recently distanced themselves from the emulation of Japan's policy making, not only in the politics of labor market reform but also in a wide range of socioeconomic policies. They have endeavored to develop their own version of reform and to examine other advanced industrialized countries as references especially since the late 1990s, a period during which Japan's economy recorded sluggish growth rates. In the case of labor market reform, Korea has adopted reform agendas intended to increase labor market flexibility as well as protection for outsiders far more extensively than Japan, which makes it difficult to posit the effects of policy makers' learning of Japan's labor market reform on Korea's reform. In addition, some of Korea's labor legislation has preceded Japan's, which suggests that Korea's reform has gone beyond the emulation of Japan. Learning effects are important to understanding how countries respond to similar pressures to change by looking to other examples. Nonetheless, the institutional arrangements of the labor market have more explanatory power with respect to the politics of labor market reform in Japan and Korea than the mechanism of learning does.

Another important point to clarify is that the labor market reform discussed in this book does not apply to the foreign workforce in Japan and Korea. Since the late 1980s and early 1990s, Japan and Korea have adopted a back-door (or side-door) policy for the hiring of unskilled foreign workers in response to the pressing problems of labor shortage in labor intensive sectors, the so-called 3D industries (dirty, difficult, and dangerous).[19] As a result, the size of the foreign population in the two countries has increased rapidly over the past two decades, constituting around 2 percent of the population. As of 2010, in Japan the number of foreign residents had doubled since 1985, reaching 2.1 million, and the number of foreign residents in Korea had climbed to 1.2 million, increasing four times since 1990 (Chung 2010, 650; Immigration Bureau of Japan, Statistics Information; Kong, Yoon, and Yu 2010, 256; Korea Immigration Service 2010, 264).[20] Despite the rapidly increasing number of foreign workers in the Japanese and Korean labor markets, the majority of unskilled foreign workers, both documented and undocumented, have been employed in low-end agriculture, manufacturing, and service jobs. Thus, Japanese and Korean labor markets might be identified as "tripartite structures," whose layers are differentiated by three distinct groups in the workforce: (1) well-paid and well-protected regular workers, (2) underpaid and under-protected non-regular workers, and (3) unskilled foreign workers placed outside of legal protection. While it is true that the increasing size of the foreign workforce affects the structure of the Japanese and Korean labor markets, this book does not take into account the foreign workforce as a primary aspect of analysis, for several reasons.

First, the series of labor market reforms in Japan and Korea discussed in this book do not apply to the majority of foreign workers because of the presence of the legal framework stipulating specific employment contract conditions and terms only applicable to foreign workers in the two countries. Most unskilled foreign workers in the Japanese manufacturing sectors are not covered by labor laws since they are identified as "trainees" rather than "workers." In Korea, unskilled foreign workers, employed under the conditions of the Employment Permit System (equivalent to the guest worker system), are eligible for legal protection (e.g., the minimum wage and social protection programs), but they are regulated by different types of labor rules and policies.

Second, a significant number of unskilled foreign workers are undocumented in the Japanese and Korean labor markets, which indicates that a large proportion of the foreign workforce is excluded from any application and coverage of labor laws. It is thus difficult to evaluate the effects of policy changes on these foreign workers. Since the majority of unskilled foreign workers have filled jobs at the very lowest tiers of the labor market, the increasing size of the unskilled foreign workforce might contribute to the exacerbation of poor employment and working conditions and low wage levels for non-regular workers (or outsiders) in the long term, given the possibility of the replacement of these workers with much cheaper unskilled foreign workers. Yet the extent to which non-regular workers and unskilled foreign workers confront a zero-sum relationship, competing for the same kinds of jobs in the labor market, is not clear. More practically, the presence of the foreign workforce has not been a primary concern for reform actors—namely, business, labor, and government—in the politics of labor market reform in Japan and Korea. Thus, this book focuses on examining the politics of labor market reform in the context of the dualistic labor market, composed of the regular workforce and the non-regular workforce, leaving aside the unskilled foreign workforce.

This book examines the politics of labor market reform in Japan and Korea, giving particular attention to employment protection, wage bargaining and industrial relations, and social protections, all of which are regarded as the focal point of labor market reform not only in Japan and Korea but also in other advanced industrialized countries. It provides critical lessons on patterns of adaptation during hard times. With recent economic crises in the United States and the European Union, these two cases and their lessons become far more relevant than ever, particularly where labor market rigidities are central to the story (as in several European countries, like Greece, Italy, and Spain). An in-depth comparative case study of Japan and Korea enriches a theory of labor market reform by offering an analytical framework based on empirical data beyond western Europe and North America. In addition, it complements the existing studies on institutional changes and the development of capitalism in East Asia by elucidating the role of the labor market. Compared with other market institutions (e.g., financial systems and corporate governance), the labor market has been relatively under-studied in the field of East Asian political economy since scholars assume a secondary role for the labor market in order to understand a model of development in East Asia.[21] As will be demonstrated in the following chapters, the labor market has been one of the most contested market institutions in recent economic reform politics and has crucial consequences and implications for the national political economy.

# JAPANESE AND KOREAN LABOR MARKETS AND SOCIAL PROTECTIONS IN COMPARATIVE PERSPECTIVE

During the 1990s and 2000s, Japan and Korea promoted labor market reforms that differed substantially from those of other advanced industrialized countries, and despite being a somewhat similar pair of market economies in many important ways, they approached labor market reform with two different strategies and with two dissimilar sets of consequences. This chapter elaborates three key institutional aspects of the labor market and social protection—employment protection, industrial relations and wage bargaining, and social protection programs—in Japan and Korea in comparison with those in other advanced industrialized countries. In particular, it shows the ways in which a set of labor market institutions and social protection programs have adapted to new challenges in their national political economies and how they have interacted with one another in the process of labor market reform.[1]

The first section illustrates the similarities and differences in employment protection regimes, the diverging patterns of labor market reform, and the sharp rise in inequality and dualism in the Japanese and Korean labor markets. The second section examines decentralized industrial relations, wage-bargaining institutions, and the features of the wage structure in the two countries. The third section describes various social protection programs associated with labor market reform. A concluding section summarizes cross-national variations in the pattern of labor market reform and convergence in the rise in inequality and dualism, but with different degrees of inequality and dualism along the lines of employment status (e.g., regular workers versus non-regular workers) and firm size (e.g., large firms versus SMEs) in Japan and Korea.

# Employment Protection

## Employment Protection Regimes in Comparative Perspective

The labor market is located at the intersection of several key institutional domains of the national political economy. A wide array of formal and informal labor rules and regulations shape firms' strategies for production and investment. For workers, the labor market offers jobs and social protections to support themselves and their family members. Meanwhile, it has been a critical policy issue for governments to identify a viable labor model that would satisfy the dual tasks of achieving sustainable growth and achieving equitable distribution. Thus, the labor market has always been the locus of political contestation between business, labor, and government over the rules and regulations governing employment contracts, working conditions and hours, and social protections that affect employers' production and investment strategies and workers' quality of life.

In the face of economic crisis, advanced industrialized countries have undertaken labor market reform, from the 1980s and onward, as a primary policy tool for rapid economic turnaround, job creation, and sustainable economic growth (Iversen 2005; Levy 2005; Palier 2005; Palier and Thelen 2010). Labor market reform is a multifaceted concept associated with a broad range of changing rules and regulations in the labor market, encompassing individual labor rights (e.g., employment contracts, working conditions, and work hours), collective labor rights (e.g., workers' basic rights to organize, strike, and bargain collectively), and social protection programs (e.g., active and passive labor market programs and social welfare benefits) (Caraway 2009; Etchemendy 2004; Levy 1999 and 2005; Miura 2002b; Murillo and Schrank 2005; Palier and Thelen 2010). Among various reform agendas, policy makers in most advanced industrialized countries prioritized lowering the level of employment protection for workers, such as easing hiring and firing practices, deregulating working conditions, and promoting the flexible allocation of work hours. Especially in many continental European countries, a high level of employment protection was regarded as a huge financial burden on labor adjustments for employers during economic downturns and was blamed as the main culprit behind economic malaise (OECD 1994 and 1999a; Siebert 1997).[2] By advancing a series of labor market reforms, policy makers intended to respond to the mounting pressures for change in their national political economies.

Since employment protection is considered one of the most crucial institutional pillars of the labor market, several strands of the existing literature attempt to explain cross-national variations in the level of employment protection. First, the varieties of capitalism (VOC) approach points out that different institutional arrangements of capitalism lead to the two distinctive types of market economies: coordinated market economies (CMEs) (e.g., countries in East Asia, continental Europe, and Scandinavia) and liberal market economies (LMEs) (e.g., the United Kingdom and the United States) (Hall and Soskice 2001). It explains that CMEs are centered on nonmarket-based strategic coordination among key economic actors over the long term, whereas LMEs are based on the principle of a laissez-faire economy. In the realm of the labor market and social protections, the VOC approach posits that CMEs tend to develop strong employment protection regimes with generous social protections anchored in long-term economic transactions, which facilitates cooperation between employers and skilled workers, whereas LMEs are more likely to institutionalize weak employment protection regimes with meager social welfare programs because of the nature of short-term economic transactions based on the market principle (Estévez-Abe, Iversen, and Soskice 2001).

Second, the power resource theory, focusing on the strength of labor as the determining factor in policy outcomes, claims that the power of organized labor and a pro-labor left government account for strong employment protection and generous social welfare benefits (e.g., Scandinavian countries). Meanwhile, it points out that weak employment protection and meager social welfare programs in countries like the United Kingdom and the United States can be attributed to weak labor and the lack of strong left political parties (Bradley et al. 2003; Huber and Stephens 2001).

Last, building upon the legal theory approach, other scholars argue that the origins of the legal system explain the variations in the regulation of labor, regulation that ranges from employment laws and collective relations law to social security laws (Botero et al. 2004). This strand of research claims that countries whose judicial systems originate from the common law system (e.g., the United Kingdom and the United States) are more likely to develop less-protective labor regulations and to bring forth better labor market outcomes (such as high labor force participation rates and low unemployment rates) than those based on legal systems with other origins (e.g., the socialist, French, and Scandinavian laws).

Empirically speaking, most countries remain grouped in the same categories across the different theoretical frameworks. As a few exceptions to note, while the VOC approach predicts a high level of employment protection in CMEs, Denmark and Switzerland (as exemplary cases of CMEs) have developed much lower levels of employment protection than other CMEs (see figure 1.1). Contrary to the theoretical predictions of the power resource theory, Japan and Korea, two primary examples of weak labor—labor there is even weaker than in the United Kingdom and the United States, measured by union organization rates—have developed a medium-high level of employment protection for regular workers, a level much higher than that of the United Kingdom or the United States.

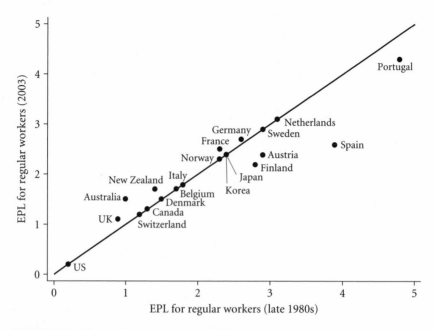

**FIGURE 1.1**   Employment protection regimes for regular workers
*Source*: OECD (2004, 117).
*Note*: EPL refers to the scores of employment protection legislation measured by OECD; for Korea and New Zealand, the scores of the late 1980s are replaced by those of the late 1990s because of the availability of data.

From the theoretical perspective, all these approaches take a rather static view of the labor market since they focus more on the level of employment protection itself at a given moment as opposed to changes in the level of employment protection.[3] For instance, the legal theory approach cannot account for variation in the politics of labor market reform within countries with legal systems of the same origins, unless countries reform the institutional foundations of the judicial system. While the VOC approach acknowledges the possibility of institutional changes derived from the concept of institutional complementarities, it emphasizes instead an institutional equilibrium in market economies, as opposed to the mechanism of institutional change. The power resource theory may account for radical labor market reform in countries with weak labor and gradual policy changes in countries with strong labor. Nevertheless, it falls short of explaining why countries like Japan have not advanced sweeping labor market reform, despite the political and organizational weakness of labor. It is crucial to understand the origins of the different levels of employment protection, but this study emphasizes the content and direction of changes in employment protection in response to global and national economic crises. Thus, this study analyzes how these labor market institutions have changed, as opposed to how they were originally established.

As presented in figures 1.1 and 1.2, CMEs like Germany, Japan, and Korea developed strong employment protection regimes compared with LMEs (e.g., the United Kingdom and the United States). Even under adverse economic conditions, CMEs have rarely changed the high levels of employment protection for regular workers over the past two decades. However, they extensively liberalized the labor market for temporary employment, accelerating the trend toward the rise of dualism—the division of labor into a dwindling group of regular workers (or insiders) with the privileges of internal labor markets and an increasing number of non-regular workers (or outsiders) more directly exposed to market forces (Brinton 2011; Palier and Thelen 2010; Rueda 2007; Thelen 2012).[4]

Japan and Korea shared similar institutional characteristics of strong employment protection regimes for regular workers and relatively weak employment protection for temporary workers, like other CMEs. For regular employment, both countries ranked medium-high in the rigidity of employment protection,

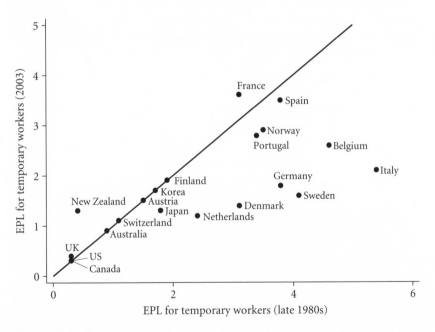

**FIGURE 1.2** Employment protection regimes for temporary workers
*Source*: OECD (2004, 117).
*Note*: EPL refers to the scores of employment protection legislation measured by OECD; for Korea and New Zealand, the scores of the late 1980s are replaced by those of the late 1990s because of the availability of data.

measured by the OECD employment protection legislation (EPL) Index, with scores of 2.4 for both Japan and Korea (as of 2003). Although these two countries ranked at a medium level in employment protection for temporary workers, Japan had a slightly lower level of employment protection for temporary workers than Korea, whose gap in the levels of protection between regular workers and temporary workers was much greater than that in any other advanced industrialized country except for the Netherlands (OECD 2004, 110–117).

In fact, labor market flexibility (or weak employment protection) does not always refer to job insecurity. For instance, in the early 1980s, the Netherlands advanced extensive labor market liberalization for temporary employment—especially part-time workers—in order to reduce unemployment rates and to enable female workers to balance work and life (Becker and Schwartz 2005; Visser and Hemerijck 1997). The Dutch model of labor market liberalization for temporary employment was based on the principle of "flexicurity" (flexibility plus security), and it sufficiently compensated for labor market flexibility for part-time workers by increasing wages (almost equivalent to the level of wages of regular workers) and expanding social protections for these workers. As a result, the Netherlands experienced reduced economic disparity between insiders and outsiders, a drastic decline of unemployment rates, and a rapid rise of part-time employment (35.7 percent of employment in the Dutch labor market as of 2005) (Levy 1999; OECD 2006a, 264). Similarly, Denmark had a relatively lower level of employment protection for regular workers compared with other Scandinavian countries and continental European countries because its economic structure centered on a large number of small-sized firms. Yet the Danish government developed generous social protections for workers, such as active labor market programs, in order to effectively absorb the costs of labor adjustments during economic downturns (Estévez-Abe, Iversen, and Soskice 2001; Iversen and Wren 1998). Contrary to the Netherlands and Denmark, Japan and Korea did not develop extensive social protections to compensate for those affected by labor market reform, which contributed to the rapid rise in labor market inequality and dualism in the two countries over the past two decades. Thus, labor market flexibility was interpreted as meaning a high possibility of job insecurity for workers, at least in Japan and Korea.

## The Content and Scope of Labor Market Reform in Japan and Korea

How, then, did Japan and Korea respond to the pressure of labor market reform when strong employment protection was considered a detrimental factor to a quick turnaround of the national political economy by hindering employers from adjusting to economic challenges? Figure 1.1, presenting a composite indicator of the level of employment protection for regular workers, emphasizes the similarities of the Japanese and Korean labor markets. Yet if we more closely examine disaggregated dimensions of employment protection and legislative changes in the two countries, we can observe interesting cross-national variations in the employment protection system for regular employment and the pattern of reform.

As illustrated in table 1.1, Korea had a much higher score for "regular procedural inconvenience" (3.3 as of 2003) than Japan did (2.0 as of 2003). Korea's Labor Standards Law, which was substantially revised in February 1998, required employers to notify labor unions or other worker representatives sixty days before dismissal (in contrast, Japan had no such specifications) and to consult procedures on the necessary grounds for dismissal and standards of selection in cases of dismissing regular workers for managerial reasons (OECD 1999a, 92; OECD 2004, 110–112). The length of the advance notification, which had been regarded as a roadblock to labor restructuring, was further shortened from sixty to fifty days in 2006 and again from fifty to thirty days in 2010 (see chapter 5 for details). On the other hand, Japan had much higher scores for "notice and severance pay for no-fault individual dismissals" (1.8 as of 2003) and "difficulty of dismissal" (3.5 as of 2003) than Korea did (0.9 and 3.3, respectively). In particular, dismissal for regular workers with a longer period of tenure was far more difficult in Japan because of high severance pay and compensation requirements for employers. In addition, an increase of the "difficulty of dismissal" score from 3.3 to 3.5 referred to the strengthening of employment protection for regular workers in the early 2000s, as opposed to the increasing trend of greater flexibility for non-regular workers in the Japanese labor market. To summarize, Korean employers confronted much more difficulty in consulting with labor unions or other worker representatives before conducting labor restructuring, whereas

**TABLE 1.1** Employment protection regimes for regular workers in Japan and Korea, summary scores by three main areas

| | REGULAR PROCEDURAL INCONVENIENCES | | NOTICE AND SEVERANCE PAY FOR NO-FAULT INDIVIDUAL DISMISSALS | | DIFFICULTY OF DISMISSAL | |
|---|---|---|---|---|---|---|
| | LATE 1980S/1990S | 2003 | LATE 1980S/1990S | 2003 | LATE 1980S/1990S | 2003 |
| Japan | 2.0 | 2.0 | 1.8 | 1.8 | 3.3 | 3.5 |
| Korea | 3.3 | 3.3 | 0.9 | 0.9 | 3.0 | 3.0 |

Source: OECD (2004, 112).

Note: Japanese and Korean data represent the late 1980s and late 1990s, respectively. There was no data for the late 1980s for Korea because it joined the OECD in 1996. In addition, Korea did not experience any substantial changes between the late 1990s and 2003 since all major legislative changes took place in February 1998.

Japanese employers were faced with much higher severance pay and unfair dismissal compensation for regular workers with long enterprise tenure.[5]

While table 1.1 compares the different types of administrative and procedural requirements for employers conducting labor restructuring for regular workers, table 1.2 presents the patterns of reform along the two dimensions of employment status (regular workers versus non-regular workers) and reform content (protection versus liberalization) in Japan and Korea in more detail. It is important to distinguish between regular workers and non-regular workers to understand the political dynamics of labor market reform in Japan and Korea, whose labor market structures have been divided between internal labor markets for regular workers and external labor markets for non-regular workers.[6] As opposed to a notion of labor as homogenous group (e.g., blue-collar skilled workers in the manufacturing industry), an increasing number of scholars point to the emergence of more diversified and heterogeneous groups of workers (such as part-time and temporary workers in the service sector, white-collar clerical workers, and highly skilled professionals) in the labor market, driven by de-industrialization and rapid technological changes. According to these scholars, diverse political and economic interests across these heterogeneous groups of workers were the key determinant of recent political changes in the process of labor market and social welfare reform in advanced industrialized countries (Häusermann 2010; Mares 2006; Palier and Thelen 2010; Rueda 2007; Thelen 2012).

Following the concept in the literature of labor as diverse groups of workers, this study disaggregates labor into two distinct groups of the workforce in the context of labor market reform, despite cross-national variations in legal definitions and real employment practices in the labor market. The first group is composed of regular workers with indefinite employment contracts and the privileges of job security, high wages, and generous social welfare benefits, whereas the second group is composed of non-regular workers in underpaid and under-protected employment conditions with definite contracts (e.g., part-time, temporary and fixed-term contract positions). In the context of the large firm-centered economic structure in Japan and Korea, regular workers in SMEs are often considered outsiders along the dimensions of firm size because of the different levels of job security, wages, and social protections between regular workers in large firms and those in SMEs (Ariga, Brunello, and Ohkusa 2000; Hwang 2006). Thus, although employment status is a primary dimension in dividing the workforce into insiders and outsiders in the context of legal definition, this book regards firm size as another crucial factor in identifying insiders and outsiders with respect to labor management practices at the firm level.

As shown in table 1.2, Japan prioritized the institutionalization of the secondary labor market composed of non-regular workers over the past two decades,

**TABLE 1.2**  Major legislative changes in the Japanese and Korean labor markets, 1986–2011

| | JAPAN | | KOREA | |
|---|---|---|---|---|
| | REGULAR WORKERS | NON-REGULAR WORKERS | REGULAR WORKERS | NON-REGULAR WORKERS |
| **LABOR MARKET FLEXIBILITY** | | | | |
| Protection | Labor Contract Succession Law (2000) Labor Standards Law (2003) Overtime Payment under the Labor Standards Law (2008) | Part-Time Work Law (2007) | | Non-Regular Worker Protection Law (2006) |
| Liberalization | Discretionary Work Hours Rule under the Labor Standards Law (1987–1999) | Worker Dispatch Law (1986–2003) Labor Standards Law (2003) | Labor Standards Law (1997, 1998, and 2006) Discretionary Work Hours Rule under the Labor Standards Law (1997) | Worker Dispatch Law (1998–2006) |
| **WORKER'S BASIC RIGHTS** | | | | |
| Protection | No change | No change | Labor Union and Industrial Relations Law (1998–2011) | Labor Union and Industrial Relations Law (1998–2011) |
| Liberalization | No change | No change | No change | No change |

*Source:* Nihon Hōurei Sakuin [Index of Japanese Laws], http://hourei.ndl.go.jp/SearchSys/; Kokkai Shūgiin [House of Representatives of Japan], *Shūgiin no Ugoki [Legislative Activities in the House of Representatives of Japan]* (various years); the parliamentary debates of the Japanese National Diet (various issues); Ūian Jŏngbo System [Legislative Database of the Korean National Assembly], http://likms.assembly.go.kr/bill/jsp/main.jsp; the parliamentary debates of the Korean National Assembly (various issues).

by extensively liberalizing the rules and regulations governing employment contracts and working conditions for these workers in response to the pressure for greater flexibility. Meanwhile, it retained (or even reinforced) employment protection for regular workers during the same period. The revisions of the Worker Dispatch Law in the late 1990s and early 2000s allowed employers to expand the hiring of dispatched workers—short-term contract workers employed through private employment agencies—in most occupational categories with contract terms that included an extended period of employment (for three to five years). Meanwhile, the Labor Contract Succession Law and the revision of the Labor Standards Law in the early 2000s further strengthened employment protections for regular workers, heading in the opposite direction from labor market liberalization (see chapter 4 for further details).[7]

If the assumptions of power resources theory hold, which attribute pro-labor policies to the strength of organized labor, Japan's labor unions, notoriously docile and weak, should have confronted far more sweeping labor market reform, with employers' massive downsizing of the regular workforce, than Korean counterparts well known for radical and militant strategies, though low union organization rates.[8] This did not happen in the process of Japan's labor market reform. Although employers consistently pressured the government to advance labor market reform for greater flexibility, they showed, at best, only a lukewarm attitude toward the relaxation of employment protection for regular workers, even footing the bill for firms to retain regular workers during economic downturns.

By contrast, Korea promoted across-the-board labor market liberalization for all workers—especially targeting regular workers in the large chaebŏl firms—by revising the Labor Standards Law in the late 1990s and 2000s. It simultaneously attempted to improve not only workers' basic rights but also protections for non-regular workers. Of course, Korea's policy makers did not promote labor market liberalization that only applied to regular workers in the chaebŏl sector. Yet given the different levels of job security for chaebŏl workers and SME workers even before reform, we can infer that Korea would prefer its labor market reform to focus on the relaxation of employment protection for chaebŏl workers under the coverage of strong internal labor markets, rather than further relaxing protection for SME workers already exposed to a much higher risk of job insecurity.

While Japan and Korea did not opt for the neoliberal model of reform, represented by easy hiring and firing practices in response to the fluctuations of the business cycle, they diverged remarkably in the pattern of labor market reform. Japan adopted a two-prong reform strategy: the liberalization of the labor market for outsiders with the persistence of protection for insiders. Meanwhile, Korea prioritized the liberalization of the labor market for all workers, with the mechanism of political and economic compensations for labor.

This book does not argue that labor market reform itself can transform the whole set of institutional arrangements of the labor market. While changes in the legal framework affect economic incentives and political strategies of employers and workers, informal rules and regulations as well as other market institutions associated with the labor market may facilitate or hinder its institutional transformation. As will be illustrated in chapter 5, despite Korea's comprehensive labor market reform intended to increase flexibility for all workers, large chaebŏl firms preferred to rely on the hiring and firing of non-regular workers for labor adjustments, as opposed to laying off regular workers, since they wanted to avoid any potential conflicts with militant chaebŏl unions in corporate restructuring. Contrary to policy makers' original reform intention, labor market inequality and dualism have been further reinforced in Korea over the past two decades. Thus, this book underlines labor market reform as shaping the overall direction of institutional changes in the labor market, while acknowledging the institutional resilience of the labor market even after reform.

## The Sharp Rise in Labor Market Inequality and Dualism

While Japan and Korea diverged in the pattern of labor market reform, these two countries converged in the reinforcement of labor market inequality and dualism, but with different degrees of economic disparity. Labor market dualism is not a new phenomenon in the two countries, whose developmental strategies and economic structures centered on a few large business conglomerates (i.e., Japan's *keiretsu* and Korea's chaebŏl), combined with large enterprise unions. During the period of rapid industrialization, large Japanese and Korean employers adopted "segmentalist approaches" to the labor market, represented by strong employment protection, efficiency wages, and generous welfare benefits for skilled workers, in order to reduce labor turnover rates and secure these skilled workers, as large American employers had done in the late nineteenth and early twentieth centuries (H-K. Song 1991; Swenson 2002; Thelen 2004; Thelen and Kume 1999).[9] Such employers' strategies for the labor market coupled with the government's public policies in favor of the interests of insiders led to the establishment of a dualistic labor market in Japan and Korea, divided between regular workers in large firms and regular workers in SMEs as well as non-regular workers (Abe 2003; Ariga, Brunello, and Ohkusa 2000; E. Jung and Cheon 2006).[10] As long as all workers, regardless of employment status and firm size, could share the benefits of sustainable economic growth and development, labor market inequality and dualism were not singled out in the two countries. The demise of the high-speed developmental model in the face of changing political and economic conditions, however, started to pose a serious challenge to the institutional arrangements of the Japanese and Korean labor markets.

As shown in figure 1.3, the proportion of the non-regular workforce (defined by employment contract terms and status) increased in Japan and Korea over the past two decades. While the non-regular workforce still constituted a greater proportion of the workforce in Korea (46 percent of the workforce as of 2007) than in Japan (33.5 percent of the workforce as of 2007), the magnitude of change in the size of the secondary labor market was far greater in Japan.[11] Until the

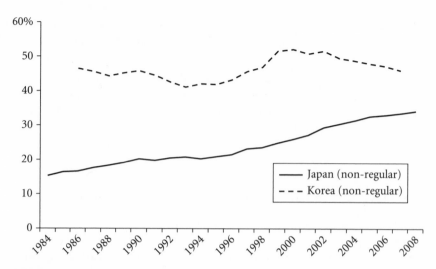

**FIGURE 1.3**  Proportion of the non-regular workforce in Japan and Korea
*Source:* Japanese Ministry of Internal Affairs and Communications, Shūgyō Kōjō Kihon Chōsa [Basic Survey on Employment Structure]; Korean National Statistical Office, Goyong Gujo Gibon Josa [Basic Survey on Employment Structure].

early 1990s, Japan's secondary labor market was relatively small (20.2 percent of the workforce as of 1990), composed mostly of middle-aged female part-time and temporary workers, but it experienced a dramatic expansion since the mid-1990s, a period during which Japan's economy fell into much deeper trouble after the collapse of the asset bubble and a series of labor market reforms for non-regular workers took place.[12]

In Japan, most job creation has been concentrated in non-regular employment since the late 1990s, whereas the number of regular workers has continued to decline during the same period (especially after 1997).[13] Specifically, the proportion of Japan's female non-regular workers, whose largest portion were part-time workers in the service sector, dramatically increased from 37.06 percent to 55.26 percent of the female workforce between 1987 and 2007, and the proportion of Japan's male non-regular workers rose from 9.1 percent to 19.97 percent of the male workforce during the same period, mostly driven by the increase of young male non-regular workers, who failed to join the internal labor market during the so-called "ice age of employment" in the 1990s and 2000s.[14] This book does not dispute the mounting pressure of economic distress on job security for regular workers as frequently reported by the news media covering "*risutora*" (restructuring or layoffs), yet it argues that Japan's labor market reform somewhat shielded insiders (especially middle-aged male regular workers in large firms) from these forces of change in the labor market.[15] Japan transferred the costs of labor adjustments to outsiders, most of whom were female and young and old workers.[16]

During the 1980s and 1990s, Korea's secondary labor market was already almost twice the size of Japan's. Amidst the 1997 Asian financial crisis, the proportion of the non-regular workforce climbed to more than 50 percent of the labor force (see figure 1.3). Contrary to its Japanese counterpart, the proportion of Korea's non-regular workforce composed of temporary and daily workers gradually declined to 44.42 percent (as of 2007) after peaking at 52.2 percent in 2000, as its economy quickly recovered from the financial crisis.[17] In the context of gender, the percentage of female non-regular workers modestly declined from 61.54 percent to 58.2 percent of the female workforce between 1987 and 2007, whereas the percentage of male non-regular workers slightly increased from 36.54 percent to 37.01 percent of the male workforce during the same period, which might indicate that Korea's male breadwinners were exposed to unstable employment conditions in the labor market equally to its female workers.[18]

Some labor market outsiders may prefer to take advantage of temporary or part-time employment status for various reasons (e.g., flexible employment and working conditions and favorable social welfare benefits). In Japan, non-regular employment for married female workers was promoted for the purpose of social welfare and tax benefits. A married female worker was regarded as a dependent of her husband and exempted from paying social welfare insurance contribution for herself if she earned less than 1.3 million yen a year, which was approximately equivalent to the level of an average part-time worker's earning (Osawa 2002, 272). Meanwhile, others may want more stable employment contracts, like those of insiders, seeing the different levels of job security, wages, and social protections between insiders and outsiders.[19] In the cases of Japan and Korea, non-regular employment is equivalent to underpaid and under-protected jobs, a "forced choice" without any other alternative employment options except, perhaps, for married female workers who prefer to balance work and life (Genda 2003; E. Jung 2006; E. Jung and Cheon 2006). Therefore, a majority of non-regular workers in the Japanese and Korean labor markets are more likely to prefer to shift their employment contracts from non-regular to regular employment, as opposed to advocating the relaxation of employment protection for regular workers to equalize job security, working conditions, and wages with non-regular workers.[20]

While the division between regular and non-regular workers became more salient in Japan and Korea, changes in the employment structure along the dimension of firm size should be also taken into consideration, given the large firm-centered economic structure in the two countries. In terms of the change in the composition of the workforce across firm size, the proportion of the workforce in large Japanese firms with more than five hundred workers rarely changed

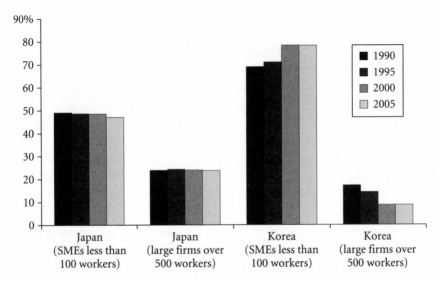

**FIGURE 1.4**   Changes in the workforce in the Japanese and Korean labor markets
*Source:* Japanese Ministry of Health, Labor and Welfare, Rōdōryoku Chōsa
[Labor Force Survey]; Korean National Statistical Office, Saŏpche Gicho Tonggye
Josa Bogosŏ [Report on Enterprise Statistics].

(around 24 percent) between 1990 and 2005, whereas its Korean counterpart
almost halved from 17.2 percent to 8.7 percent (see figure 1.4).[21] Of course, it is
difficult to underestimate the consequences of the 1997 Asian financial crisis on
massive labor adjustments for large Korean firms. Several large chaebŏl groups
within the top thirty (e.g., the Hanbo Group and Jinro Group) filed for corporate
bankruptcy, and even survivors were forced to streamline inefficient business
organization through corporate restructuring, including layoffs of regular workers. Nevertheless, we can infer that large Korean firms aimed to reduce the share
of the workforce even before the financial crisis, through small-scale downsizing
in the early 1990s, and the size of the workforce under the privileges of internal labor markets (e.g., job security, high wages, and generous welfare benefits)
shrank more drastically over the subsequent two decades.

Yet Korea's shrinking number of regular workers in large firms further strengthened internal labor markets even after labor market reform. It is reasonable to
expect that large firms can provide much stronger employment protection for
their workers than SMEs, due to the availability of financial and organizational
resources in response to the fluctuations of the business cycle. As illustrated in
figure 1.5, workers in large firms had much longer tenure (namely, more stable
employment conditions) than average workers in the Japanese and Korean labor

markets. However, Korea experienced a far more drastically widening gap in enterprise tenure years between workers in large firms (with more than five hundred employees) and average workers, whereas Japan presented a consistent magnitude of the gap in enterprise tenure years during the same period. This trend indicates a much greater degree of labor market inequality and dualism along the dimension of firm size in Korea than in Japan over the past two decades.

In the face of economic crisis, Japan and Korea promoted a series of labor market reforms for greater flexibility, but each took a different path. Japan opted for labor market liberalization for outsiders with the persistence of protection for insiders, further deepening labor market inequality and the segmentation of the dualistic labor market between insiders and outsiders through its insider-favored reforms. Meanwhile, Korea adopted comprehensive labor market liberalization for all workers, but its far-reaching reform ironically consolidated labor market inequality and the segmentation of the dualistic labor market along the dimensions of employment status as well as firm size, as opposed to alleviating the problems of economic disparity between insiders and outsiders. In the realm

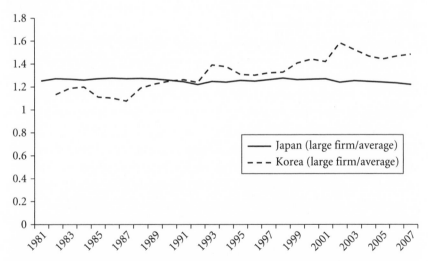

**FIGURE 1.5**  Gaps in enterprise tenure by firm size in Japan and Korea, 1981–2007
*Source:* Japanese Ministry of Health, Labor and Welfare, Chingin Kōjō Kihon Chōsa [Basic Survey on Wage Structure]; Korean National Statistical Office, Goyong Gujo Gibon Josa [Basic Survey on Employment Structure].
*Note:* Gaps in enterprise tenure are calculated by tenure in large firms divided by the average tenure of the labor market. Because of different statistical categories in each survey, Japan's large firms are companies with more than one thousand workers and their Korean counterparts are defined as those with more than five hundred workers.

of employment protection, Japan and Korea utilized different reform strategies in response to economic challenges, but they also experienced converging outcomes in the reinforcement of labor market inequality and dualism, albeit to varying degrees along the lines of employment status and firm size.

# Industrial Relations and Wage-Bargaining Institutions

In response to the economic crisis, employers and policy makers also attempt to introduce various measures for labor adjustments in industrial relations and wage bargaining, such as the increasing costs for going on strike and the decentralization of wage bargaining. In Japan and Korea, a decentralized wage-bargaining mechanism at the firm level is the most important determinant of wage settlement, which is distinct from wage-bargaining institutions at the industry and/or national levels in other CMEs (e.g., continental European and Scandinavian countries). Over the past two decades, these two countries experienced similar trajectories of decentralized wage bargaining as well as rising wage differentials across the labor market.

Since wage-bargaining mechanisms closely affect macro-economic policy outcomes (e.g., economic growth and unemployment), institutional changes and developments in wage bargaining have always drawn scholarly attention in the field of comparative political economy (Calmfors and Driffill 1988; Hall and Franzese 1998; Iversen 1999; Mares 2006). The neo-corporatist literature posits that centralized wage bargaining led by business organizations and labor federations encompassing the entire economy contributes to a virtuous cycle of wage restraints, price stability, and low unemployment, whereas decentralized wage bargaining at the firm level is a less effective mechanism for wage restraints across firms and industries, and its impacts on the national political economy are rather marginal at best (Calmfors and Driffill 1988; Mares 2006; Schmitter and Lehmbruch 1979).[22] Although centralized wage bargaining is an important tool to orchestrate diverse interests across firms and industries, one group of scholars points to wage coordination as a more important factor in macro-economic outcomes (especially wage restraints) (Hall and Franzese 1998; Soskice 1990). The conceptual distinction between centralization and coordination of wage bargaining is worthwhile for understanding the role of informal institutional settings in wage bargaining. The centralization of wage bargaining focuses on the levels—firm, industry, and/or nation—at which wage bargaining takes place, whereas coordination refers to the political capacities of upper-level associations to orchestrate the determination of wage settlements across the entire economy (Hall and Franzese 1998, 509; OECD 2004, 151). The levels of centralization and coordination are highly correlated with one another, but some countries, like Japan and Italy, develop a high political capacity for coordination (through the informal mechanism of wage bargaining) despite the low level of centralization.

As shown in table 1.3, CMEs developed high levels of centralization and coordination in wage setting, whereas LMEs established decentralized and uncoordinated wage-bargaining mechanisms. In contrast to other CMEs, Japan and Korea are ranked at the very bottom levels of wage centralization, similar to LMEs. Yet these two countries differed remarkably in levels of wage coordination: a high level of coordinated wage bargaining in Japan, like other CMEs, versus a very low level of coordinated wage bargaining in Korea, like LMEs. As will be further discussed

**TABLE 1.3**  Wage-setting institutions

| WAGE CENTRALIZATION (1995–2000) | WAGE COORDINATION (1995–2000) |
|---|---|
| Finland (5) | Finland (5) |
| Norway (4.5) | Belgium (4.5) |
| Ireland (4) | Norway (4.5) |
| Portugal (4) | Austria (4) |
| Austria (3) | Denmark (4) |
| Belgium (3) | Germany (4) |
| Germany (3) | Ireland (4) |
| Netherlands (3) | Italy (4) |
| Spain (3) | **Japan (4)** |
| Sweden (3) | Netherlands (4) |
| Australia (2) | Portugal (4) |
| Denmark (2) | Switzerland (4) |
| France (2) | Spain (3) |
| Italy (2) | Sweden (3) |
| Switzerland (2) | Australia (2) |
| Canada (1) | France (2) |
| **Japan (1)** | Canada (1) |
| **Korea (1)** | **Korea (1)** |
| New Zealand (1) | New Zealand (1) |
| UK (1) | UK (1) |
| US (1) | US (1) |

Source: OECD (2004, 151, table 3.5).

Note: The scale is 1–5. High scores refer to a high level of wage centralization and wage coordination. OECD (2004, 151) defines these scores of centralization and coordination as follows. Regarding the centralization of wage bargaining, if wage bargaining is dominant at the company and plant level, it obtains a score of 1; if wage bargaining is dominant at the combination of industry and company/plant level, it obtains a score of 2; if wage bargaining takes place at the industry level, it obtains a score of 3; if wage bargaining takes place at the industry level with recurrent central-level agreements, it obtains a score of 4; if the predominant form of wage bargaining takes place at the central level, it obtains a score of 5. With respect to the coordination of wage bargaining, in the case of fragmented company/plant bargaining, the score of coordination is 1; in the case of fragmented industry and company-level bargaining, the score is 2; if industry-level bargaining with moderate coordination among major bargaining actors takes place, it is given a score of 3; if certain forms of coordination by several peak associations, peak confederations, large firms, or government wage arbitrations take place in the labor market, it is given a score of 4; in the case of coordination by an encompassing union confederation, peak confederations, or government imposition of a wage schedule/freeze, the score of coordination is 5.

in chapter 3, in the mid-1950s, Japan established *shuntō* (or spring offensive), an informal inter- and intra-industry wage-coordination mechanism led by a few large firms in leading export-oriented sectors (as pattern setters in wage bargaining), which was functionally equivalent to centralized wage-bargaining institutions (Kume 1998, 49–72). In contrast, Korea never developed similar wage-coordination mechanisms across firms and industries despite its policy makers' attempt to build up one emulating Japan's *shuntō* during the 1990s (J. Song 2012c).

Although the index of wage coordination was still high, the role of Japan's *shuntō* as wage-coordination mechanism became marginalized during its protracted recession, when it was faced with intense downward pressures on decentralized wage bargaining (Nakamura 2005b; Weathers 2003).[23] As illustrated in figure 1.6, Japan and Korea experienced widening wage differentials across firm size, regardless of the presence or absence of wage-coordination mechanisms. Even during the period of high-speed economic growth, Japan's *shuntō* did not aim at reducing the wage gap across firms of all sizes, driven by the difference in productivity between large firms and SMEs. The primary function of *shuntō* was to equalize wage increase rates over the entire economy, which allowed unorganized SME workers to benefit from a similar range of wage increases offered for workers in large export-oriented firms. The magnitude of widening wage differentials across firm size was far more drastic in Korea, which had never established any wage-coordination mechanism, than in Japan. Although the authoritarian government tightly controlled Korea's wage differentials until the mid-1980s, wage inequality was exacerbated after the 1987 democratic transition and the 1997 Asian financial crisis pushed by the strength of large chaebŏl unions (see chapters 3 and 5 for details).

One of the most pressing issues with respect to wage settlements in Japan and Korea is that the very low levels of union organization and coverage of collective bargaining exacerbated economic disparity between unionized insiders and unorganized outsiders (including both unorganized SME workers and non-regular workers). While most advanced industrialized countries also confronted the declining trend in union organization rates, indicating the weakening power of labor unions in wage bargaining, the coverage of collective bargaining remained relatively intact, despite a few exceptions (e.g., New Zealand and the United Kingdom). For instance, as presented in table 1.4, France and Spain were ranked at the very lowest levels of union organization rates, but collective bargaining in the two countries covered over 90 percent of the workforce, which may alleviate the problem of the widening economic gap across the labor market in those countries. But in Japan and Korea, most union memberships were concentrated in large firms, and large enterprise unions exclusively representing the interests of insiders widened the economic gaps

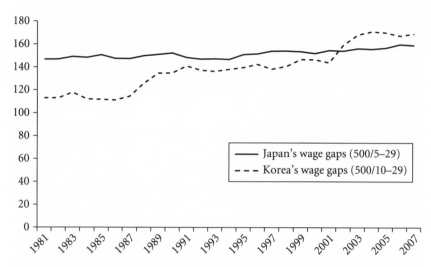

**FIGURE 1.6**  Wage differentials across firm size in Japan and Korea, 1981–2007
*Source:* Japanese Ministry of Health, Labor and Welfare, Maitsuki Rōdō Tōkei Chōsa [Monthly Labor Statistics]; Korean National Statistical Office, Maewŏl Nodong Tonggye [Monthly Labor Statistics].
*Note:* Because of the lack of data availability for average wages for regular workers across firm size, I extrapolated Japan's wage gaps between 1980 and 1992 based on average wages for regular and part-time workers.

between insiders and outsiders, although national labor federations attempted to organize non-regular workers in order to enlarge their organizational structures. In the context of wage equality, non-regular workers, mostly excluded from the coverage of collective bargaining at the firm level, received around 60 percent of the wages of regular workers in Japan and Korea (Eun, Oh, and Yoon 2008; Jones 2008).

The structure of seniority-based wages under the pressure of an aging workforce also imposed heavy financial burden on firms in the Japanese and Korean labor markets. Seniority-based wages depend on the presence of a large youthful workforce in the labor market, paid below-market wages in their youth in exchange for the promise of higher wages in later years (Schoppa 2006, 51). However, both Japan and Korea confronted the intense labor costs associated with seniority-based wages in a rapidly aging workforce.[24] Thus, it came to be in the primary interests of employers to make way for more productive young workers by moving older workers out of jobs through modifications in the employment structure of the labor market or the replacement of the seniority-based wage structure with a performance-based one. While Japan and Korea faced the common problem of the aging workforce and seniority-based wages, Korea's

**TABLE 1.4**  Union organization rates and collective bargaining coverage

| | UNION ORGANIZATION RATES (%) | | COLLECTIVE BARGAINING COVERAGE (%) | |
|---|---|---|---|---|
| | 1980 | 2000 | 1980 | 2000 |
| Australia | 48 | 25 | 80 | 80 |
| Austria | 57 | 37 | 95 | 95 |
| Belgium | 54 | 56 | 90 | 90 |
| Canada | 35 | 28 | 37 | 32 |
| Denmark | 79 | 74 | 70 | 80 |
| Finland | 69 | 76 | 90 | 90 |
| France | 18 | 10 | 80 | 90 |
| Germany | 35 | 25 | 80 | 68 |
| Italy | 50 | 35 | 80 | 80 |
| **Japan** | **31** | **22** | **25** | **15** |
| **Korea** | **15** | **11** | **15** | **10** |
| Netherlands | 35 | 23 | 70 | 80 |
| New Zealand | 69 | 23 | 60 | 25 |
| Norway | 58 | 54 | 70 | 70 |
| Portugal | n.a. | 15 | n.a. | 40 |
| Spain | 7 | 15 | 60 | 80 |
| Sweden | 80 | 79 | 80 | 90 |
| Switzerland | 31 | 18 | 50 | 40 |
| UK | 51 | 31 | 70 | 30 |
| US | 22 | 13 | 26 | 14 |

*Source:* OECD (2004, 145).

seniority-based wage profile was far steeper than its Japanese counterpart despite the modest decline of the seniority-based wage curve in Korea between 1990 and 2005, which might indicate the greater degree of the financial burden of increasing labor costs on Korean employers (see figure 1.7).

While Japan and Korea shared institutional similarities with other CMEs in terms of strong employment protection regimes (especially for regular workers), the institutional trajectories of industrial relations and wage-bargaining mechanisms in the Japanese and Korean labor markets developed similarly to the institutional configurations of LMEs. Japan and Korea, both of which had already established decentralized industrial relations based on large enterprise unions, had to cope with the severe pressure to further decentralize wage bargaining during economic downturns as well as rapidly increasing labor costs pushed by the combination of the seniority-based wage structure and the aging labor force. As a result, wage differentials across employment status as well as firm size have been further exacerbated in the two countries over the past two decades.

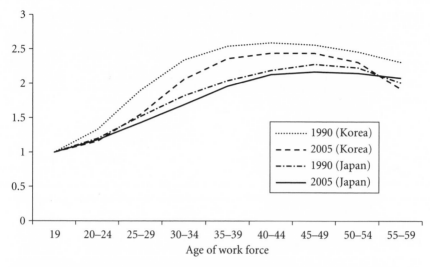

**FIGURE 1.7** Seniority-based wage curve in the Japanese and Korean labor markets
*Source:* Japanese Ministry of Health, Labor and Welfare, Maitsuki Rōdō Tōkei Chōsa [Monthly Labor Statistics]; Korean National Statistical Office, Maewŏl Nodong Tonggye [Monthly Labor Statistics].

## Social Protection

While social protection itself had important implications for employers and workers by defining employers' social insurance contributions and individual citizens' access to different levels and types of social welfare benefits, it played a crucial role in facilitating labor market reform by providing compensations for those affected by reform (Iversen and Stephens 2008; Levy 1999 and 2005; Levy, Miura, and Park 2006; Mares 2006; Palier 2005). Amid a series of labor market reforms in the 1990s and 2000s, Japan and Korea expanded social protection programs in order to absorb the costs of labor adjustments. However, the institutional characteristics of social protections centered on employment-based entitlements favored the interests of insiders, leading to the reinforcement of labor market inequality and dualism.

As illustrated in table 1.5, Japan and Korea developed a small welfare state (measured by the levels of public social expenditure) with meager welfare benefits. In the context of social protection related to the labor market, Scandinavian countries most actively intervened in compensating for labor adjustments by establishing various active labor market programs, such as retraining of the unemployed. While continental European countries developed large welfare states like Scandinavian countries, they had relatively minor public-sector employment because of policy concern about fiscal stability (Iversen and Wren

**TABLE 1.5** Public spending on labor market programs and social protections

| RANKING | PUBLIC SOCIAL EXPENDITURE (% OF GDP, 2000) | LABOR MARKET PROGRAM EXPENDITURE (% OF GDP, 2005) | SHARE OF ALMP* SPENDING IN LABOR MARKET PROGRAM EXPENDITURE (2005) | AVERAGE OF NET REPLACEMENT RATES OVER 60 MONTHS OF UNEMPLOYMENT WITHOUT SOCIAL ASSISTANCE (2005) | PUBLIC SECTOR EMPLOYMENT (1995) |
|---|---|---|---|---|---|
| 1 | Sweden (29.48%) | Denmark (4.26%) | UK (77.1%) | Denmark (68%) | Norway (32%) |
| 2 | Denmark (28.89%) | Belgium (3.45%) | Sweden (52.4%) | Finland (64%) | Sweden (31.8%) |
| 3 | France (28.34%) | Netherland (3.35%) | New Zealand (47%) | Belgium (62%) | Denmark (31.2%) |
| 4 | Germany (27.17%) | Germany (3.32%) | Norway (46.3%) | UK (61%) | Finland (26.3%) |
| 5 | Austria (26.02%) | Finland (2.79%) | Switzerland (45%) | Austria (59%) | Canada (19.8%) |
| 6 | Switzerland (25.4%) | France (2.52%) | Ireland (43.2%) | France (57%) | Belgium (19.2%) |
| 7 | Finland (24.5%) | Sweden (2.52%) | Australia (42.5%) | Ireland (55%) | UK (18.8%) |
| 8 | Belgium (24.25%) | Spain (2.23%) | Denmark (40.8%) | Australia (51%) | Australia (18.7%) |
| 9 | Italy (24.07%) | Austria (2.13%) | Italy (39.7%) | New Zealand (51%) | US (15.6%) |
| 10 | Norway (23%) | Portugal (1.98%) | Netherlands (39.7%) | Portugal (44%) | Austria (14.6%) |
| 11 | Netherlands (21.77%) | Switzerland (1.69%) | **Korea (37.1%)** | Norway (41%) | Netherlands (13.9%) |
| 12 | UK (21.69%) | Norway (1.62%) | **Japan (36.8%)** | Netherlands (40%) | Germany (13.4%) |
| 13 | Portugal (20.5%) | Ireland (1.46%) | France (35.7%) | Spain (37%) | Switzerland (12.6%) |
| 14 | Spain (19.91%) | Italy (1.36%) | Spain (35%) | Germany (33%) | New Zealand (12.5%) |
| 15 | New Zealand (19.21%) | Australia (1.06%) | Portugal (34.8%) | Sweden (29%) | **Japan (8%)** |
| 16 | Australia (18.56%) | Canada (0.95%) | US (34.2%) | Switzerland (24%) | **Korea (7%)** |

| RANKING | PUBLIC SOCIAL EXPENDI-TURE (% OF GDP, 2000) | LABOR MARKET PROGRAM EXPEN-DITURE (% OF GDP, 2005) | SHARE OF ALMP* SPENDING IN LABOR MAR-KET PROGRAM EXPENDITURE (2005) | AVERAGE OF NET REPLACEMENT RATES OVER 60 MONTHS OF UNEM-PLOYMENT WITH-OUT SOCIAL ASSIS-TANCE (2005) | PUBLIC SECTOR EMPLOYMENT (1995) |
|---|---|---|---|---|---|
| 17 | Canada (17.33%) | New Zealand (0.83%) | Canada (33.7%) | Canada (17%) | |
| 18 | **Japan** **(16.13%)** | UK (0.68%) | Finland (31.9%) | **Japan** **(8%)** | |
| 19 | US (14.19%) | **Japan** **(0.68%)** | Belgium (31.3%) | Italy (7%) | |
| 20 | Ireland (13.63%) | US (0.38%) | Germany (29.2%) | **Korea** **(6%)** | |
| 21 | **Korea** **(5.61%)** | **Korea** **(0.35%)** | Austria (29.1%) | US (6%) | |

Source: Column 1: OECD (2006b, 181); columns 2 and 3: OECD (2007a, 270–276); column 4: Benefits and Wages, OECD Indicator (OECD 2007b, 103); column 5: Estévez-Abe (2008, 50), except for Korea. Korea's public employment is based on OECD Observer, http://www.oecdobserver.org/news/fullstory.php/aid/2874/Public_sector_jobs_.html, accessed October 8, 2010.
* ALMP: active labor market policies.

1998; Martin and Thelen 2007). Instead, large-scale early retirement programs for middle-aged regular workers were extensively employed in many continental European countries in order to facilitate firms' restructuring through state-funded compensations for these insiders (Levy 1999; Levy, Miura, and Park 2006; Mares 2003). Ranked at the very bottom levels in spending and benefits, social protection programs in Japan and Korea were not as extensive and generous as those in continental European and Scandinavian countries, and they were not sufficient to absorb the costs of labor adjustments.

It is a valid point that the size of welfare states, measured only by the level of public spending on social welfare programs, may not precisely capture the institutional features of social protection in Japan and Korea. In fact, various "informal" social protection programs, such as economic and social regulations (e.g., agricultural subsidies, cartel policies, and employment protection) and firm-based welfare benefits (such as housing subsidies, educational expenses, and family benefits), served as crucial mechanisms of social protection for workers as well as the general public by supplementing the underdeveloped state-funded welfare programs in these two countries (Estévez-Abe 2008; Gao 2001; P. H. Kim 2009 and 2010; Kume 1998; H-K. Song and Hong 2006; Uriu 1996).[25]

As presented in table 1.6, Japan and Korea were ranked at a medium level in non-statutory social welfare expenditure by private sectors, contrary to their very bottom ranking in public spending expenditure. Nevertheless, workers' entitlements to welfare benefits are largely determined by employment status and occupation in the Japanese and Korean labor markets (e.g., full-time workers versus part-time workers and workers in large firms versus workers in SMEs), not by the criterion of citizenship. Therefore, Japanese and Korean workers seem to be directly exposed to a much higher degree of commodification—namely, the reliance on market income to maintain the quality of their lives—by firm-based welfare benefits.[26] Moreover, changing economic conditions and business environments substantially weakened the role of social and economic regulations and firm-based welfare benefits as alternative mechanisms of social protection for workers in the two countries (Murasugi 2010; Nishikubo 2010; H-K. Song and Hong 2006).

While Japan and Korea expanded social protection programs to facilitate labor market reform and provide a safety net for workers, the institutional

**TABLE 1.6**  Non-statutory social welfare spending by private sectors (% of GDP)

| COUNTRY | 1980 | 1990 | 2000 | 2005 |
|---|---|---|---|---|
| Australia | 0.993 | 0.832 | 3.474 | 2.551 (7) |
| Austria | 1.121 | 1.055 | 0.997 | 1.023 (16) |
| Belgium | 0.891 | 1.556 | 2.378 | 4.47 (5) |
| Canada | 1.569 | 3.275 | 4.998 | 5.498 (3) |
| Denmark | 1.357 | 1.647 | 2.087 | 2.392 (10) |
| Finland | 0.868 | 1.071 | 1.161 | 1.098 (15) |
| France | 0.575 | 1.684 | 2.355 | 2.69 (6) |
| Germany | 1.102 | 1.454 | 1.657 | 1.845 (11) |
| Italy | n.a. | 0.535 | 0.447 | 0.559 (18) |
| **Japan** | **n.a.** | **n.a.** | **3.052** | **2.488 (9)** |
| **Korea** | **n.a.** | **0.118** | **2.035** | **1.761 (12)** |
| Netherlands | 3.638 | 5.628 | 6.584 | 7.484 (2) |
| New Zealand | 0.068 | 0.191 | 0.479 | 0.434 (20) |
| Norway | 0.574 | 0.71 | 0.783 | 0.796 (17) |
| Portugal | 0.367 | 0.635 | 1.097 | 1.54 (13) |
| Spain | 0.201 | 0.242 | 0.28 | 0.485 (19) |
| Sweden | 1.138 | 1.221 | 2.104 | 2.54 (8) |
| Switzerland | n.a. | 0.977 | 1.186 | 1.114 (14) |
| UK | 3.325 | 4.745 | 6.817 | 5.312 (4) |
| US | 4.19 | 7.093 | 8.694 | 9.66 (1) |

Source: OECD Social Expenditure, http://stats.oecd.org/Index.aspx?datasetcode=SOCX_AGG, accessed June 8, 2011.
Note: ranking in parentheses; n.a. means "not available."

configurations of social protection in favor of insiders consolidated the widening gap of social benefits between privileged insiders and outsiders with little or no coverage. These policy outcomes were very similar to the defects of the Christian democratic welfare system in continental Europe. Japan relaxed the eligibility requirements for the Employment Insurance Program for dispatched workers in the wake of the global financial crisis of 2008 by reducing the required period of enrollment. However, Japan still privileged the interests of insiders, especially laid-off regular workers with longer tenure. In the case of Korea, policy makers rapidly expanded universalistic social protection programs for workers amid the 1997 Asian financial crisis, rather than retrench social protections. In 1999, Korea integrated occupationally segmented health insurance programs into one unified state-run model and expanded the coverage of the national pension program, which had initially been introduced for firms with more than ten workers in 1988, to the urban self-employed, the last target of the program expansion. It also broadened the coverage and benefits of the Employment Insurance Program to SME workers, non-regular workers, and even the self-employed on a voluntary basis in the late 1990s and the decade following (Hwang 2006; Korean Ministry of Labor 2008a; Wong 2004; Yang and Klassen 2010).[27] Despite Korea's unprecedented expansion of social protection programs toward citizenship-based universalistic programs, a large number of SME workers and non-regular workers were still excluded from these social protection programs because of policy loopholes as well as insiders' indifference to the expansion of these programs for outsiders (J. Cho, Kim, and Kwon 2008).

Table 1.7 shows that employment status (regular versus non-regular workers) and firm size (large firms versus SMEs) are the two most important determinants of the eligibility and level of social welfare benefits in Japan and Korea. In the case of Korea, even regular workers (e.g., regular workers in SMEs) have not been fully covered by social protection programs, despite the government's

**TABLE 1.7**   Coverage of social welfare programs in Japan and Korea, 2005

| | JAPAN | | KOREA | |
|---|---|---|---|---|
| | REGULAR WORKERS | NON-REGULAR WORKERS | REGULAR WORKERS | NON-REGULAR WORKERS |
| Employment Insurance Program | 99.2% | 60.0% | 63.8% | 34.5% |
| Public Pension Program | 98.7% | 46.6% | 75.7% | 36.3% |
| National Health Insurance | 99.7% | 48.6% | 75.9% | 37.7% |

Source: Japanese Ministry of Health, Labor and Welfare, Shūgyō Keitai no Tayōka ni Kansuru Sōgō Jitai Chōsa [General Survey on Diversified Types of Employment]; Korean National Statistical Office, Gyŏngje Hwal'dong Ingu Josa [Economically Active Population Survey].
Note: This table was originally published in J. Song (2012b, 429, table 1). Copyright © 2012 Wiley Periodicals, Inc. Used with permission by Wiley Periodicals, Inc.

rapid expansion of eligibility for coverage. In other words, Japan and Korea intentionally and unintentionally reinforced the segmentation of welfare benefits through social protection reform by disadvantaging outsiders who needed social protection most under the pressure of economic distress and labor market reform.

## Summary

This chapter describes institutional changes and developments in the three key aspects of the Japanese and Korean labor markets and social protections in comparative context. Each section of the chapter demonstrates the institutional arrangements of the labor market and social protection as well as country-specific details. While Japan and Korea advanced labor market reform for greater flexibility, they diverged in the pattern of reform: reform for outsiders in Japan versus reform for all workers in Korea. Yet despite different reform strategies, a shrinking number of insiders in Japan and Korea have benefited from the privileges of job security, high wages, and generous social protections along the dimensions of employment protection and firm size. In particular, the different levels of job security between workers in large firms and those in SMEs were far more intensified in Korea than that in Japan. In the realm of industrial relations and wage bargaining, both countries experienced the decentralization of wage bargaining, increasing wage differentials across firm size, and wage disparities between regular workers and non-regular workers. Korea, which had never developed any mechanism of wage bargaining across firms and industries, confronted far more drastic wage disparity along the dimension of firm size than Japan did. Similarly, Japan and Korea further reinforced insider-favored social protection programs, but Korea experienced a much higher degree of labor market inequality and dualism along the lines of employment status and firm size regarding social protections, indicating much more serious problems of economic disparity in the labor market and social protections.

* * *

This chapter has presented several key dimensions of the labor market and social protection systems in Japan and Korea. Well known for the institutional similarities of their national political economies, these two countries developed similar labor market arrangements (e.g., strong employment protections for regular workers, decentralized wage bargaining, and small welfare states). Yet despite these similarities, Japan and Korea presented different trajectories of labor market reform. Under the pressure for reform, Japan adopted labor market liberalization for outsiders, while retaining a high level of employment protection for insiders, which led to the strengthening of labor market inequality and dualism between insiders and outsiders. In contrast, Korea promoted labor market liberalization for all workers, targeting regular workers in the large chaebŏl sector, in exchange for the improvement of workers' basic rights to unions as well as protections for non-regular workers. Nevertheless, Korea was not able to avoid the deepening of labor market inequality and dualism, which resulted in the reinforcement of economic disparity between chaebŏl workers and the others in the labor market. The remainder of this book identifies and examines the causal processes of the institutional convergence and divergence of labor market reform, focusing on the institutional arrangements of the labor market as the key determinant of the trajectories of reform.

# THE POLITICS OF LABOR MARKET REFORM IN HARD TIMES

That countries adopt diverging paths of labor market reform raises an important question for policy makers as well as scholars, considering the frequency of global and national economic crises around the world and the necessity of reform for economic adjustment. This chapter focuses on the institutional arrangements of the labor market to explain the political process and outcome of labor market reform. It argues that the features of the employment protection system determine the patterns of reform and that the configurations of industrial relations shape the trajectories of labor market inequality and dualism.

The first section analyzes three possible explanations for the politics of labor market reform: the political partisanship of the government, the role of political institutions, and economic crisis. While these explanations provide useful insights in accounting for the politics of labor market reform, they do not sufficiently answer empirical questions arising from the two cases of Japan and Korea as well as general patterns of reform across advanced industrialized countries. The second section, then, turns to building a theoretical framework to explain labor market reform, inequality, and dualism. The third section explains the ways in which the variables of employment protection systems and industrial relations shape the patterns of labor adjustments and institutional changes in the labor market in times of economic crisis, focusing on the cases of Japan and Korea. The final section summarizes the core argument presented in this chapter.

# Three Possible Explanations for the Politics of Labor Market Reform

What causal mechanisms might undergird the three explanations for the politics of labor market reform?[1] By testing these frameworks against empirical evidence drawn from Japan and Korea, I demonstrate that they fall short in providing adequate explanations for the variations in the politics of labor market reform.

# Political Partisanship of the Government

A first possible explanation for the politics of labor market reform is the political partisanship of the government. A strand of research on this points out that labor-friendly socioeconomic policies (e.g., strong employment protection and generous social welfare programs) to shield workers from the vagaries of the market can be attributed to left governments closely tied with labor unions (Bradley et al. 2003; Esping-Andersen 1990; Garret 1998b; Huber, Ragin, and Stephens 1993; Huber and Stephens 2001; Korpi 2006). Recently, departing from the simple dichotomy of the left–right ideological spectrum of the political partisanship of the government, a group of scholars points to the political partisanship of the government combined with insider-outsider differences as a key variable to account for the diverging patterns of reform in advanced industrialized countries, especially the rise in labor market inequality and dualism (Iversen and Soskice 2009; Iversen and Stephens 2008; Palier and Thelen 2010; Rueda 2007).[2] Yet even scholars within this camp disagree as to whether social democratic governments (or left governments) foster or prevent the increase in labor market inequality and dualism. Rueda (2007) claims that social democratic governments have accelerated labor market inequality and dualism between insiders and outsiders because they have prioritized the interests of insiders—their core constituencies in electoral competition—over those of outsiders (e.g., temporary and unskilled workers). He argues that a lack of policy responsiveness by social democratic governments to widening economic disparity further deepens labor market inequality and dualism, although he points to employment protection legislation and corporatism as two additional factors to mediate the consequences of inequality and dualism in the labor market (Rueda 2007, 27–35).[3]

Meanwhile, other scholars argue that social democratic governments, combined with specific skills-training systems and wage-coordination mechanisms, have effectively preempted the rise in labor market inequality and dualism by expanding social protections for those most affected by labor market reform, such as active labor market policies for outsiders (Iversen and Soskice 2009; Iversen and Stephens 2008). Contrary to Rueda (2007), these scholars claim that social democratic governments, in support of protecting the interests of labor (including both insiders and outsiders), have been able to maintain a high level of economic equality amid labor market reform, whereas Christian democratic governments, composed of more diverse groups of political constituencies ranging from business to religious groups, have exacerbated labor market inequality and dualism in most continental European countries.

While the political partisanship of the government provides a compelling story for explaining cross-national variations in the politics of labor market reform in western Europe, its theoretical framework is not consistent with empirical findings drawn from Japan and Korea. Contrary to the prediction of the theory of political partisanship, Japan's conservative LDP government maintained employment protection for insiders, whereas Korea's center-left governments prioritized the relaxation of stringent rules on employment protection for insiders. In Japan and Korea, the political partisanship of the government is an important factor in explaining the improvement of employment protection and working conditions for outsiders (such as part-time, temporary, and fixed-term contract workers). For instance, the conservative LDP focused more on labor market liberalization for outsiders, whereas left parties (e.g., the Social Democratic Party of Japan—previously known as the Japan Socialist Party—and the Democratic Party of Japan) advocated protective measures for these workers. Similarly, in the case of Korea, the two center-left governments made political efforts to enhance protection for outsiders (e.g., job security and social protection programs). Nevertheless, the political partisanship theory falls short in accounting for why Japan liberalized the labor market for outsiders while preserving protection for insiders, whereas Korea adopted labor market liberalization across the board.

In addition, although Rueda's framework of insider-outsider difference might explain the trend of increasing labor market inequality and dualism, it cannot sufficiently account for the sharp rise in labor market inequality and dualism in Japan and Korea. As predicted by Rueda's framework on the linkage between political partisanship and labor market policy, Korea experienced a growing economic gap between insiders and outsiders during the reign of the two center-left governments. Contrary to Rueda's theoretical proposition, however, it was not the center-left governments that accelerated labor market inequality and dualism by advocating the interests of insiders in the process of Korea's labor market reform. As will be elaborated in chapter 5, the two center-left governments lowered the level of employment protection for insiders and improved employment protection and social welfare benefits for outsiders. This reform did not bear fruit, though, since the strength of large chaebŏl unions blocked the implementation of labor market reform for insiders at the firm level, and decentralized industrial relations (based on large chaebŏl unions) further reinforced social protection programs in favor of the interests of insiders. As Iversen and Soskice (2009) and Iversen and Stephens (2008) claim, the absence of social democratic parties linked with workers and labor unions to defend the interests of the working class may explain the increase in labor market inequality and dualism in Japan and Korea, since neither of the countries developed strong social democratic parties. While the variable of social democratic parties seems to offer a persuasive analytical framework to account for the drastic rise in labor market inequality and dualism in the two countries, it cannot sufficiently explain why Japan and Korea took diverging reform paths for insiders: persistent protection for insiders in Japan versus liberalization for insiders in Korea.

Why, then, does the theory of political partisanship of the government fail to account for the politics of labor market reform in Japan and Korea? The key assumption of the theory of political partisanship is the presence of "programmatic" party systems in electoral competition, which indicates a political linkage between voters and political parties through policy platforms (Kitschelt 2000). However, political party systems in Japan and Korea are defined as "non-programmatic" (e.g., clientelistic or charismatic/personalistic party systems), limiting the explanatory power of the political partisanship argument (B-K. Kim 2000a; Kitschelt 2000; Scheiner 2006). In the cases of Japan and Korea, political linkages between left parties and labor unions and workers are not as strong as those in western Europe (Carlile 1994; Y. Lee 2009).[4]

In addition, while the ideal policy position of a political party, measured by the left–right ideological spectrum, differentiates party platforms among different parties, Japanese and Korean political parties have often taken more flexible policy approaches, not strictly bound by coherent party platforms and election manifestos. Scholars of Japanese politics point to the strategic adaptability of the LDP to political challenges (known as "creative conservatism"): the flexible shift of its positions to preempt policy agendas of the leftist party, such as social welfare and environmental issues (Calder 1988; Pempel 1982). In Korea, a few controversial issues (e.g., national security policies toward North Korea) critically divide voters as well as political parties, but for most other policy areas political parties have emulated each other's agendas. Thus, the theory of political partisanship of the government, the distinction between conservative parties and left parties, does not travel well beyond the boundaries of western Europe, especially when applied to the politics of labor market reform in Japan and Korea.

## Political Institutions

A second possible explanation for the politics of labor market reform stems from the political institution approach, which presumes that a range of political institutions set the rules of the game and shape the incentives and strategies of actors in policy making. In particular, the analytical frameworks of the neo-corporatist institution and the electoral system have drawn scholarly attention to accounting for cross-national variations in labor policy making. First, the neo-corporatist institution approach predicts that the corporatist institutions of policy making—composed of business, labor, and government—will lead to safeguarding the interests of organized labor by allowing labor to participate in the process of reform and effectively pressuring governments to expand social protection programs for those affected by reform. By contrast, in the absence of the corporatist political institution, policy makers may pursue more drastic reform by restricting the access of interest groups (especially labor unions) to decision making and paying less attention to compensations for reform losers (Martin and Thelen 2007; Visser and Hemerijck 1997).

The neo-corporatist institution approach seems to account for cross-national variations in the pattern of reform (e.g., radical reform in LMEs versus incremental reform in CMEs) and the degree of increasing labor market inequality and dualism (e.g., the rise in labor market inequality and dualism in continental European countries versus a high level of equality in Scandinavian countries). Yet the variable of the corporatist institution cannot sufficiently explain the political dynamics of labor market reform in Japan and Korea.[5] Despite the declining political capacity of labor deliberative councils (or *rōdō shingikai*), composed of the political representatives of business, labor, and public interests, in labor policy making, Japan's policy makers have rarely challenged employment protection for insiders, while prioritizing the liberalization of the rules and regulations governing employment and working conditions for outsiders (Miura 2002b; J. Song 2010 and 2012b).[6] In Korea, the Tripartite Commission, composed of the representatives of business, labor, and government, served to formulate the liberalization of the labor market for insiders, as opposed to protecting the interests of insiders in reform politics (Y. Lee 2009; Rho 1999; J. Song 2012a and 2012c). In addition, regardless of the development (or the weakening) of the corporatist policy-making institution, Japan and Korea were not able to avoid widening economic disparity between insiders and outsiders.[7]

Second, the electoral system approach asserts that a set of electoral formulas—e.g., majoritarian and proportional representation (PR) systems, district magnitudes, and candidate nomination procedures—determine the characteristics of electoral competition and distribution/redistribution policy outcomes (Carey and Shugart 1995; Cox 1990; Estévez-Abe 2008; Horiuchi and Saito 2003; Iversen and Soskice 2006; Martin and Swank 2008; Ramseyer and Rosenbluth 1997). Among these institutional configurations of the electoral system, different electoral incentives shaped by majoritarian and PR electoral rules have attracted scholarly attention to explain cross-national variations in policy outcomes.

In focusing on the relationship between the different types of capitalism and electoral systems, an increasing number of scholars of varieties of capitalism (VOC) point to the political dimensions of the VOC—especially electoral systems—as the key variable to explain different political responses to recent economic challenges in advanced industrialized countries (Cusack, Iversen, and Soskice 2007; Estévez-Abe 2008; Iversen and Soskice 2006; Martin and Swank 2008).[8] By examining the origins and development of the linkage between market institutions and electoral systems, these scholars point to an institutional affinity between the mode of capitalism and the electoral rule. According to the VOC framework, CMEs based on the economic interests of co-specific asset holders tend to develop proportional representation (PR) electoral systems because the principle of political consensus building embedded in PR systems is more likely to protect the interests of employers and workers investing in co-specific assets. Meanwhile, LMEs centered on general (or transferable) assets are more closely related to the establishment of majoritarian systems in electoral competition (see Cusack, Iversen, and Soskice 2007). The political dimension of the VOC approach seems to provide a compelling argument to explain the ways in which two different sets of countries—CMEs with PR electoral systems and LMEs with majoritarian systems—have maintained the distinct types of capitalism, as opposed to convergence to the model of LMEs under the pressure of economic globalization.

However, the electoral rule approach has analytical limitations in explaining the variation in the politics of labor market reform across CMEs. First, although CMEs in continental Europe and Scandinavia share the similar electoral systems of PR, they have remarkably diverged in the degree of increasing labor market inequality and dualism. Most continental European countries have experienced sharply increasing economic disparity between insiders and outsiders in the process of labor market reform, whereas Scandinavian countries have maintained a high level of equality. Second, Japan and Korea are more complicated cases in applying the logic of electoral systems because of the institutional characteristics of the mixed electoral system. Although Japan and Korea are identified as the primary examples of CMEs based on group-based coordination in the VOC framework (Hall and Soskice 2001; Soskice 1999), these two countries have adopted electoral rule that mixes the majoritarian system and the PR system, distinctly different from other CMEs with PR electoral systems (Grofman et al. 1999; Reed 2003; Shugart and Wattenberg 2001). The mixed electoral system makes it difficult to examine the effects of the electoral system on policy outcomes; the theory's insights are drawn from the simple dichotomy of the majoritarian and PR electoral systems. Also, the similar institutional arrangements of the mixed electoral system cannot sufficiently account for cross-national variations in the patterns of reform in Japan and Korea.

## Economic Crisis

A third possible explanation for the politics of labor market reform is the economic crisis approach. This approach points out that economic crisis catalyzes swift and sweeping policy responses by suppressing the political resistance to reform and by departing from the legacies of old political and market institutions (Drazen and Grilli 1993; Fajertag and Pochet 2000; Gourevitch 1986; Kruger 1993; Przeworski 1991; Williamson and Haggard 1994). In particular, the different characteristics of the crisis—Japan's protracted recession after the collapse of the asset bubble versus Korea's intense financial crisis—are considered the key to the variation in the politics of labor market reform in these two countries. This analytical framework postulates that the severity of economic crisis combined with strong external pressure from international actors (e.g., the International Monetary Fund and the US government) caused Korea's immediate and extensive labor market reform in exchange for receiving the financial rescue packages.[9] As the economic crisis approach predicts, Korea embarked on comprehensive labor market liberalization for all workers under the severe pressure of the financial crisis, whereas Japan, confronting a slow-moving economic recession over a decade, adopted labor market liberalization for outsiders with the persistence of protection for insiders (Corsetti, Pesenti, and Roubini 1998; Haggard 2000; Y. C. Kim and Moon 2000; Radelet and Sachs 1998; H-K. Song 2003).

This book agrees that the different characteristics of the economic crisis have significant effects on the diverging paths of reform in Japan and Korea. Nevertheless, the crisis itself cannot sufficiently explain several important dimensions of the reform. First, even before the 1997 Asian financial crisis, Korea's policy makers prioritized comprehensive labor market reform, focusing on the weakening of employment protection for insiders, in order to streamline business organizations and conduct labor restructuring (especially in large chaebŏl firms), although a general strike led by two national labor federations in January 1997 postponed the implementation of reform with a two-year grace period

(Y. C. Kim 1998; B-K. Kim and Lim 2000; Koo 2000). In addition, considering its quick economic recovery from the financial crisis (as shown in figure I.1 in the introduction) and the presence of pro-labor presidents during the period of 1998–2007, we might expect to see a reverse course of reform to strengthen the level of protection for insiders, which did not happen in Korea.

Second, some might point to the different awareness or perception of the economic crisis in Japan and Korea as the key factor for different reform strategies, highlighting that Japan's slow-moving economic recession did not alarm its policy makers to the point of urgency in implementing comprehensive labor market reform, whereas Korea's economic shock caused extensive and prompt responses from the government. Yet, although the collapse of the asset bubble led to Japan's decade-long recession, the consequences of its protracted crisis on the economy were as severe as or even more severe than those of its Korean counterpart, especially since the late 1990s.[10] The magnitude of the bad debts of the Japanese banking sector amounted to almost one-third of the gross domestic product (GDP) in 1999 and its average growth rates between 1992 and 2001 were a record 1 percent (Amyx 2004, 2–3). A series of bank runs and corporate bankruptcies in the late 1990s contributed to soaring unemployment rates in Japan, which more than doubled from 2.1 percent in 1991 to 5.4 percent in 2002.[11] During the first half of the 1990s, Japan's policy makers might not have considered comprehensive labor market reform an imperative because of the characteristics of its endogenous and protracted recession. As elaborated in the studies on Japan's financial and corporate reforms, however, around the late 1990s and early 2000s, they realized the necessity of more extensive market reform in order to resuscitate Japan's faltering economy (Amyx 2004; Tiberghien 2007). Thus, it is difficult to claim that the limitations of Japan's labor market reform resulted from policy makers not considering the economic malaise sufficiently serious. Even more puzzling was that Japan retained (or even strengthened) extensive employment protection for insiders amid a series of labor market reforms for greater flexibility for outsiders in the late 1990s and 2000s. To explain these questions in the politics of labor market reform in Japan and Korea, other causal factors should also be taken into account.

## Employment Protection Systems and Industrial Relations

This section analyzes the ways in which the institutional arrangements of the labor market—employment protection systems and industrial relations—affect the politics of labor market reform. Table 2.1 presents the theoretical argument

**TABLE 2.1**  Theory of labor market reform, inequality, and dualism

| | | INSTITUTIONALIZATION AND COVERAGE OF THE EMPLOYMENT PROTECTION SYSTEM | |
| --- | --- | --- | --- |
| | | HIGHLY INSTITUTIONALIZED AND LARGE COVERAGE | LESS INSTITUTIONALIZED AND SMALL COVERAGE |
| Configurations of industrial relations | Decentralized | Selective reform for outsiders with a high degree of labor market inequality and dualism | Comprehensive reform for all workers with a high degree of labor market inequality and dualism |
| | Centralized | Selective reform for outsiders with a low degree of labor market inequality and dualism | Comprehensive reform for all workers with a low/medium degree of labor market inequality and dualism |

of this book. First, the institutional features of the employment protection system—the institutionalization and coverage of the system—explain the diverging patterns of labor market reform: reform for outsiders with the persistence of protection for insiders versus reform for all workers. In the face of economic crisis, labor market flexibility is always a primary reform agenda item for employers as well as policy makers as a way of alleviating the financial burden of labor costs on employers by allowing them to opt for various labor adjustment strategies. But the available range of reform options is highly constrained by the existing institutional characteristics of the employment protection system, which have shaped production and investment strategies, human capital investment through skills training systems, and public policies in the labor market.

More specifically, in a system where the institutionalized practices of employment protection cover a large proportion of the workforce, reform is more likely to focus on the liberalization of the labor market for outsiders on the margin, while preserving protection for privileged insiders. It is not surprising that insiders prefer to maintain a high level of employment protection even under intense economic strain. Yet some employers, if not all, may share similar preferences for labor market reform with insiders, namely employment protection for insiders, since they would prefer to maximize the benefits of their production and investment strategies centered on protection for insiders and to ensure that the core institutional tenets of the system remain intact. In addition, faced with the institutional constraints of employment protection covering a large proportion of the workforce, employers may adopt more feasible reform options, while minimizing the political and economic costs of labor market reform (e.g., stalemate or intense confrontation). Under such institutional conditions, policy makers, worrying about the political costs of reform for insiders (as a majority of the workforce), are also more likely to liberalize the labor market for outsiders, most of whom are already excluded from the coverage of the employ-ment protection system.

By contrast, where the less-institutionalized practices of employment protec-tion cover a small segment of the workforce, leaving the remainder unprotected, reform is more likely to focus on the relaxation of employment protection for all workers, particularly targeting the small segment of the workforce enjoy-ing the privileges of internal labor markets (e.g., job security, high wages, and generous social protections). For insiders, the persistence of employment pro-tection is imperative during severe economic distress. However, given such insti-tutional characteristics of the employment protection system, employers may have a much stronger temptation to streamline inefficient production facilities and dismiss insiders for greater labor market flexibility, as opposed to making long-term investments in the institutionalization and extension of the employ-ment protection system. In particular, if employment protection systems cover a small proportion of the workforce, policy makers are more likely to advance comprehensive labor market reform for all workers by taking advantage of the small share of the workforce under protection, with the hope of rapid economic turnaround.

Second, while certain patterns of labor market reform (e.g., reform for out-siders) may account for a sharp rise in labor market inequality and dualism, the configurations of industrial relations affect the degree of increasing labor mar-ket inequality and dualism in the process of labor market reform by formulating specific types of social protections. It is inevitable that reform losers—either dispersed groups or concentrated ones—will be created as a consequence of changing rules and regulations. The remaining policy problem is how to pro-vide social protections for those affected by labor market reform. By shaping the preferences and strategies of employers and workers (especially insiders), the institutional configurations of industrial relations determine the develop-ment of social protections as political and economic compensations for these reform losers.

The key assumption is that centralized industrial relations are based on the institutionalization of business associations and labor federations that would encompass the entire economy and have the political and organizational capac-ity to coordinate interests internally as well as between one another, which allows both business and labor to adopt "solidaristic" approaches to the labor market and social protections (Olson 1965 and 1982; Swenson 2002; Thelen 2004). Accordingly, countries with centralized industrial relations are more likely to preempt the rise in labor market inequality and dualism by expanding social protection programs over the entire economy in order to absorb the costs of labor adjustments.

By contrast, countries with decentralized industrial relations tend to deepen labor market inequality and dualism since decentralized industrial relations (based on large enterprise unions) prevent employers and well-organized insiders from adopting "solidaristic" approaches to the labor market and social protections. Decentralized industrial relations based on fragmented business and labor organizations incentivize employers and insiders to consolidate insider-friendly social protections because of their narrowly defined economic interests as well as the lack of a coordinating capacity beyond the boundary of firm and workplace, which results in the deepening of the economic disparity between insiders and outsiders. Most insiders can ensure the privileges of internal labor markets without looking for other political allies, such as fellow SME workers and non-regular workers or politicians and political parties. Thus, all things being equal, countries with decentralized industrial relations are more likely to reinforce labor market inequality and the segmentation of the dualistic labor market than those with centralized industrial relations.

In sum, the institutionalized practices of employment protection covering a large proportion of the workforce are more likely to lead to labor market reform in favor of the interests of privileged insiders, while resulting in the sacrifices of outsiders for greater flexibility. Meanwhile, the less-institutionalized practices of employment protection covering a small share of the workforce become far more vulnerable to the forces for change, allowing employers and policy makers to advance the full-scale liberalization of the labor market for all workers. In the politics of reform, the configurations of industrial relations may alleviate or exacerbate the problems of labor market inequality and dualism by shaping the development of the compensation mechanism in the labor market and social protections.

## Effects of Employment Protection and Industrial Relations on the Politics of Labor Market Reform

This section elaborates how the institutional variables of employment protection systems and industrial relations determine labor market reform, inequality, and dualism in Japan and Korea. It argues that the variation in the institutionalization and coverage of employment protection accounts for diverging patterns of reform—reform for outsiders in Japan versus reform for all workers in

Korea—and the similarities in decentralized industrial relations explain the two countries' convergence in reinforced labor market inequality and dualism.

## Employment Protection Systems and Labor Market Reform

Employment protection systems describe a broad range of rules and regulations governing job security, working conditions and hours, and compensation for workers in the labor market. To assess the characteristics of employment protection, this study focuses on the institutionalization and coverage of the system. "Institutionalization" of the employment protection system refers to the extent to which employers, workers, and policy makers have invested in the establishment and survival of the system, and "coverage" indicates the proportion of the workforce that has benefited from the privileges of internal labor markets (especially job security).[12] While institutionalization and coverage are somewhat correlated, the institutionalized practices of employment protection do not always lead to extensive coverage. A high degree of employment protection may be applicable only to a small segment of the workforce.

Then how can we measure the institutionalization and coverage of employment protection? Different legal definitions and labor practices on the ground make it difficult to compare employment protection systems across nations. To complement the lack of a comparable cross-national indicator of employment protection, this study uses three different indicators that would measure the institutional features of the system. First, the proportion of the workforce covered by the employment protection system measures the extent to which employment protection applies (namely the coverage of employment protection). A large share of the workforce being covered by employment protection indicates the predominance of the employment protection system in the labor market. Thus, the larger the size of the workforce covered by employment protection, the more extensive the coverage of employment protection. Second, this study uses the composite OECD EPL Index for regular employment as one of the indicators of the level of employment protection for insiders, which is stipulated by administrative and legal frameworks at the national level.[13] Lastly, the number of years of tenure (the length of service within enterprises) is utilized as another indicator to measure the levels of stable employment within enterprises.[14] The number of years of tenure reflects the costs of dismissal, which are derived from the level of strict legal restrictions on employment protection. Nevertheless, the number of years of tenure also reflects labor turnover rates (or labor mobility) within enterprises interacting with labor management practices at the firm level, which may not be the sole outcome of legal restrictions on employment protection for workers. In addition, the institutionalization of employment protection at the firm level (or stable employment within enterprises) has always been considered more important for workers in countries like Japan and Korea, where employment practices at the firm level have influenced the levels of job security, wages, and social protections more than formal rules and regulations defined by administrative and legal frameworks at the national level (Estévez-Abe, Iversen, and Soskice 2001, 163–169). In this study, the OECD EPL Index for regular employment and enterprise tenure years are two indicators to measure the levels of institutionalization of employment protection, while the proportion of the workforce under employment protection measures the coverage of the system.

Figure 2.1 presents the different proportions of the workforce covered by employment protection in the Japanese and Korean labor markets over the past two decades. Considering the characteristics of the dualistic labor market—internal labor markets for regular workers versus external labor markets for non-regular workers—the regular workforce can be regarded as insiders who have benefited from job security, high wages, and social protections, even if it is true that regular workers in SMEs are not as privileged as those in large firms. While the size of the regular workforce in the Japanese labor market rapidly declined, especially after the late 1990s, Japan still had a larger share of the

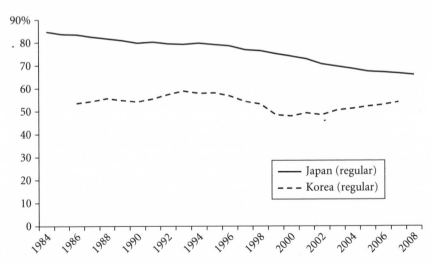

**FIGURE 2.1**  Proportion of the regular workforce in Japan and Korea
*Source*: Japanese Ministry of Internal Affairs and Communications, Shūgyō Kōjō Kihon Chōsa [Basic Survey on Employment Structure]; Korean National Statistical Office, Goyong Gujo Gibon Josa [Basic Survey on Employment Structure].

workforce covered by employment protection than Korea, indicating the more extensive coverage of employment protection for the workforce.

As shown in figure 2.2, most OECD countries demonstrate a strong positive correlation between the OECD EPL Index for regular employment and average enterprise tenure years, except for the case of Korea. Despite identical levels of employment protection legislation for regular employment and similar labor management practices (known as permanent employment practices), Japan and Korea present remarkable differences in the average number of enterprise tenure years. As of 1995, Japan ranked second in enterprise tenure years (11.3 years), just behind Italy (11.6 years), whereas Korea was at the lowest rank (5.7 years), behind even the United States (7.4 years), an archetypical model of easy firing and hiring practices. These institutional discrepancies between the OECD EPL Index for regular employment and average years of enterprise tenure point out the different degrees of the institutionalization of employment protection in the Japanese and Korean labor markets: a high degree of the institutionalization of employment protection in Japan versus a low degree of the institutionalization of employment protection in Korea.

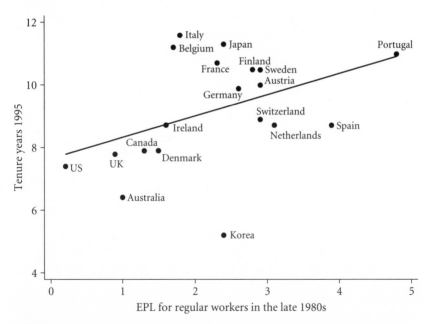

**FIGURE 2.2**   OECD EPL Index for regular employment and average enterprise tenure years
Source: OECD (1997, 139) and OECD (2004, 112).
Note: EPL refers to employment protection legislation; for Korea, the EPL Index of the late 1990s was used because of the data availability.

Changes in average enterprise tenure years over time further buttress important differences between the two countries' experiences in the institutionalization of employment protection. As of 2007, Japan's average number of enterprise tenure years (11.8 years) was almost twice its Korean counterpart (6.2 years), which casts doubt on the myth of Korea's permanent employment practices (see figure 2.3). Even for workers in large Korean firms with more than five hundred employees, the average number of enterprise years was 9.2, shorter than Japan's average over its entire workforce. In other words, workers in large Korean firms did not even have the same level of job security within enterprises as those in Japan's SMEs, although they were ensured a far greater degree of job security than their fellow Korean SME workers.

In addition, the political mechanism of institutionalizing employment protection differed remarkably in the two countries, derived from the legacies of labor politics and developmental strategies. Japan's employment protection systems have been centered on the implicit and explicit agreement of employers, insiders,

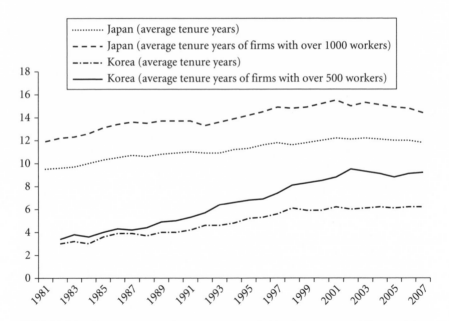

**FIGURE 2.3**  Average enterprise tenure years in the Japanese and Korean labor markets, 1981–2007
*Source*: Japanese Ministry of Health, Labor and Welfare, Chingin Kōjō Kihon Chōsa [Basic Survey on Wage Structure]; Korean National Statistical Office, Goyong Gujo Gibon Josa [Basic Survey on Employment Structure]. This figure was originally published in J. Song (2012a, 168, figure 1). Copyright © The East Asia Institute. Used with permission by Lynne Rienner Publishers, Inc.

and policy makers on job security for insiders, in exchange for alternative labor adjustment mechanisms (e.g., flexible work arrangements, wage restraints, and the hiring of outsiders) and public policy programs (Gordon 1998; Kume 1998; Miura 2002b; Moriguchi and Ono 2006; Shinoda 2008). Japan's employment protection systems (well known as permanent employment practices) do not cover all workers; core coverage is estimated between 20 percent and 35 percent of the workforce (namely, male regular workers in large firms), excluding most female workers and non-regular workers (Reed 1993, 81). However, regular workers in SMEs have also greatly benefited from job security because of various institutional protections for these workers (e.g., social and economic regulations and government policies) in the Japanese political economy, although the level of employment protection for SME workers was not as high as it was for workers in large firms (Cheng and Kalleberg 1996; Gao 2001). A majority of regular workers in the Japanese labor market, whose proportion was 61.3 percent of the workforce as of 2010, still receive a relatively high level of employment protection (Noble 2011).[15]

By contrast, Korea's employment protection systems, which had been originally imposed by the authoritarian regime, were consolidated by the organizational power of large chaebŏl unions after the 1987 democratic transition (Hwang 2006; E. Jung and Cheon 2006; Dae-whan Kim, Choi, and Yun 2010). Although it was often thought that chaebŏl workers enjoyed the privileges of insiders during the period of industrialization in the 1960s and 1970s, internal labor markets for blue-collar production workers in the chaebŏl sector were established after democratization, pressured by chaebŏl unions, most of which were organized in the wake of the Great Workers' Strikes during the summer of 1987. The proportion of the workforce in the top thirty chaebŏl, considered as "core" insiders in the labor market, was very small, around 7 percent as of 1996.[16] In addition, contrary to their Japanese counterparts, Korea's employers rarely made commitments to the institutionalization of employment protection even for regular workers (especially blue-collar production workers) during the period of development and industrialization (as will be further elaborated in chapters 3 and 5).

The different levels of the employment protection system are also salient along the dimension of age group. It is not surprising that young workers tend to have shorter enterprise tenure years than older workers because their length of service in the labor market differs. Yet across all different age groups, Japan had much longer average enterprise tenure years (especially for middle-aged and elderly workers) than Korea, as shown in figure 2.4. Although Japan's young male workers have experienced a slightly declining number of enterprise tenure years over the past two decades, which reflects the "ice age of employment"

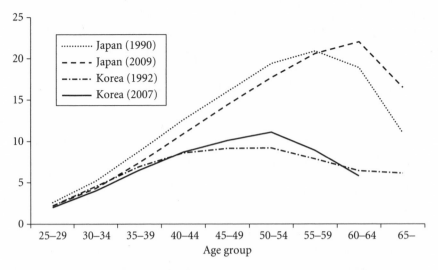

**FIGURE 2.4**  Average enterprise tenure years for Japanese and Korean male workers by age group
*Source*: Japanese Ministry of Health, Labor and Welfare, Chingin Kōjō Kihon Chōsa [Basic Survey on Wage Structure]; Korean Ministry of Labor, Goyong Hyŏngtae byŏl Siltae Josa [Basic Survey on Employment Practices] and Imkŭm Gujo Gibon Tonggye Josa [Basic Survey on Wage Structure].
*Note*: For Korea 2007 data only, the age group of sixty and over is used.

during the late 1990s and 2000s, its older male workers were relatively shielded from the pressure for changes in the labor market, contrary to the mass media coverage of the death of Japan's permanent employment practices. Meanwhile, Korea's male workers seemed to confront a much higher risk of job insecurity in their early middle age (the age group of fifty to fifty-four years) compared with their Japanese counterparts whose enterprise tenure years only started to decline after their retirement ages at sixty.

Despite similarities in employment protection regimes at the national level measured by the OECD EPL Index, the institutional features of employment protection, measured by the proportion of the workforce covered by employment protection as well as enterprise tenure years at the firm level, differed remarkably in Japan and Korea. These subtle but important differences in the characteristics of employment protection led to the variations in the pattern of labor market reform by constraining a feasible range of reform options for employers, workers, and policy makers in times of economic crisis.

Given the large proportion of the workforce covered by the institutional-ized practices of employment protection in Japan, insiders, employers, and policy makers formed a political coalition in support of persistent protection for insiders, with the liberalization of the labor market for outsiders. Since Japanese employers made a long-term commitment to the institutionaliza-tion of employment protection for insiders, in exchange for industrial peace, a specific-skills training system, and managerial discretion over the workplace, some if not all employers tended to preserve protection for insiders in order to continue to benefit from the existing system of employment protection. Employers might also restrict an available range of labor market reform, expecting the opposition of insiders and policy makers, although reform for outsiders might not be an optimal solution for them. Japan's policy makers, worrying about the political backlash of privileged insiders as a majority of the workforce, were less willing to undermine the institutional foundations of job security for insiders. Based on such preferences and the calculations of insiders, employers, and policy makers for reform, Japan experienced the liberalization of the labor market for outsiders with persistence of protection for insiders.

In contrast, Korea's employers and policy makers advanced sweeping labor market reform for all workers under the less-institutionalized practices of employment protection covering a small segment of the workforce. For both groups, a high level of employment protection for insiders (as a small segment of the workforce) was regarded as burdensome in a time of economic distress. Promising rapid economic turnaround, policy makers opted for far-reaching labor market reform for all workers. Employers, who did not expect to benefit from the existing system of less-institutionalized practices of employment pro-tection, also supported the liberalization of the labor market for all workers. Meanwhile, Korean insiders were not able to find any political allies in support of continued employment protection.

## The Configurations of Industrial Relations and Economic Disparity

The configurations of industrial relations—measured by union organization rates, collective bargaining coverage, and wage-bargaining institutions—have more explanatory power for the rise in labor market inequality and dualism than any other factors. In Japan and Korea, decentralized industrial relations based on large enterprise unions exacerbated labor market inequality and the segmenta-tion of the dualistic labor market along the dimensions of employment status and firm size, since such institutional structures of industrial relations prevented employers and organized insiders from adopting "solidaristic" approaches to labor market and social protection reforms.

As illustrated in chapter 1, in contrast to other CMEs, these two countries developed decentralized industrial relations based on large enterprise unions, whose collective bargaining did not encompass all workers across firms and industries (although Japan developed an intra- and inter-industry wage-coordination mechanism). Union organization rates in Japan and Korea continued to drop from 25.2 percent to 18.1 percent and from 17.2 percent to 10.5 percent respectively between 1990 and 2008 (Japan Institute for Labor Policy and Training, Labor Statistics [www.jil.go.jp]; Korea Labor Institute 2008, 19). A trend of declining union membership furthered labor market inequality and dualism because unionized insiders were heavily concentrated in large firms in the two countries. As of 2008, 45.3 percent of firms with more than one thousand workers were unionized in Japan, whereas only 1.1 percent of firms with less than ninety-nine workers were unionized (Japan Institute for Labor Policy and Training, Labor Statistics [www.jil.go.jp]). Similarly, 45.4 percent of Korean firms with more than three hundred workers were unionized, but only 3.1 percent of firms with thirty to ninety-nine workers were unionized in 2008 (Korea Labor Institute 2008, 6).

In neither Japan nor Korea did the coverage of collective bargaining go beyond the boundary of the individual firm. In the process of labor market reform, employers and insiders at the firm level were not interested in the development of social protection programs for those affected by reform at the national level, since neither of them were willing to pay for additional social insurance contribution in order to absorb the costs of labor adjustments. Decentralized industrial relations—exclusively representing the interests of insiders in large firms—intensified the widening economic disparity between a small segment of unionized insiders and the others. Despite the diverging patterns of labor market reform, Japan and Korea under the similar institutional configurations of decentralized industrial relations confronted widening economic disparity in the labor market over the past two decades.

## Summary

The institutional arrangements of the labor market—the characteristics of the employment protection system and the configurations of industrial relations—led to both convergence and divergence in the politics of labor market reform in Japan and Korea. First, Japan could not encroach upon the privileges of insiders. With such a large proportion of the workforce covered by the highly institutionalized practices of employment protection, employers and policy makers were constrained in reform efforts. In addition, scholars of Japan point out that its employment protection system for insiders became the cultural and social norm in Japan (Reed 1993; Vogel 2006). Under these institutional and normative constraints, Japanese employers might need to calculate not only the economic costs of labor restructuring for insiders, but also the reputational costs of labor restructuring for insiders (e.g., their own public image) (Ahmadjian and Robinson 2001).[17] These aspects of Japan's employment protection system made the institutional arrangements of the labor market far more resilient than Korea's even under the pressure to change. Thus, Japan opted for labor market reform that would minimize the costs of reform for insiders, while transferring the costs of reform to outsiders, whose differences from insiders were far more enlarged by Japan's decentralized industrial relations and the underdevelopment of social protections for outsiders.[18]

In contrast, Korea's employment protection systems, which were less institutionalized and covered a small proportion of the workforce, became much more vulnerable to the forces of change since neither employers nor policy makers had a higher stake in the persistence of the employment protection system for insiders in reform politics. Rather, Korean employers and policy makers prioritized comprehensive labor market reform in order to increase labor market flexibility for all workers in times of economic distress. Korea's chaebŏl unions and workers were unable to block labor market reform at the national level without any political allies in support of protection for insiders. However, they were able to overrule policy makers' intention of across-the-board labor market liberalization with its strong potential to disrupt industrial relations. These unions and workers blocked the implementation of reform and ensured protection for insiders at the firm level, which further reinforced labor market inequality and dualism between chaebŏl workers (as "core" insiders) and the others in the Korean labor market.

* * *

This chapter has developed a theoretical framework that explains the politics of labor market reform in the face of challenges in national political economies. It has argued that the institutional arrangements of the labor market determine the political dynamics of labor market reform, inequality, and dualism. Under the institutionalized practices of employment protection covering a large proportion of the workforce, insiders, employers, and policy makers are more likely to form a political coalition in order to promote reform for outsiders, while privileging the interests of insiders and minimizing the political and economic costs of reform (e.g., political backlash at election time or industrial disputes) on these workers. In contrast, if employment protection systems have been less institutionalized with the coverage of the very small segment of the workforce, employers and policy makers are more likely to advance labor market reform for greater flexibility across the board. Decentralized industrial relations based on large enterprise unions are more likely to reinforce labor market inequality and dualism because such institutional configurations incentivize employers and insiders to opt for "segmentalist" approaches to the labor market and social protections.

The following three chapters assess the theoretical framework developed in this chapter to explain the politics of labor market reform in Japan and Korea. These two cases elaborate the ways in which the institutional features of the labor market account for the convergence and divergence of labor market reform over the past two decades.

# 3

# THE INSTITUTIONAL ORIGINS OF THE LABOR MARKET AND SOCIAL PROTECTIONS IN JAPAN AND KOREA

Japanese and Korean labor markets and social protections were established during the period of rapid industrialization.[1] Although this book does not focus exclusively on the path-dependent institutional trajectory of labor market reform, it is still important to examine the conditions under which certain labor market and social protections were introduced because these institutional arrangements have had crucial consequences for recent reform by shaping the interests and strategies of reform actors.

The first three sections below describes the origins and development of the labor market and social protections in postwar Japan, with an analytical focus on employment protection, industrial relations and wage bargaining, and social protections. They elaborate how these institutional arrangements were formulated and consolidated in the Japanese political economy during the period of high-speed growth. The following three sections outline the origins and development of the labor market and social protections in Korea, tracing them back to the period of the authoritarian regime (1961–1987). They present the ways in which the authoritarian government unilaterally imposed a set of labor market institutions and social protection programs on business and labor in order to achieve its ultimate national goal of rapid economic growth. The final section compares similarities and differences of the labor market and social protections in the two countries, followed by a discussion of recent challenges for Japan and Korea that have provoked intense pressure in their national political economies over the course of the 1990s and 2000s.

# Japan: Institutionalization of Employment Protection for Insiders

Beginning in the early twentieth century, the period in which Japan began to industrialize, large firms introduced seniority-based wages, corporation-provided employee benefits, and firm-based training systems in order to stabilize high labor mobility and to retain a skilled workforce (Gordon 1985; Moriguchi 1998; Thelen 2004; Thelen and Kume 1999). The perfection of the Japanese model of the labor market, however, came with the institutionalization of strong employment protection and intra- and inter-industry wage coordination in the postwar period. In Japan, three institutional pillars of the labor market—permanent employment practices, seniority-based wages, and enterprise unions—were regarded as "three treasures" that contributed to Japan's postwar economic "miracle," in conjunction with cooperative industrial relations at the firm level. In particular, strong employment protection systems at the firm level—so-called permanent employment practices—were considered a linchpin upholding the institutional stability of the Japanese labor market.[2]

When the US occupation authorities lifted all legal restrictions on collective labor rights (e.g., rights to organize labor unions, strike, and bargain collectively) in the immediate postwar years, a wave of militant labor strikes and industrial conflicts swept over Japan, driven by unions' vehement demands for wage increases, collective bargaining agreements, and the democratization of management (Gordon 1998; Moriguchi 1998; Moriguchi and Ono 2006).[3] Amid intense industrial disputes in the late 1940s and early 1950s, a group of workers, opposing militant and radical labor movements led by leftist union leaders and worrying about firms' productivity growth, organized moderate "second enterprise unions" (*daini kumiai*) and paved the way for cooperation with employers at the firm level (Estévez-Abe 1999; Gordon 1998; Hyodo 1997; Moriguchi 1998; Moriguchi and Ono 2006).[4] Beginning in the late 1950s and early 1960s, most large firms and their enterprise unions—exclusively representing regular workers—gradually agreed to guarantee employment protection for regular workers (or insiders), in exchange for assured managerial authority over the introduction of new technology, the rationalization of production, discretion in skills training, and job allocation (Gordon 1998; Hiwatari 1999; Kume 1998 and 2005; Shinoda 2008).[5]

Japan's firm-based training system further consolidated the institutional foundations of employment protection for insiders, especially in large firms (Kume 1998; Miura 2002b). In the early twentieth century, when Japan embarked on industrialization, its state-owned enterprises in heavy industries institutionalized firm-based skills training systems in order to supply the skilled workforce.[6] Soon after, large private firms, such as shipbuilding and steel companies, emulated these training systems in the workplace, which gradually spread to SMEs (Gordon

1985; Thelen 2004; Thelen and Kume 1999 and 2001). Human asset specificity embedded in the firm-based skills training systems required business and labor to make long-term mutual commitments to job security and better economic rewards (e.g., high wages and generous benefits) for regular workers (Becker 1993; Estévez-Abe 2008, 177; Estévez-Abe, Iversen, and Soskice 2001; Kasza 2006, 56; Thelen 2004). Considering the long-term investments involved in promoting firm-based skills training systems, it might have been too costly for Japanese employers to give up their prior commitments to job security for these workers, even during economic downturns.[7]

Yet the limited options for shedding regular workers in times of economic distress forced Japanese firms to develop alternative labor adjustment strategies to maximize the usage of these workers. In order to increase intra-firm (or functional) labor market flexibility, employers emphasized upgrading skills and multi-skill training systems for regular workers. In addition, labor adjustment methods like work transfer, including *shukkō* (temporary work transfer to affiliate firms) or *tenseki* (permanent work transfer), and the firing of non-regular workers (or outsiders) were extensively employed to safeguard job security for male regular workers in large firms (equivalent to "core" insiders) (Brinton 1993; Dore 1986; Gottfried 2008; Hiwatari 1999; Rebick 2005; Reed 1993; Shinotsuka 1989; Weathers 2001). Amid the two oil crises of the 1970s, a majority of Japanese firms implemented the employment adjustment strategy of dismissing outsiders, most of whom were female part-time and temporary workers (Brinton 1993; Shinotsuka 1989).[8] According to statistical data, as of October 1976 the percentage of female workers was reduced by 17 percent, whereas the percentage of male workers only declined by 6 percent in the aftermath of the first oil crisis (Shinotsuka 1989, 58).

In fact, a large number of SMEs were unable to maintain their commitments to strong job security for regular workers during economic downturns in the Japanese labor market (Cheng and Kalleberg 1997; Koike 1988). What prevented SME employers from laying off regular workers during economic distress were (1) the case laws of Japan's Supreme Court, which strictly restricted employers' rights to dismiss, (2) the government's employment subsidy programs that helped firms to retain regular workers in economic downturns, and (3) various economic and social regulations protecting SMEs from fierce market competition (Gao 2001; Estévez-Abe 2008; Kasza 2006; Miura 2002b).[9] In Japan, employment protection was engaged with much broader social and economic perspectives than any other social welfare policies, and the mutual commitments of business and labor to employment protection for regular workers were further strengthened by the government's public policies (Estévez-Abe 2008; Kasza 2006).[10] Some scholars point out that enterprise unions and organized insiders took a passive role in forging a political compromise with employers at the firm level because they lacked the political capacity to oppose or resist what management proposed to discuss

(Gordon 1998; A. Suzuki 2004). Nonetheless, it cannot be disputed that the level of employment protection for insiders remained high during the past few decades, even if the political power of labor was extremely weak in Japan.

## Japan: Informal Wage Coordination

Despite decentralized industrial relations led by large enterprise unions, Japan developed an informal wage-coordination institution, the so-called *shuntō* (or spring offensive), in the mid-1950s, functionally equivalent to centralized wage bargaining in other CMEs (Hiwatari 1999; Hiwatari and Miura 2001; Kume 1998 and 2005; Miura 2002b; A. Suzuki 2004). Employers and their enterprise unions in large export-oriented firms led intra- and inter-industry wage coordination as the de facto political representatives of business and labor in wage bargaining. At the start, radical public-sector unions, affiliated with the leftist labor federation Sōhyō (General Council of Trade Unions of Japan), dominated *shuntō*, demanding high wage increases during the period of rapid growth in the 1950s. However, as large export-oriented firms and their enterprise unions in the private sectors affiliated with Dōmei (Japanese Confederation of Labor) took a leading role in wage setting in the mid-1960s, wage moderation gradually became institutionalized (Hiwatari 1999; Kume 1998 and 2005; A. Suzuki 2004). During the 1960s and 1970s, the shipbuilding and steel industries played a pivotal role in leading informal intra- and inter-wage coordination, and since the early 1980s, the automobile and electronics industries have led informal wage coordination in *shuntō*. Unlike centralized wage bargaining mechanisms developed in the continental European and Scandinavian countries, Japan's *shuntō* did not narrow wage differentials across firm size (Hiwatari 1999; Milly 1999; Weathers 2003).[11] However, the equalization of wage increase rates across firms and industries provided an important wage increase guideline for unorganized workers in SMEs.

The 1975 *shuntō* was another critical turning point in the context of Japan's wage bargaining and industrial relations (Shimada 1983).[12] In 1974, Japan's nominal wages increased by 29.3 percent, an increase driven by inflation from the first oil crisis in 1973, which imposed intense financial pressures on all Japanese firms.[13] Confronting intense economic distress and inflation, large employers, labor unions (representing the interests of insiders), and the government agreed to make a political compromise at the national level between employment protection, wage restraints, and price stability in the 1975 *shuntō*. In the midst of the first oil crisis, moderate union leaders affiliated with the IMF-JC (Japan Council of the International Metalworkers Federation) played a more central role in leading the spring offensive, replacing the political leadership of Sōhyō, whose organization was dominated by radical and militant public-sector labor unions. In particular, large enterprise unions in leading export-oriented private firms, concerned more about the long-term international competitiveness of their companies than their short-term economic gains, were willing to make political concessions to Nikkeiren (Japanese Federation of Employers' Associations) and the government by restraining wage increase demands in exchange for employment protection and an anti-inflation macroeconomic policy (Gao 2001, 226–230; Kume 1998, 164–173).[14] Within the business community, eight leading firms playing the role of pattern-setters in *shuntō*—Nippon Steel and NKK (steel), Toyota and Nissan (automobiles), Mitsubishi Heavy Industries and Ishikawajima-Harima (shipbuilding and engineering), and Toshiba and Hitachi (electronics)—also established an informal meeting of personnel managers for the purposes of information sharing and wage coordination in 1976 (Weathers 1999, 965; Weathers 2003, 124). In Japan, no formal tripartite system was established, but Sanrōkon (Roundtable Conference on Industry and Labor) functioned as a de facto tripartite forum where business, organized labor, and government discussed various labor and economic policies, particularly during the mid-1970s (Kume 1998; A. Suzuki 2004).[15]

Japan's cooperative industrial relations, based on political compromise between job security for insiders and wage restraints for employers, became institutionalized immediately following the first oil crisis in 1973. The two oil crises of the 1970s led large enterprise unions, particularly those in export-oriented private sectors, to abandon politically confrontational stances toward employers and opt for more cooperative strategies at the firm level (Tsujinaka 1993). After peaking in 1974, the number of labor strikes dramatically subsided in the second half of the 1970s as illustrated in figure 3.1. In addition, the union leadership of

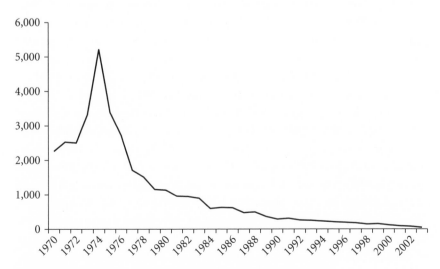

**FIGURE 3.1**  Number of labor disputes in Japan, 1970–2003
*Source:* International Labor Organization, labor statistics (http://laborsta.ilo.org/).

labor movements at the national level gradually came out of the export-oriented private sector rather than the public sector, in conjunction with the privatization of major public enterprises, such as the Japan National Railway and Nippon Telegraph and Telephone, during the late 1970s and early 1980s (Mochizuki 1993). The dominance of moderate export-oriented private-sector unions, most of which cared more about their firms' competitiveness and profitability in the domestic and international markets than short-term economic benefits, accelerated cooperative political attitudes of labor toward business and government.

## Japan: Occupationally Segmented Social Protection Programs

During the 1950s and 1960s, Japan established its core institutional pillars of various social protection programs. In 1961, Japan made its old-age public pension program universal by extending coverage from civil servants and workers in large firms to all citizens, including SME workers, farmers, and the self-employed. However, the old-age pension program, occupationally segmented along the lines of employment status and firm size, structured economic disparity between insiders and outsiders from the beginning. Such institutional features of the pension program allowed large firms and their regular workers to opt out of the Employees' Pension Insurance and to establish the Employees' Pension Fund with tax benefits so as to avoid sharing the risk pool with high-risk pension subscribers (e.g., SME and non-regular workers) (Estévez-Abe 2008, 173–176). In 1973, Prime Minister Tanaka Kakuei announced "the first year of welfare" (*fukushi gannen*) by emphasizing the rapid expansion of Japan's welfare state. During the first oil crisis, however, the Japanese government had to retreat from its policy stance on the expansion of state-funded welfare programs, putting the focus instead on the role of community, family, and corporation as primary welfare providers during the late 1970s and 1980s and proposing the concept of the "Japanese model of the welfare system" (Kasza 2006, 58).

Although Japan introduced the Unemployment Insurance Program for firms with more than five regular workers in 1947, focusing on passive labor market policies (e.g., unemployment benefits for workers during the period of six months), unemployment was not a primary policy concern for the government during the 1950s and the 1960s because of Japan's rapid economic growth and consequent labor shortage, especially in SMEs (Estévez-Abe 2008, 107; Milly 1999, 106–111).[16] It was only after the first oil crisis in 1973 that Japan reformed the Unemployment Insurance Program to become the Employment Insurance Program in 1974, in order to respond to the rise of unemployment during economic downturns and the necessity of industrial restructuring in the Japanese economy.

In contrast to the previous focus on passive policy measures for unemployment, the Employment Insurance Program introduced several active labor market policies, which would subsidize employers to provide re-skilling and alternative employment opportunities for regular workers (Estévez-Abe 2008, 161; Milly 1999, 18). Still, Japan's policy makers prioritized the maintenance of full employment as a primary social safety net for workers. In making a political effort to keep regular workers on the job even in economically inefficient sectors as well as during economic downturns, policy makers actively implemented a wide range of policy supports in order to prevent massive unemployment.

Employment and wage subsidies as well as public works projects served as complements to the underdeveloped social protection programs and the small public-sector employment in the Japanese labor market (Estévez Abe 2008, 30–50). During the mid-1970s, the government introduced a series of policy measures to prevent unemployment by legislating the Employment Stability Fund (1976) and the Special Emergency Measure for Promoting Employment for Old-Aged Workers (1976) (Matsubuchi 2005, 21). In addition, labor market programs for the declining and depressed industries—e.g., the Special Emergency Law for the Coal Mining Industry (1959), the Depressed Industry Subsidy Program (1961), and the Special Emergency Law for Workers in the Depressed Industrial Sector (1977)—served to absorb the costs of economic adjustments to workers by offering financial support for these sectors (Matsubuchi 2005, 17). As another mechanism for social protection, the government extensively and strategically utilized public works projects.[17] By allocating massive public works projects, Japan's policy makers provided workers and firms with more jobs and business opportunities in economically depressed regions and rural areas (Estévez-Abe 2008; G. Park 2011). As Kasza points out, Japan's construction industry was one of the largest employers in the labor market, hiring approximately 10 percent of the Japanese workforce, and almost 40 percent of investment in the construction sector came from the government's public works projects in the postwar period (Kasza 2006, 101). Despite the underdevelopment of state-funded social welfare programs compared with other CMEs, an intricate web of social protection in the Japanese political economy effectively shielded workers from the vagaries of the market in the postwar period.

## Korea: Imposed Employment Protection and Repressive Industrial Relations

With the goal of transforming poverty-stricken Korea into a second Japan within a generation, the Park Chung Hee regime (hereafter "the Park regime"), which had come to power through a military coup in 1961, imposed the Japanese model of capitalism on the Korean political economy. Following Japan's state-led developmental strategy, the Park regime organized the Economic Planning Board (EPB) as a pilot agency of state-led development (à la the Japanese Ministry of International Trade and Industry), nationalized the commercial banking sector in order to control financial resource allocation for industrialization, and contributed to the creation of the chaebŏl by concentrating economic resources into a few politically selected large firms (B-K. Kim 2002).[18]

The labor market was considered the secondary market institution to support Korea's export-oriented growth model. The Park regime depoliticized the working class by severely restricting workers' basic rights (e.g., prohibiting unions' political participation and restricting strikes and collective bargaining) and implemented a repressive labor control policy in order to preempt any labor unrest that might disturb the state-led developmental strategy (Jang-jip Choi 1997; Koo 2001; Y. Lee 2009). Simultaneously, the authoritarian Park regime played a pivotal role in establishing the institutional arrangements of the labor market by consciously emulating the Japanese model. Contrary to its Japanese counterpart, however, there was no implicit or explicit political consensus between employers, workers, and policy makers. It was the authoritarian government that designed and imposed a set of labor market institutions on business and labor during the period of high-speed growth.[19]

The Park regime imposed a political exchange for job security and wage restraints on business and labor in order to preempt the possibility of industrial disputes over unemployment and distributional conflicts, which were regarded as detrimental to Korea's export-oriented growth model. But employment protection for workers was only ensured in exchange for wage restraints dictated by the authoritarian government (see the following section for details).[20] The Park regime made an explicit political commitment to employment protection for workers by prohibiting layoffs without "justifiable" cause in the Labor Standards Law, and it also funneled massive financial resources to chaebŏl in order to expand their businesses and create more jobs, even during serious economic downturns. Under authoritarian rule with repressive labor control, the legal clause might not be sufficiently secure to guarantee employment protection for workers; nevertheless, employment protection was one of the Park regime's most important policy tasks because massive unemployment could lead to serious political and social unrest, possibly triggering the collapse of the regime itself.

Despite these political efforts, the boom-and-bust nature of Korea's economic cycle exposed workers to high economic uncertainty and vulnerability since its economy was highly linked with the fluctuations of the business cycle in the global market. The only feasible policy option to sustain employment protection for workers was to carry on rapid economic growth and keep firms alive even in financial distress, regardless of any political and economic costs to the society.[21] Therefore, when the first oil crisis severely hit the Korean economy in 1973, the Park regime utilized an immense Heavy and Chemical Industrialization (HCI) drive to bail out ailing large firms and to generate more employment opportunities for workers by diversifying investments, rather than subscribing to a conservative monetary policy (Haggard 1994, 23–30; B-K. Kim 2002, 5–6; Woo 1991, 106–111).[22] During the recession of 1973–1974, the HCI drive encouraged large firms to create more jobs and consequently assisted them in retaining the workforce. According to Sung-jung Kim and Seong (2005, 91), firms with over two hundred workers increased their number of workers by 164,872, while firms with less than fifty workers experienced a total decline of 74,726 employees during this period. This indicates that large Korean firms could provide employment protection for their workers only through the expansion of their businesses.

The viability of labor market model imposed by the Park regime can also be attributed to the multifaceted institutional arrangements of the labor market and industrial relations, which preempted labor unrest and saved the state's need to use coercive measures. In the first place, pro-state and pro-business union leadership (ŏyongnojo) prevented workers from making any political resistance to the state and to firms. A few co-opted leaders at the Federation of Korean Trade Unions (FKTU)—the only national labor federation legally recognized by the authoritarian government—and its affiliated industrial federations collaborated with the Park regime to demolish autonomous and democratic labor movements in return for political and economic incentives, such as political appointment and material compensation for union officials (Bum-sang You 2005, 124–140).[23] Similarly, the state closed its eyes to labor management practices in which employers paid union officials' wages and other union expenses to buy off industrial peace at the firm level, which was finally prohibited as of July 2010 after several rounds of intensive reform debates.[24]

In addition, national security agencies—e.g., the Korean Central Intelligence Agency (KCIA)—as well as the Ministry of Labor (MOL) were extensively engaged in monitoring labor unions in order to thwart any potential industrial disputes. Despite the presence of co-opted union leadership, the KCIA never lost sight of union leaders and labor movements, dispatching its agents to the FKTU to monitor union activities (Bum-sang You 2005, 124–125). The MOL, whose main administrative task was to execute labor control policy to support Park's export-oriented growth strategy, as opposed to protecting and improving workers' rights, also fell under the tight control of the KCIA.[25] The political role of the MOL can be clearly deduced from the fact that between 1963 and 1987 six out of fourteen labor ministers were former security personnel in the military, the National Police Agency, or the Ministry of Home Affairs (see figure 3.2).[26] These effective labor administrative tools enabled the state to competently manage industrial relations without much coercion.

Lastly, organizationally weak and ideologically underdeveloped political parties, with few links to societal interest groups, could not assist workers in claiming political and economic rights. Park's institutional design of the party system strictly confined the ruling Democratic Republican Party to an auxiliary function in policy making, debilitating political incentives and preventing political parties from deepening their links to societal interest groups. Neither did opposition parties have any organizational links to grassroots groups.[27] Although the New Democratic Party (Shinmindang), the major opposition party, supported the 1979 sit-in and hunger strike spearheaded by Y. H. Industry Company's female workers at its party headquarters, there were few efforts on the part of opposition parties to forge political coalitions with societal interest groups (Sun-hyuk Kim 1996, 89–90).

The Chun Doo-hwan regime (1980–1987), which seized power through another military coup after the assassination of President Park, perfected the

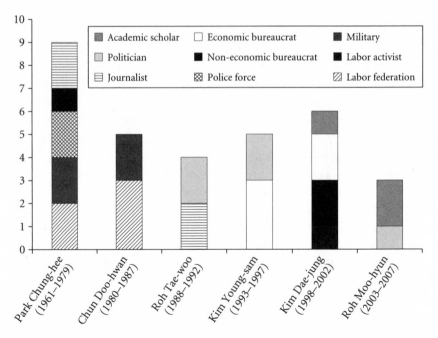

**FIGURE 3.2**  Labor ministers in Korea, 1961–2007

*Source:* B-K. Kim (1994, 196); Korean Ministry of Labor (http://www.molab.go.kr). This figure was originally published in J. Song (2012c, 240, figure 8.1). Copyright © 2012 by the Board of Trustees of the Leland Stanford Junior University. Used with permission by the Board of Trustees.

labor control policies bequeathed by the Park regime. Building upon Park's prohibition on political participation by labor unions, the 1980 revision of the labor laws reinforced the political restrictions on labor unions: a limitation of the number of labor unions to one per workplace; a ban on the intervention of third parties—not only by political parties but also by labor federations—in labor disputes at the firm level; and the abolishment of industrial federations to fortify decentralized enterprise unions (B-K. Kim and Lim 2000, 115–116). The Chun regime completed Park's labor model by legalizing *samkŭm* (three prohibitions on workers' basic rights). During the era of rapid economic growth, the authoritarian state imposed a political exchange between job security and wage restraints on business and labor, but the underdevelopment of political consensus between employers, workers, and policy makers became the primary source of conflict in times of political and economic challenge after democratization.

## Korea: State-led Wage Coordination and Skills Formation System

Although the Park regime emulated the Japanese model of the labor market, it rarely attempted to build a wage-coordination mechanism. Instead it imposed wage restraints on workers. Given the Park regime's political pledge to guarantee employment protection for workers and accomplish rapid growth for future rewards (e.g., deferred wage increases), workers were forced to accept wage increases that fell short of keeping pace with labor productivity growth.[28] The EPB, the control tower of the state-led developmental strategy, dictated a wage-control policy for business and labor by setting an upper limit to wage increases and threatened to revoke the government's financial subsidies to firms that did not comply with this guideline in wage bargaining. In addition, it ordered the MOL to closely monitor wage-bargaining processes and outcomes at the firm level (Liu 2006, 103–104; H-K. Song 1991, 262–266). Yet Korea's rapid economic growth since the mid-1960s delivered substantial real wage increases to workers, although the rates of these increases were lower than those of labor productivity growth, except in the late 1970s (H-K. Song 1993, 81; Tak 1974, 111).

The Park regime's industrial policy, in alliance with a few politically chosen large firms, gave rise to the establishment of the dualism in the labor market between chaebŏl and SMEs. But the authoritarian government intervened in the labor market to artificially equalize the wage levels of chaebŏl workers and SME workers and to suppress wage differentials across firm size. When the Park regime embarked on the HCI drive in 1973, the average wage of workers at firms with ten to twenty-nine employees was 66.4 percent of that of workers at firms with over five hundred employees, but this gap closed dramatically to 91.74 percent by 1979.[29] Without the government's intervention to restrain overly increasing wages in the chaebŏl sector, wage equality across firm size could not have been achieved. The Park regime allowed SME workers market wages while preventing chaebŏl workers from exerting their organizational capacities to raise their wages even higher.

In contrast to the trend of decreasing wage differentials across firm size, wage inequality across different industrial sectors remained large. In a comparison of firms with over five hundred employees in the labor-intensive garment industry and the skill-intensive industrial chemical industry, workers in the former sector, where unskilled female workers comprised a disproportionate number of the labor force, received on average only 42.8 percent of the wages of workers in the latter industry, which was composed of a majority of skilled male workers during the late 1970s.[30] This meant that in spite of the Park regime's political intervention in the labor market, a labor shortage heightened wage levels in heavy and chemical industries, where chaebŏl aggressively diversified their investments with the political and financial support of the government.

The authoritarian state was also in charge of educating and training low-skilled and semi-skilled workers and intervened in the institutionalization of skills training systems in order to secure the stable supply of the skilled workforce for its state-led HCI drive (Jeong 2002, 28–29, 211–212; Yang 2004). Emulating the German vocational training system, the Korean government established skills training systems targeting SMEs during the 1970s and 1980s, but SME employers regarded young trainees only as a cheap labor force (Jeong 2002, 193). Chaebŏl confronted the similar problem of the shortage of skilled workers. Beginning in the early 1970s, chaebŏl vigorously integrated and diversified businesses into heavy and chemical industries, transforming themselves into large business conglomerates with dozens of associated and subsidiary companies. The labor shortage, deriving from the HCI drive launched in 1973, created serious difficulties in recruiting and retaining skilled workers in the chaebŏl. Unlike large Japanese firms that made long-term mutual commitments to the founding of firm-based training systems, chaebŏl failed to solve collective action problems in institutionalizing firm-based or industry-based training systems, resorting to poaching skilled workers from other chaebŏl. Korea's two business associations—the Federation of Korean Industries (FKI) and the Korean Employers' Federation (KEF)—did not have the political and organizational capacities to coordinate their member firms over this issue (S. Kim 1983; Sung-jung Kim and Seong 2005).[31] The lack of politically competent business associations complicated the problems of high labor turnover rates and the underdevelopment of firm-based skills training systems even in the chaebŏl sector, which contributed to employers' weak commitments to job security for their regular workers in economic downturns because of their low investments in these workers.

Given incompetent business associations and chaebŏl caught with collective action problems in institutionalizing skills training systems at the firm or industry levels, the Park regime once again took the initiative in promoting the Japanese model of firm-based training systems. It enacted the National Skills Training Legislation in 1974, which required large chaebŏl firms to establish in-house training systems for the stable supply of the skilled workforce, yet it did not effectively stop chaebŏl from poaching workers from other chaebŏl. The state's initiative and involvement in the labor supply alleviated firms' burden of educating and training workers in the short run, but it removed their economic incentives to invest in skills training systems in the long run. In Korea, even large chaebŏl did not institutionalize firm-based training systems until the mid-1980s, indicating the underdevelopment of firm-based training systems and weak economic incentives for business to retain a surplus of the regular workforce during economic downturns. They were dependent upon external labor markets to hire workers if necessary, as opposed to the establishment of internal labor markets to train and retain skilled workers (H-K. Song 1991).

## Korea: Underdeveloped Social Protection Programs

During the 1960s and 1970s, social protection did not draw much attention in Korea because of its stage of late economic development. There was no universal coverage for health insurance and pension programs, except for a few occupationally targeted social protection programs for the core constituencies of the authoritarian regime. Korea introduced the old-age pension program for civil servants and the military in 1960 and 1963, respectively (P. H. Kim 2009, 187; Klassen and Yang 2010, 6).[32] In the early 1970s, Korea's policy makers attempted to expand the old-age national pension program to cover all citizens, not only to gain political legitimacy, but also to mobilize financial resources for the state-led HCI project. Yet the economic recession immediately following the first oil crisis postponed the introduction of the pension program for more than a decade until the Roh Tae-woo government (1988–1992) launched the program for firms with more than ten employees in 1988.[33] Although social welfare bureaucrats underscored the necessity of the Employment Insurance Program, more powerful economic bureaucrats in policy making, prioritizing economic growth over social welfare programs, blocked policy debates on the introduction of the program by arguing that Korea was not ready to provide unemployment benefits for workers, considering its low level of economic development (P. H. Kim 2009, 196). Except for the National Health Insurance Program for firms with more than five hundred workers, there were no social protection programs for workers.[34] Unlike Japan, where politicians were very keen on social welfare programs in the context of political support and electoral competition, Korea, under the control of the authoritarian regime, did not provide strong incentives for politicians and political parties to broaden social safety nets in order to appeal to voters.

Instead the authoritarian state transferred the responsibility of providing social welfare benefits primarily to private sectors, especially large firms, emulating Japan (P. H. Kim 2009 and 2010; Sung-jung Kim and Seong 2005; H-K. Song 2003; H-K. Song and Hong 2006). By legislating the retirement allowance system, workers (mostly white-collar regular workers in large firms) were able to receive lump-sum retirement cash benefits to prepare for post-retirement. The coverage of the retirement allowance program expanded from 5 percent to 24.3 percent of the economically active population between 1966 and 1985 (P. H. Kim 2009, 188).[35] Except for a very small group of workers in large firms as well as the core constituencies of the authoritarian regime (e.g., military and civil servants), a majority of the Korean population was excluded from social protection programs during the period of rapid economic growth in the 1960s and 1970s.

## Japan and Korea Compared

During the period of high-speed growth, Japan and Korea established similar institutional configurations of the labor market and social protections, but they diverged in the political mechanism of developing these institutional pillars. First, Japan and Korea institutionalized relatively strong employment protection systems for regular workers, although the origins and development of the system remarkably differed in the two countries. In Japan, the institutionalization of employment protection was formulated and consolidated on the basis of mutual commitments between employers and regular workers (or insiders) as a consequence of a political exchange between employment protection for regular workers and wage restraints and managerial authority over labor practices for employers. In addition, the government's public policies, ranging from employment and wage subsidies and public works projects to case laws restricting the dismissal of regular workers, buttressed the principle of job security for insiders in the Japanese labor market.

By contrast, in Korea, it was the authoritarian government that stipulated the Labor Standards Law to prevent massive unemployment and channeled immense financial resources to large firms in severe economic distress.

Neither employers nor workers were engaged in establishing the institutional foundations of the employment protection system in the labor market. Although large Korean employers started to develop internal labor markets for white-collar clerical workers, they rarely focused on the institutionalization of internal labor markets for blue-collar production workers until the mid-1980s (Hwang 2006; E. Jung and Cheon 2006; H-K. Song 1991). Korea's employment protection at the firm level, exemplified by the permanent employment system, was not as deeply rooted in the labor market as its Japanese counterpart, or at an inchoate stage of institutional development at best. These differences in the institutional configurations of employment protection affected the diverging political patterns of labor market reform, as will be discussed in chapters 4 and 5.

Second, although the locus of wage settlement was at the firm level in both the Japanese and Korean labor markets, the two countries differed in terms of the development of wage coordination. In Japan, large employers and their enterprise unions in leading export-oriented private sectors established an intra- and inter-industry wage-coordination mechanism over the entire economy, *shuntō* (or spring offensive). Despite the lack of centralized political authority of business associations and labor federations in wage bargaining, an informal wage-coordination mechanism between business and labor as well as within each group affected wage bargaining across firms and industries (Kume 1998, 49–72). By contrast, under an authoritarian regime with a repressive labor control policy, neither large Korean employers nor workers had the economic incentives or political capacity to establish a wage-coordination mechanism to encompass the entire economy, which would have required them to pay the political and economic costs to institutionalize one. Instead, the authoritarian state imposed a guideline of wage increases on employers and workers, although the state itself was not that effective in restraining the consequences of market forces on wage increases driven by labor shortage (H-K. Song 1991, 245–291). As discussed in chapter 1, the underdevelopment of wage coordination in the Korean labor market further accelerated the widening of wage differentials across firm size after the late 1980s (see figure 1.6). Yet in the face of the downward pressure of decentralized wage bargaining at the firm level, Japan, with the institutional arrangement of wage coordination across firms and industries, was also not able to avoid the increasing wage differentials across firm size after the 1990s.

Third, Japan and Korea shared similarities in terms of the institutional features of social protection. Both countries rarely focused on the development of a large welfare state, contrary to other CMEs. Eligibility for state-funded social protections was closely tied to employment status and occupation in the two countries, which caused widening economic disparity between insiders and outsiders in the process of recent labor market and social protection reforms. In the case of Japan, the underdeveloped state-funded social protections were extensively complemented by various social and economic regulations to prevent layoffs of regular workers in economic downturns as well as the government's public policies to absorb the costs of labor adjustment, such as employment and wage subsidy programs and public works projects. Meanwhile, Korea's policy makers did not focus on expanding social protection for workers. Considering the level of its economic development during the 1960s and 1970s, Korea prioritized its limited financial resources for economic development, not for social protection. Additionally, the authoritarian rule did not provide strong political incentives for politicians and political parties to develop generous social protection programs for workers or the general public.

Japan and Korea developed many similar institutional configurations of their labor markets and social protections, such as strong employment protection, decentralized industrial relations, and small welfare states; as a result, the existing literature places these two countries in the same category. However, subtle but important discrepancies in the process of establishing and maintaining these institutional arrangements of the labor market, represented by the different characteristics of employment protection systems and the development (or underdevelopment) of wage coordination mechanisms, affected the diverging political pathways of labor market reform in the two countries over the past two decades.

* * *

This chapter has elaborated the ways in which a set of labor market institutions and social protection programs were established and developed in Japan and Korea during the period of industrialization. The similarities and differences of the political dynamics in developing these institutional features affected the process and outcome of recent labor market reform in the two countries. In the case of Japan, permanent employment practices, which evolved as the consequence of a political compromise between employers, regular workers, and policy makers, consolidated a high level of employment protection at the firm and national levels in the postwar period. While *shuntō*, led by leading export-oriented private firms, played an important role in coordinating wage bargaining over the Japanese economy, its decentralized industrial relations, based on large enterprise unions, and social protections closely tied to employment status and occupation formed a dualistic labor market along the lines of firm size and employment status. Nonetheless, its sustainable economic growth, lasting until the late 1980s, did not aggravate the serious problems of inequality and dualism in the Japanese labor market.

In Korea, the authoritarian government emulated the Japanese model of the labor market without looking for political consensus between employers and workers over these institutional configurations. These political processes of institutional development substantially weakened employers' commitments to job security even for insiders at the firm level. Like Japan, Korea's large firm-centered industrial policies as well as a small welfare state, with benefits linked with employment status and occupation, structured the dualistic labor market and social protection system. Nevertheless, the authoritarian state artificially pre-empted the rise of inequality and dualism through interventionist policies in the Korean labor market.

Over the past two decades, the institutional arrangements of the labor market and social protections have been under intense strain driven by a series of political and economic challenges in the two countries. In Japan, the collapse of the bubble economy has caused a protracted recession since the early 1990s, leading to a series of bank runs and corporate bankruptcies as well as soaring unemployment rates. In the face of intense economic distress in the domestic market, a large number of manufacturing firms continued to increase offshore production and global outsourcing, while reducing the weight of domestic production (Schoppa 2006). The breakdown of the LDP-dominant political system in 1993 began to destabilize a set of political institutions involved in policy making. In the labor market and social protections, the mechanism of informal wage coordination gradually lost its power in wage bargaining, and thus wage differentials along the lines of employment status and firm size increased more rapidly. Japanese firms increasingly adopted performance-based wage systems in order to reduce the pressure of a seniority-based wage system combined with an aging workforce, and they retrenched their spending on various benefits programs. Similarly, Korea had to respond to the consequences of political democratization and the financial crisis and their influences on its political economy. The 1987 democratic transition began to break down the state-imposed institutional configurations of the labor market, leaving business, labor, and the government with the arduous task of finding an alternative model of the labor market, and the 1997 Asian financial crisis exposed the Korean market economy to a much higher degree of economic vulnerability to changes in the global market. Under these political and economic circumstances, Japanese and Korean governments over the past two decades have initiated a series of labor market reforms to resuscitate sluggish economies, to alleviate the burden of firms' financial distress, and to create more jobs. The following two chapters demonstrate the empirical evidence to support my analytical framework—the effects of the institutional arrangements of the labor market on the politics of reform—presented in chapter 2, using data drawn from Japan and Korea.

# JAPAN: LIBERALIZATION FOR OUTSIDERS, PROTECTION FOR INSIDERS

The 1990s were a critical turning point for Japan, a country whose economic system was centered on the nonmarket-based strategic coordination of capitalism.[1] After the bursting of the asset bubble in the early 1990s, the Japanese economy plunged into a protracted recession and its state-led developmental strategy combined with nonmarket-based strategic coordination, long seen as the model of Japan's postwar economic "miracle," turned out to be problem-ridden. In addition, the collapse of the conservative political system in 1993, dominated by the Liberal Democratic Party (LDP), which had ruled Japan since 1955, heightened political uncertainty in elections. Although the LDP was able to regain power within less than a year, it had to seek coalitions with small parties in order to form a ruling bloc and ensure a legislative majority in the Diet.[2] These political and economic challenges have imposed severe pressure on the stability of the Japanese model of capitalism over the following two decades.[3]

To resuscitate the country's faltering economy, Japan's policy makers promoted a series of reforms, including labor market reform, financial reform, corporate reform, and fiscal reform (Amyx 2004; Aoki, Jackson, and Miyajima 2007; Gourevitch and Shinn 2005; Schaede 2006 and 2008; Schoppa 2006; Tiberghien 2007; Vogel 2006). Among these, labor market reform in particular offers a very intriguing empirical case. First, despite its economic quagmire over the past two decades, Japan did not initiate across-the-board labor market reform meant to transform its rigid labor institutions into a neoliberal model represented by easy hiring and firing practices. While Japan adopted labor market liberalization for non-regular workers, it maintained (and even reinforced) its high level of employment protection for regular workers. Second, contrary to the beliefs about Japan's postwar egalitarian and middle-class society (*ichioku sōchūryū shakai*), its labor market reform deepened inequality and dualism along the lines of employment status (e.g., regular workers versus non-regular workers) and firm size (e.g., large firms versus SMEs). Last, all these processes and outcomes of reform did not provoke any serious political confrontations between business, labor, and government, unlike reform in Korea (as will be elaborated in chapter 5). This chapter explains the ways in which the institutional features of the Japanese labor market—the institutionalized practices of employment protection covering a large proportion of the workforce and the configurations of decentralized industrial relations—affected selective labor market reform for outsiders and increasing labor market inequality and dualism between insiders and outsiders over the past two decades.

I begin with a series of institutional changes in the Japanese model of capitalism and the consequences of these changes on the labor market, and I elaborate how Japan's labor market institutions adjusted to economic distress and changing business environments during the 1990s and 2000s. The second section below lays out the positions of business associations and organized labor on labor market reform and labor adjustment strategies. It describes the similarities and differences of policy positions on labor market reform across business and labor as well as within each group across different industrial sectors, focusing in particular on the automobile, electronics, and steel industries. The third section examines in detail the political procedures of Japan's labor market reform by closely analyzing episodes of reform of employment contracts, working conditions and hours, and social protections. It elaborates the political interactions between societal interest groups, bureaucrats, and politicians and political parties, whose interests and strategies for reform were shaped by the existing institutional arrangements of employment protection systems and industrial relations. Although the key factor in labor market reform is the interaction of employment protection systems and decentralized industrial relations, this section also takes into account the effects of recent political changes (e.g., the centralized policy-making authority, coalition governments, and the divided control of the Diet) on Japan's reform. Finally, I summarize the empirical findings and provide implications for the future of Japan's labor market.

## Institutional Changes and Continuities in the Japanese Model of Capitalism

Japan has been classified as one of the primary examples of coordinated market economies (CMEs), composed of the interdependent institutional pillars of debt financing, stable inter-firm relations, cooperative industrial relations and wage moderation, and specific skills-based training systems (Aoki 2001; Gourevitch and Shinn 2005; Hall and Gingrich 2004; Hall and Soskice 2001; Soskice 1990 and 1999; Streeck and Yamamura 2001; Yamamura and Streeck 2003). But Japan's decade-long economic recession has challenged the institutional arrangements of its CME, if not completely dismantled them.[4]

As presented in figure 4.1, the ratios of stable shareholdings and cross shareholdings in the stock market held by the financial institutions and other affiliated firms, which had ensured long-term business strategies by shielding Japanese firms from hostile takeovers and short-term profit seeking, have drastically declined since the mid-1990s. In particular, when Japan's banking sector confronted the swelling amount of non-performing loans driven by a series of corporate bankruptcies in the late 1990s and early 2000s, it was under intense pressure to improve the soundness of its financial status and increase its prime capital ratios by selling off the shares of stable shareholdings and cross shareholdings for large Japanese firms.[5] The traditional boundary of the *keiretsu* (loose grouping of large business conglomerates) was also blurred because of firms' cooperation and transactions across different *keiretsu* as well as business reorganization (Schaede 2006 and 2008). The 1997 lifting of the legal ban on holding companies, which had been imposed by the Supreme Command of the Allied Powers (SCAP)

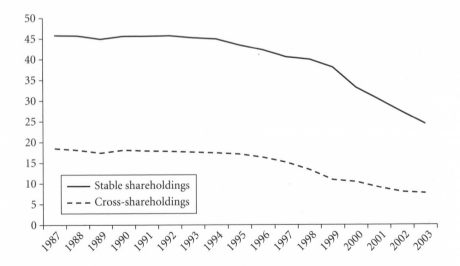

**FIGURE 4.1**  Share of stable shareholdings and cross shareholdings in the Japanese stock market, 1987–2003
*Source*: Nissei Kiso Kenkyūsho [Japan Life Insurance Basic Research Institute], http://www.nli-research.co.jp, accessed November 15, 2007.

in order to break up *zaibatsu* (family-owned large business conglomerates in prewar Japan), allowed large Japanese firms to create a new form of corporate governance and corporate grouping in response to new business environments. The revisions of the Commercial Code and accounting standards were proposed to facilitate corporate restructuring during economic downturns as well.[6]

All these institutional changes in the financial system and corporate governance had important consequences for the institutional configurations of Japan's labor market by weakening the long-standing protections for Japanese firms as well as pressuring firms to focus more on shareholder value and short-term economic profits than on stakeholders' interests and long-term business transactions. The drastic decline of such institutional protections, which had enabled Japanese employers to weather the severe pressure of massive downsizing and corporate restructuring even during economic downturns, posed a severe strain on the institutional stability of the labor market, making it more difficult to retain the workforce (Tiberghien 2007).

*Shuntō*, an informal intra- and inter-industry wage-coordination mechanism led by large firms in leading export-oriented private sectors, underwent significant institutional changes in the face of the mounting pressures of economic distress and intensified global market competition. The decentralizing pressure of wage bargaining in economic distress began to weaken the role of *shuntō* as a wage-coordination mechanism; this phenomenon has been particularly noticeable in the private railway and steel industries since the early 1990s (*Nikkeiren Times*, various issues). Except for a few large competitive firms in leading export-oriented private sectors, most Japanese firms and industries confronted intense financial distress after the collapse of the bubble economy. While Nikkeiren (Japanese Federation of Employers' Association) and Rengō (Japanese Trade Union Confederation) have continued to participate in *shuntō* for wage bargaining over the past two decades, wage increase rate differentials across firm size have gradually enlarged since the mid-1990s because most SMEs have been unable to follow the guidelines for wage increases implicitly set by large firms in the export-oriented sectors.[7] Nakamura Keisuke, a leading scholar on Japan's industrial relations, asserts that the primary function of *shuntō* as wage-coordination mechanism almost disappeared over the course of the late 1990s and 2000s because large firms were no longer able to play the role of "pattern setters" in wage bargaining on behalf of SMEs and sheltered industries.[8] Even large enterprise unions representing the interests of insiders were pressured to accept a trade-off between job security and wage restraints during the protracted economic recession. An increase in hiring cheap non-regular workers (outsiders), driven by labor market reform, further weakened the bargaining leverage of regular workers and unions because of the alternative employment option for employers.[9]

Confronting intense financial strains due to rising labor costs driven by a rapidly aging labor force under the structure of seniority-based wages, large firms competitively introduced performance-based wage systems or a combination of performance and seniority-based wages in order to offset the pressure of increasing labor costs (Thelen and Kume 2003).[10] Various benefits, ranging from housing subsidies and medical cost subsidies to education subsidies for employees' children, were also retrenched or restructured in order to reduce employers' financial burdens under the pressures of economic distress. These programs had provided crucial social protections for workers to complement the small state-funded welfare program in Japan. Since the late 1990s, the ratio of non-mandatory welfare benefits to salary has gradually declined, and a majority of firms have decided to outsource their firm-based welfare services or to revamp their own benefits programs (Murasugi 2010; Nishikubo 2010).

Despite all these important institutional changes in the national political economy and labor market, Japan maintained the key tenets of employment protection for insiders (e.g., full-time permanent workers) at the firm and national levels, although its recession imposed severe strain on the institutional stability of job security for insiders. Japan extensively liberalized the labor market for outsiders (e.g., part-time, temporary, and fixed-term contract workers) as a primary policy tool to enhance labor market flexibility in economic distress. Meanwhile, employment protection for insiders—in particular, male regular workers in large firms—remained relatively intact amid a series of labor market reforms over the 1990s and 2000s.[11] Such reform measures combined with decentralized industrial relations enlarged the insider-outsider differences in the Japanese labor market in terms of job security, wages, and social protections. Before analyzing the political processes and outcomes of reform at the national level, the following section will examine the positions of business and labor on labor market reform and labor adjustment strategies under the constraints of the institutionalized practices of employment protection and decentralized industrial relations based on large enterprise unions.

## Positions of Business and Labor on Labor Market Reform and Labor Adjustment

Japan's decade-long recession pressured both employers and workers to find an alternative way to adjust to rapidly changing economic conditions. This section examines the positions of business associations and labor unions on labor market reform and labor adjustment strategies across class and industrial sector, and the effects of such policy stances on reform politics. In particular, it elaborates the ways in which Japanese businesses and organized labor shared similar preferences for the liberalization of the labor market for outsiders with persistent protection for insiders, and focused on the development of economic compensation at the firm level in the process of implementing labor adjustments.

As will be further elaborated, under the constraints of institutionalized practices of employment protection for regular workers as a majority of the workforce, Japan's business associations and employers were reluctant to propose comprehensive labor market reform for regular workers, since they were concerned about the opposition of regular workers as privileged insiders as well as policy makers worrying about political backlash. In addition, they preferred to keep the benefits of cooperative industrial relations and firm-specific skills training systems, centered on the institutional arrangement of employment protection for insiders, which further restricted the available range of reform options for greater labor market flexibility. Meanwhile, organized labor, which was forced to accept labor market reform for greater flexibility during economic downturns, decided to transfer the costs of reform to outsiders in exchange for keeping insiders' privileges intact. Yet Japan's decentralized industrial relations, based on large enterprise unions, accelerated the rapid increase in labor market inequality and dualism between insiders and outsiders since neither business nor labor had any political and economic incentives to develop social protections as a mechanism of compensation for those affected by labor market reform at the national level.

## Business Community's Positions on Labor Market Reform and Labor Adjustment

Soskice (1990 and 1999) identifies Japan as a CME on the basis of employers' ability to orchestrate wage coordination despite its decentralized industrial relations. However, Japan's business associations substantially lacked the political authority to monitor and punish its member firms and affiliated industrial associations compared with their counterparts in other CMEs. Nippon-Keidanren (Japanese Business Federation), the largest and the most influential business association, is composed of both globally competitive and protection-dependent firms, and such a heterogeneous structure of organizational membership has made it difficult for Nippon-Keidanren to propose coherent policy proposals to the government on behalf of the business community.[12] If its members cannot come to an agreement on certain policy proposals, Nippon-Keidanren simply removes controversial policy agendas from the bargaining table or, at best, submits a very broad outline of proposals to the government.[13] Regarding this problem of interest aggregation within the business community, Vogel (1999) and Pempel (1998 and 1999) point out that no leading interest group has emerged to advocate for

Japan's bold economic reform because firms themselves are closely interlinked across various industrial sectors.

In the context of labor market reform, Japanese employers and business associations advocated the increase in labor market flexibility under adverse economic conditions and intense global market competition, but they diverged in policy preferences and priorities for reform. Nikkeiren, which merged into Nippon-Keidanren in May 2002, served as the political representative of the business community in labor policy making in postwar Japan.[14] Since the early 1990s, it has insisted that it is essential to increase labor market flexibility in order to enable Japanese firms to survive under the pressure of intense global competition, rapid technological transformations, and new business environments (*Nikkeiren Times,* various issues). Its policy stance gained momentum in the business community when Nikkeiren published its position paper on Japan's employment system in 1995. The position paper officially announced that management's strong commitment to employment protection for workers (i.e., the permanent employment system) would be restricted to "core" regular workers, and that management would expand the hiring of professionals and non-regular workers (e.g., part-time, temporary, and fixed-term contract workers) for greater flexibility in rapidly changing business conditions (Japanese Federation of Employers' Association [Nikkeiren] 1995).[15] Although an increase in the hiring of non-regular workers during an economic slowdown was not a new strategy in Japan (as described in chapter 3), what Nikkeiren explicitly signaled was that Japanese employers would institutionalize a secondary labor market (or external labor market) composed of non-regular workers excluded from permanent employment practices, which departed from the Japanese model of the labor market. In addition, by claiming that Japanese firms had no other choice but to move production facilities overseas if they could not control increasing labor costs, Nikkeiren emphasized the necessity of wage restraints, of the introduction and expansion of a performance-based wage system, and of managerial rights in the flexible allocation of work hours (*Nikkeiren Times,* various issues).

The pressure of labor market liberalization was far more intense from SME employers. Nihon Shōkō Kaigisho (Japanese Chamber of Commerce and Industry), representing the interests of SMEs concentrating in the domestic market, attempted to block any deregulation policy that would bring forth intense market competition by eliminating protective measures for SMEs (Pempel 2006, 54).[16] Meanwhile, it forcefully demanded that the government remove all legal restrictions on hiring dispatched workers, employed on short-term contracts and through private employment agencies, in order to increase greater flexibility and to curtail labor costs for SMEs (Imai 2006; Miura 2002b).

Another important business association, Keizai Dōyūkai (Japanese Association of Economic Executives), whose charter limited its membership to "progressive" (namely, market-oriented) individual businessmen, supported the dramatic transformation of the Japanese model of capitalism into a neoliberal one, including the change in labor management practices.[17] Because members of Keizai Dōyūkai, such as Shiina Takeo and Miyauchi Yoshihiko, joined various government committees to discuss market-oriented economic reform agendas (e.g., the Deregulation Committee), Keizai Dōyūkai was regarded as the spearhead of Japan's market-oriented reform (Noble 2006). Nevertheless, Keizai Dōyūkai's view on Japan's market-oriented reform was considered too progressive even for the Japanese business community, and thus its influence on policy outcomes was more limited than expected.

Not all Japanese employers wanted to make strong commitments to the high level of employment protection for insiders as they had done in the past. At the firm and industrial levels, employers' positions on labor market reform were further divided along the dimensions of market profitability and the positions of their firms and industrial sectors in the product market. High-performing firms and industries (e.g., the automobile sector) preferred to benefit from the advantages of the Japanese model of the labor market, represented by strong employment protection for insiders, firm-based skills training systems, and cooperative industrial relations. In particular, firm-specific skills—positive externalities of strong employment protection—were one of the primary sources of market competition for leading Japanese firms in the global market, since these skills allowed employers to develop incremental technological innovation (Hall and Soskice 2001; Estévez-Abe, Iversen, and Soskice 2001). Thus, Japanese employers focused on keeping regular workers' morale and loyalty high by avoiding labor adjustment strategies for these workers, even if they needed to foot the bill to retain them (Koike 1981; Miura 2002b). By contrast, low-performing firms and industries under the intense strain of financial distress during Japan's decade-long recession complained about the mounting problem of a surplus of the regular workforce and rising labor costs linked to the seniority-based wage system and an aging workforce. Nevertheless, Nikkeiren (and other business associations) rarely challenged employment protection for insiders in reform politics.[18]

In Japan, it was a group of employers in high-performing firms and industries (especially those in leading export-oriented sectors) who actively participated in a wide array of labor policy making on behalf of the business community. Thus, the political position of the business community was much closer to the preferences and interests of large-sized firms in leading export-oriented sectors rather than those of SMEs in sheltered industrial sectors. Since they greatly benefited from the institutionalized practices of employment protection for insiders in the context of production and investment strategies (e.g., incremental technological innovations and firm-specific skills), these employers preferred to maintain the core institutional element of the employment protection system, even if they also acknowledged the problems of the labor market rigidity.

Japan's powerful business leaders, such as the then-president of the Nippon-Keidanren and former CEO of Toyota Motor Corporation, Okuda Hiroshi, strongly advocated the maintenance of the traditional model of the Japanese management, including employers' strong commitment to employment protection for insiders (Miura 2002b). Unless these employers consented to the relaxation of employment protection for insiders, it would not be easy for the Japanese business community to pressure the government to advance comprehensive labor market reform for all workers. In addition, given policy makers' strong support for the persistence of employment protection for insiders as a majority of the workforce (especially male regular workers in large firms), Japan's employers seemed to focus more on labor market reform for outsiders as feasible.

Thus, notwithstanding the severe pressure on the institutional arrangements of the labor market over the past two decades, the Japanese business community insisted on continued employment protection for insiders, while prioritizing labor market liberalization for outsiders for greater flexibility during economic downturns. It attempted to secure the benefits of the existing system of employment protection (e.g., skills training systems and stable industrial relations) and to maximize the usage of alternative labor adjustment mechanisms (e.g., flexible working conditions and hours for insiders and the easy hiring and firing practices for outsiders), which would balance between costs and benefits of labor market reform.

### THE AUTOMOBILE, ELECTRONICS, AND STEEL INDUSTRIES

This subsection examines the similarities and differences in the labor adjustment strategies of three key industrial sectors—automobiles, electronics, and steel—all of which played a central role in leading wage coordination in *shuntō* and actively engaged in a wide range of labor policy making on behalf of business and labor. It demonstrates the common pattern of Japan's labor adjustment across these industrial sectors—the usage of outsiders as an economic buffer—and presents variations in labor adjustment, such as the method and scope of labor restructuring, depending on the characteristics of each industry and their market positions.[19]

First, except for a brief mild recession during the late 1990s, the Japanese automobile sector maintained high economic performance and market profitability compared with the other two sectors during the 1990s and 2000s. For the automobile sector, the upcoming retirement of the high-skilled baby-boom generation (*dankai sedai*) was an urgent problem.[20] Some automobile firms tried to extend the mandatory retirement age of regular workers and to rehire skilled retirees as non-regular workers after their retirement in order to retain skilled workers in production lines and pass down their technological expertise to young workers (Noble 2005). Job security for regular workers was mostly unchallenged in the automobile sector in the process of labor adjustment over the past two decades. For example, when Nissan was taken over by Renault (a French automobile company) in 1999, the new management team of Nissan-Renault ambitiously announced a comprehensive corporate restructuring plan. Yet it retained a majority of the workforce, as opposed to conducting massive labor restructuring for regular workers, except for those who voluntary left the firm (Tiberghien 2007, 183–192). Although the automobile sector, like other industrial sectors, expanded the hiring of non-regular workers and the outsourcing of production lines to subcontracting companies, it relied less on subcontracting companies as a buffer during economic downturns, and the size of non-regular employment remained relatively stable compared with other manufacturing industries (Keizer 2008, 410, 415).

Second, Japan's electronics industry confronted far more severe financial distress compared to other manufacturing sectors in the early 2000s after the bust of the information technology bubble, and it was forced to shed a surplus of the regular workforce.[21] Rather than laying off regular workers, most electronics firms recruited volunteers for an early retirement program and compensated them with generous retirement packages in order to maintain the morale of regular workers within companies (*Shūkan Rōdō Shimbun [Weekly Labor Newspaper]*, from internal documents of Denki Rengō [Japanese Electrical Electronic and Information Union]).[22] The electronics industry, which had to catch up quickly with rapid technological developments compared with other manufacturing sectors, was always a vocal supporter of labor market flexibility even for regular workers (e.g., flexible working conditions and hours for regular workers).[23] In contrast to the automobile industry, the electronics industry focused more on the standardization and modularization of production lines, which enabled employers to increase the hiring of non-regular workers to replace regular workers in corporate restructuring (Keizer 2008, 415).

Third, unlike the automobile and electronics industries, Japan's steel industry had already undergone several rounds of labor restructuring to cope with market conditions and intense competition with developing countries, such as Korea, Taiwan, and China, from the 1970s and onward. At least in production lines, the steel industry employed a substantial share of non-regular workers. Between 1972 and 1988, five major steel companies—Nippon Steel Corporation (NSC), NKK, Kawasaki Steel Corporation, Mitsui Kinzoku, and Kobe Steel—reduced the proportion of blue-collar regular workers (*honkō*) from 55.5 percent to 48.1 percent, while they increased the hiring of non-regular temporary workers (*shagaikō*) from 44.5 percent to 51.9 percent (Miyuki 2001, 42–43). During economic downturns in the 1990s, the steel industry followed previous patterns of labor adjustment, such as *tenseki* (permanent intra-firm or intra-group work transfer) and early retirement programs, in order to shed the regular workforce, in addition to an increase in the hiring of non-regular workers (Miyuki 2001).[24]

Although some industrial sectors implemented labor restructuring for regular workers in the face of severe economic distress and intensified market competition, the layoff of regular workers was not a dominant strategy of labor adjustment in the Japanese labor market, regardless of the different characteristics of the industry and economic performance. An early retirement program with generous compensation packages was also adopted as a last resort of labor restructuring for regular workers. The magnitude of the hiring of non-regular workers differed across industrial sectors, but the increase in the hiring of non-regular workers and the expansion of subcontracting systems were primary tools of increasing labor market flexibility in the three key industrial sectors. Under the institutional features of employment protection entrenched in the labor market with a large proportion of the workforce covered by the system, Japan's employers focused on greater flexibility through the increased hiring of outsiders.

## CONVERGENCE AND DIVERGENCE OF POLICY POSITIONS

As illustrated above, Japanese firms neither socialized the cost of labor adjustments, like their French and German counterparts, nor proposed labor market reform to ease the firing of insiders, despite Japan's decade-long economic quagmire. Its employers did not pressure policy makers to develop social protections over the entire economy in order to absorb the costs of adjustments for those affected by reform. As a last resort for labor adjustments after implementing a wide range of natural attrition strategies (e.g., hiring freezes, retirement, the reduction of work hours, and layoffs of non-regular workers), they proposed the "early-retirement program package" (*shokki taishoku yūsen seido*), the financial burden of which fell on their shoulders if it was necessary to shed part of the regular workforce. As shown in table 4.1, since the 1980s an increasing number of large Japanese firms have utilized early retirement programs to downsize the regular workforce, although early retirement programs with generous compensation packages were an option available only for large firms with abundant financial resources. Under the configurations of decentralized industrial relations, Japan's employers were more willing to provide early retirement compensation for insiders at the firm level, however they were not interested in extending the mechanism of such compensation to the entire workforce.

**TABLE 4.1**    Percentage of Japanese firms implementing early retirement program

| | FIRMS WITH MORE THAN 5,000 WORKERS | FIRMS WITH BETWEEN 1,000 AND 4,999 WORKERS | FIRMS WITH BETWEEN 300 AND 999 WORKERS | FIRMS WITH BETWEEN 100 AND 299 WORKERS | FIRMS WITH BETWEEN 30 AND 99 WORKERS |
|---|---|---|---|---|---|
| 1980 | 34.1 (%) | 19.8 (%) | 6.7 (%) | 3.7 (%) | 1.8 (%) |
| 1990 | 59.3 (%) | 40.4 (%) | 21.3 (%) | 8.3 (%) | 3.3 (%) |
| 2000 | 58.2 (%) | 43.0 (%) | 24.3 (%) | 10.1 (%) | 3.0 (%) |

Source: Japanese Ministry of Health, Labor and Welfare, Koyō Kanri Chōsa [Survey on Employment Management System].

Employers' dominant strategy for labor adjustments was the expansion of the external labor market for non-regular workers. According to a survey of in-house subcontracting companies (Ukeoi Jigyōsha Chōsa) conducted by the Ministry of Health, Labor and Welfare (MOHLW), firms decided to expand non-regular workers for the purposes of labor market flexibility and labor cost reduction (Kobayashi 2004, 208). This survey shows that the electronics and precision machinery industries most frequently take advantage of an in-house subcontracting system, indicating that 53.9 percent and 34.9 percent of firms in each industry adopt this system, respectively (Kobayashi 2004, 209). Even in the field of high-tech production (e.g., digital camera or flat-panel TV production), almost half of newly hired workers are employed as non-regular temporary workers (Kobayashi 2004, 215). Such employment patterns seemed to be driven by the standardization and modularization of production lines in the electronic industry, which reduced firms' reliance on skilled workers. In addition, with the implicit consent of the regular workforce, the competitive automobile sector expanded the hiring of non-regular workers (e.g., temporary and contract workers) and increased the outsourcing of its production lines to in-house subcontracting firms (*ukeoi kaisha*), in exchange for job security for the regular workforce.[25] As a result, the institutional constraints of employment protection restricted an available range of employers' labor adjustment options, although Japan's employment protection system may have weakened in the context of the decline of institutional protections for job security for regular workers over the past two decades. Japan's decentralized industrial relations further discouraged its employers to develop social protections over the entire economy.

## Organized Labor's Positions on Labor Market Reform and Labor Adjustment

With the formation of Rengō through the merger of two national labor federations based on private sector unions—Dōmei (Japanese Confederation of

Labor) and Chūritsu Rōren (Federation of Independent Labor Unions)—in 1987, Japan's labor movement became more centralized than before.[26] As of 2002, Rengō was composed of fifty-seven industry federations with 6,808,000 members, encompassing 63.6 percent of organized labor, and two small labor federations, Zenrōren and Zenrōkyō, which included 7.5 percent and 1.7 percent of organized workers, respectively (Japanese Trade Union Confederation [Rengō] 2006, 28).[27] Notwithstanding the founding of the unified national labor federation, Rengō, the low coverage of union membership and the decline of union organization from 25.2 percent to 18.1 percent between 1990 and 2008 did not solve the problems of labor market inequality and dualism along the dimensions of employment status and firm size in Japan.[28] In particular, Japan's decentralized industrial relations based on large enterprise unions, whose collective bargaining did not encompass workers over the entire economy, led to the deepening of economic disparity between unionized insiders in large firms and the rest of others (e.g., SME workers and non-regular workers).[29]

Rengō, led by export-oriented private-sector unions, has, since its inception, adopted more cooperative strategies than Sōhyō, which had centered on public-sector unions, and Rengō was exclusively invited to the process of labor policy making.[30] At first, Rengō as the political representative of organized labor at the national level was rather reluctant to discuss labor market liberalization for non-regular workers in the late 1980s and early 1990s. In addition, it was concerned that the easy hiring of non-regular workers, driven by labor market liberalization, might enable employers to replace its unionized members with under-protected and underpaid non-regular workers.

Contrary to Rengō's cautious approach to labor market liberalization for non-regular workers, Denki Rengō (Japanese Electrical Electronic and Information Union) and Jidōsha Sōren (Confederation of Japan Automobile Workers' Unions), which provided important organizational capacities and financial resources for Rengō and represented the interests of large export-oriented firms, were more willing to accept employers' demands for greater flexibility, such as the easy hiring of non-regular workers and the flexible allocation of work hours for regular workers.[31] In particular, their intense exposure to the international market made them more amenable to management's labor adjustment strategies to improve firms' competitiveness and profitability. Since the mid-1990s, Denki Rengō and Jidōsha Sōren have consented to the diversification of employment contracts and to managerial discretion in the flexible allocation of work hours at the firm level, in exchange for job security for regular workers.[32]

As the political representative of organized labor, Rengō was in a difficult situation in positioning itself in the process of labor market reform. As a leader of Japan's labor movement, Rengō needed to protect the interests of labor, regardless of employment status and firm size. Yet its core member unions in leading export-oriented sectors, such as Denki Rengō, Jidōsha Sōren, and their affiliated enterprise unions, were rather keen on the maintenance of their firms' market competitiveness and profitability, even if they had to sacrifice the protection of non-regular workers. Until the mid-1990s, Rengō adhered to marginal labor market liberalization for a small fraction of professionals in order to accommodate the economic needs of firms. Since the late 1990s, however, Rengō has been unable to stick firmly to the principle of employment protection for all workers, driven by the mounting pressure of economic distress and the demands of labor unions in export-oriented sectors for labor market liberalization for outsiders. The dominant influence of these two sectors within Rengō, coupled with decentralized industrial relations, constrained its political strategies at the labor deliberative councils under the jurisdiction of the Ministry of Labor (MOL), dividing the positions of organized labor on reform. Thus, Rengō reluctantly consented to reform for outsiders, which was a less politically expensive choice for its own organization composed of insiders in large firms. In addition, Japan's decentralized industrial relations based on large enterprise unions made insiders in large firms and their labor unions indifferent to demands for social protections beyond the boundary of firm and workplace in the process of reform for outsiders.

## Winners and Losers in the Labor Market

Over the past two decades, the majority of Japanese firms have not altered the high level of employment protection for insiders, though some insiders have had to shoulder costs of economic distress and labor adjustments. At the same time, they have rapidly expanded the usage of the non-regular workforce as an economic buffer.[33] Gender and age group, which are correlated with the structure of the dualistic labor market along the dimensions of employment status and firm size, became two other key variables to divide the workforce into insiders and outsiders in the Japanese labor market. A majority of female part-time and temporary workers as well as young and old non-regular workers—namely, unorganized outsiders—were excluded from the intricate web of job security, wage coordination, and social protections, all of which insiders were entitled to receive. According to a survey conducted by Rengō in 2004, a majority of non-regular workers were allocated to the same job tasks as the regular workforce, but in-house subcontracted workers (*ukeoi*) only received between 58.9 percent and 69.8 percent of the wages of regular workers, depending on age and rank (Japanese Trade Union Confederation [Rengō] 2006, 45; Kobayashi 2004, 210, table 5.3).[34] The institutional stability of employment protection for insiders became relatively weakened because of the institutional decoupling of Japan's coordinated market economy during the 1990s and 2000s, which caused the decline of institutional protections for firms as well as workers. Although a majority of insiders has remained under an implicit guarantee of employment protection at the firm level, the institutionalization of the secondary labor market has led to a rapidly shrinking number of insiders and, in the long run, the drastic decline of employment protection for these workers.

## The Politics of Labor Market Reform, Inequality, and Dualism

Japan always considered employment a basic social safety net, in lieu of expanding social protections for workers, and prioritized public investment expenditures in its budget allocation for both workers and the unemployed (Estévez-Abe 2008; Hiwatari and Miura 2001; Miura 2002b).[35] Various employment subsidy programs of designated industries, regions, and age groups were also widely implemented in order to alleviate the financial burden on firms of retaining regular workers during economic downturns (Hiwatari and Miura 2001; Kume 1998; Matsubuchi 2005; Uriu 1996). Faced with protracted economic recession and fiscal constraints over the past two decades, Japan has been no longer able to maintain its principle of full employment, and it has been pressured to curtail government spending on public works projects and employment and wage subsidy programs (Estévez-Abe 2008; Miura 2002b; G. Park 2011). Departing from a previous focus on employment as a basic social safety net, Japan's policy makers put much weight on labor market liberalization to satisfy firms' demand for greater flexibility in employment contracts and working conditions as well as to create more jobs in times of economic distress. As shown in table 4.2, Japan has advanced a series of labor market and social protection reforms since the mid-1980s, represented as selective labor market reform for outsiders with insider-favored social protections.

This section examines the ways in which Japan's employment protection systems and decentralized industrial relations affected its political process and outcome of labor market reform. These institutional features of the labor market were not the only factors that determined the political dynamics of Japan's reform. Several political factors, such as the collapse of the LDP-led political system, coalition governments, a centralized policy-making authority, and the divided control of the Diet, also shaped the political pathways of reform. Nevertheless, the overall direction of Japan's labor market reform—(1) labor market liberalization for outsiders with the persistence of protection for insiders and (2) the rapid rise in labor market inequality and dualism—can be better explained

**TABLE 4.2** Japan's labor market and social protection reform since the mid-1980s

| REFORM MEASURE | REFORM OUTCOME |
|---|---|
| Worker Dispatch Law (1986) | Direction and target: increasing labor market flexibility for outsiders<br>Content: legalization of the hiring of dispatched workers in a few occupational categories |
| Discretionary Work Hours Rule under the Labor Standards Law (1987) | Direction and target: increasing labor market flexibility for outsiders<br>Content: flexible allocation of work hours for professional occupations |
| Revision of the Discretionary Work Hours Rule under the Labor Standards Law (1998) | Direction and target: increasing labor market flexibility for insiders<br>Content: flexible allocation of work hours for white-collar workers in managerial positions, yet strong protective measures for insiders in the process of policy implementation at the firm level |
| Revision of the Worker Dispatch Law (1999) | Direction and target: increasing labor market flexibility for outsiders<br>Content: further liberalization of the hiring of dispatched workers by introducing the "negative system" |
| Revision of the Employment Insurance Program (2000) | Direction and target: insider-favored social protections<br>Content: more-generous and longer employment insurance benefits for regular workers with longer enterprise tenure years (e.g., middle-aged workers) |
| Labor Contract Succession Law (2000) | Direction and target: enhancing employment protection for insiders<br>Content: protection of insiders' labor contracts in cases of corporate divisions |
| Revision of the Worker Dispatch Law (2003) | Direction and target: increasing labor market flexibility for outsiders<br>Content: legalization of hiring dispatched workers in the manufacturing industry, which had been prohibited under the revision of the Worker Dispatch Law (1999) |
| Revision of the Labor Standards Law (on employment contract) (2003) | Direction and target: increasing labor market flexibility for outsiders<br>Content: extension of employment contract terms from one to three years for fixed-term contract workers |
| Revision of the Labor Standards Law (on the doctrine of abusive dismissal) (2003) | Direction and target: enhancing employment protection for insiders<br>Content: codification of the doctrine of abusive dismissal in the Labor Standards Law |
| Elderly Employment Stabilization Law (2004) | Direction and target: enhancing employment protection for insiders (especially the elderly)<br>Content: gradual extension of the retirement age of workers from sixty to sixty-five |
| Pension Reform (2004) | Direction and target: insider-favored social protections<br>Content: no extension of the pension program to part-time workers |
| Revision of the Part-Time Work Law (2007) | Direction and target: enhancing protection for outsiders (especially part-time workers)<br>Content: wage equality between regular workers and part-time workers |

(*Continued*)

**TABLE 4.2**  *(Continued)*

| REFORM MEASURE | REFORM OUTCOME |
|---|---|
| Revision of Labor Contract Law (2007) | Direction and target: enhancing employment protection for insiders |
|  | Content: dismissals would be null and void if proper procedures not taken by employer |
| Revision of the Labor Standards Law (on overtime payment) (2008) | Direction and target: enhancing protection for insiders |
|  | Content: increase in overtime payment for insiders; generous premiums for overtime payment; low threshold for overtime payment |
| Revision of the Worker Dispatch Law (2012) | Direction and target: enhancing protection for outsiders |
|  | Content: re-regulation of the hiring of dispatched workers on daily basis, and improvement of working conditions |

by the institutional arrangements of employment protection systems and decentralized industrial relations. The remainder of this section demonstrates how the Japanese government responded to the pressure of labor market reform during the 1990s and 2000s.

## Japan's Labor Market Reform during the 1990s

Beginning in the early 1990s, Japan proposed "deregulation" (*kiseiganwa*), regarding it as a panacea for all economic and social problems. Political debates on deregulation led to the establishment of a centralized policy-making authority intended to drive far-reaching and swift deregulation policies by avoiding red tape and bypassing bureaucracy-led policy making, such as deliberative councils (*shingikai*).[36] It was the Hosokawa cabinet (August 1993–April 1994)—the first non-LDP government since 1955, composed of seven coalition parties—that set up a study group to discuss the creation of a new administrative agency to take charge of deregulation. The Hiraiwa report published in 1993 under the direction of Hiraiwa Gaishi, chairman of Keidanren, proposed deregulation based on "market principles" for economic deregulation and "personal responsibility" for social regulation (Masujima 1999, 297).[37] The short-lived Hosokawa proposal was inherited by the Murayama cabinet (June 1994–January 1996), composed of a coalition of the LDP, the Japan Socialist Party (JSP), and the Sakigake Party (hereafter, Sakigake), and materialized in the Deregulation Subcommittee under the Administrative Reform Committee in 1994.

Even before Japan's protracted recession in the 1990s and 2000s, policy makers submitted several labor market reform bills to liberalize the rules and regulations governing employment contracts and working conditions for highly skilled professional workers, such as the Worker Dispatch Law (Rōdōsha hak-enhō) (1986) and the Discretionary Work Hours Rule under the Labor Standards Law (1987). However, policy makers took very careful approaches to reform because they prioritized the institutional stability of the Japanese model of the labor market, represented by permanent employment practices, seniority-based wages, and enterprise unions, and they preferred to maintain the cooperative relationship with labor in policy making.

Before the establishment of the Deregulation Subcommittee in 1994, labor deliberative councils (rōdō shingikai) under the jurisdiction of the MOL played a central role in deciding all major components of policy change based on consensus between business, labor, and public interests (usually represented by academic scholars).[38] The MOL drafted reform bills based on the policy recommendations of labor deliberative councils, and submitted them to the cabinet.[39] Unlike other deliberative councils, often criticized for their perfunctory functions of only supporting their parent ministries, labor deliberative councils were considered the locus of policy debates and coordination between business, labor, and public interests over the whole gamut of labor policy making. If labor deliberative councils could not reach an agreement over policy changes, the MOL was reluctant to draft reform bills by itself and instead simply postponed submitting them to the cabinet in order to maintain its implicit principle of unanimous decision making at the labor deliberative councils, which allowed Rengō to exert its political power over labor policy making. Meanwhile, the consensus-based decision-making structure of labor deliberative councils, which required extensive debates and negotiations among participants, irritated the Japanese business community since it preferred to accelerate labor market reform in times of severe economic distress.

The Deregulation Subcommittee, a new centralized decision-making authority, turned out to be a very useful tool for the business community to promote labor market reform for greater flexibility. The business community itself was deeply engaged in establishing a new government-led deregulation agency. Chaired by Japanese IBM CEO Shiina Takeo, who was also a member of Keizai Dōyūkai, itself composed of market-oriented business leaders, the Deregulation Subcommittee comprised sixteen members: five academic scholars, one economic commentator, seven business representatives (including one foreign CEO), one labor union representative, and one writer. After Shiina Takeo's step-down in 1995, the CEO of Orix (a leasing and financial group), Miyauchi Yoshihiko, another outspoken member of Keizai Dōyūkai, succeeded to the chair of the Deregulation Subcommittee and served in the position until September 2006.[40]

In 1994, Nikkeiren proposed several key policies for labor market reform: the elimination of an industrial minimum wage, the relaxation of restrictions on employment and working conditions for dispatched workers, the elimination of protection for female workers, and the expansion of the discretionary work hours rule (*Nikkeiren Times,* October 17, 1994). Accepting these policy demands of Nikkeiren in 1995, the Deregulation Subcommittee recommended that the MOL liberalize occupational categories for hiring dispatched workers as well as deregulate fee-paying private employment service agencies (*Asahi Shimbun,* December 6, 1995).[41] Despite the policy recommendation of the Deregulation Subcommittee, the Central Employment Security Deliberative Council under the MOL decided to add only twelve more occupational categories to the list of dispatched workers available for hire, as opposed to full-scale liberalization (*Asahi Shimbun,* December 8, 1995; *Nikkeiren Times,* January 1, 1996).

Labor market reform proceeded rather slowly when the JSP formed a political coalition with the LDP between 1994 and 1996. Unlike another small coalition partner, Sakigake, which was a splinter party from the LDP, the JSP had traditionally formed strong personal and organizational ties with labor unions, especially public-sector unions (Pempel 1998). Since the merger of Sōhyō, based on public-sector unions, into Rengō in 1989, Rengō continued to play a crucial role in providing political and organizational support for the JSP and its candidates during electoral campaigns.[42] Thus, JSP Diet members expressed concerns over labor market reform that might undermine the interests of workers and labor unions. The MOL, which had agenda-setting power in labor policy making, was unwilling to discuss extensive labor market deregulation for non-regular workers because it preferred to avoid complicating policy coordination within the coalition government (J. Song 2010).

After Socialist prime minister Murayama Tomiichi's step-down in January 1996, momentum for labor market reform came from the LDP-led Hashimoto cabinet (January 1996–July 1998). While the JSP joined the LDP-led coalition government, Prime Minister Hashimoto pressured the MOL to shift its policy position toward more extensive reform for outsiders (*Asahi Shimbun,* March 22, 1996). Just a few months after the MOL refused to fully liberalize the occupational categories in which dispatched workers are eligible to be hired, the ministry announced a tentative schedule to eliminate these restrictions (*Nihon Keizai Shimbun,* March 19, 1996). After Prime Minister Hashimoto stepped down, taking responsibility for the political setback of the 1998 Upper House election, LDP politician Obuchi Keijo succeeded to his position and inherited his labor market reform proposal for outsiders, which had been prepared by the second Hashimoto cabinet right after the JSP left the LDP-led coalition government in November 1996.

# Labor Market Reform under the Obuchi Cabinet

The Obuchi cabinet (July 1998–April 2000) promoted several labor market reform agenda items, in particular the flexible allocation of work hours for regular workers and the liberalization of the hiring of non-regular workers. The Obuchi cabinet's emphasis on administrative reforms, centralizing political authority at the top, further strengthened the political power of the prime minister and the Cabinet Office in policy coordination and decision making, which affected the political process of labor market reform, especially during the following Koizumi cabinet (April 2001–September 2006).[43]

With much deeper economic trouble in the late 1990s, the Japanese business community pressured the government even more strongly to liberalize the labor market to cope with the downturns. Most of all, it insisted on employers' rights to flexibly allocate work hours and to extensively hire outsiders (especially, dispatched workers) from external labor markets in response to business conditions. Although organized labor was rather reluctant to this, it finally consented to the increase in flexibility in return for inserting several protective measures for workers with the help of the opposition camp. On the basis of this policy stance of societal interest groups on labor market reform, Japan's policy makers reinforced the institutionalization of a secondary labor market by expanding the hiring of underpaid and under-protected outsiders, while maintaining job security for insiders (Japanese Ministry of Labor 1998 and 1999).[44]

### FLEXIBLE ALLOCATION OF WORK HOURS FOR INSIDERS

The Discretionary Work Hours Rule (Sairyō rōdōsei) under the Labor Standards Law enacted in 1987 aimed to increase the flexibility of work hours for a few professional occupations, whose employment contracts and work assignments did not fit well with those labor management practices centered on long-term employment contracts and seniority-based wages. In negotiating the gradual reduction of the standard workweek to forty hours in the late 1980s and 1990s, the Japanese business community requested more managerial discretion in allocating work hours to compensate for the pressure of increased labor costs caused by shorter work hours as well as to swiftly adjust to temporary business demand (Kume 2000; Schwartz 1998). According to a survey conducted by Nikkeiren in the mid-1990s, employers pointed to overtime payment as one of the most serious concerns in terms of controlling labor costs (Japanese Federation of Employers' Association [Nikkeiren] 1995, 21–23).

In 1994, the MOL suggested a discussion of the expansion of the Discretionary Work Hours Rule, but no substantial progress to draft a reform bill on the flexible allocation of work hours was made because of the disagreement between business and labor at the Central Labor Standards Deliberative Council (Miura 2002a; Nakamura 2005a). While business representatives advocated the immediate expansion of the Discretionary Work Hours Rule for a broad range of workers beyond its current coverage, labor representatives claimed that the existing "flexible work system" (*furekkusu taimusei*) would be sufficient to accommodate the need for flexible work hours without sacrificing workers' overtime earnings (Nakamura 2005a, 258, 262–264).[45]

Another round of the revision of the Discretionary Work Hours Rule came after the Deregulation Subcommittee turned in its policy recommendation for the introduction of flexible work hours for white-collar workers in managerial positions to the Cabinet in December 1996.[46] At the Central Labor Standards Deliberative Council, labor representatives dispatched by Rengō did not agree to revise the Discretionary Work Hours Rule for white-collar workers in managerial positions. One difficulty for these labor representatives was that large firms in leading export-oriented sectors—e.g., those in electronics and automobile industries—had already established managerial discretion in flexibly allocating work hours at the firm level (in exchange for employers' commitment to continued employment protection for regular workers) in order to enhance their companies' competitiveness and profitability in the global market.[47] Therefore, Rengō was unable to seriously oppose the expansion of the Discretionary Work Hours Rule because of the diverse interests within its organization. Despite the failure in forging a political consensus at the deliberative council, the MOL unilaterally drafted and submitted the bill to the Diet in February 1998. It overruled its implicit principle of unanimous decision making at the labor deliberative council in order to comply with the policy recommendations of the Deregulation Subcommittee under the strong political support of Prime Minister Hashimoto. The centralization of labor policy making weakened the role of the labor deliberative council, the locus of bargaining and negotiations over Japan's labor policy.

Deliberations on the revision of the Discretionary Work Hours Rule resumed in the Diet when Obuchi succeeded Hashimoto as prime minister after the 1998 Upper House election. While the LDP was the ruling party of the government, it lacked stable coalition partners to control a secure legislative majority in the Upper House between July 1998 and October 1999, which pressured the LDP leadership to make a political compromise with the opposition camp in order to facilitate legislative bargaining in the Diet. Under these political circumstances, the LDP and opposition parties—especially the Democratic Party of Japan (DPJ) lobbied by Rengō—consented to amend the legislation of the revision of the Discretionary Work Hours Rule under the Labor Standards Law. The Labor Standing Committee in the Diet decided to include the following clauses to improve protection for white-collar workers in managerial positions: (1) a one-year grace period before implementation; (2) the necessity of the workers' consent; (3) another revision to enhance protection for workers, if necessary, after the implementation; and (4) strict guidelines on the implementation of the system agreed upon by the Central Labor Standard Deliberative Council.[48] In particular, the condition of a unanimous decision between management and unions (or other worker representatives) imposed severe restrictions on management when adopting the Discretionary Work Hours Rule for white-collar workers at the firm level.

In the process of the revision of the Discretionary Work Hours Rule under the Labor Standards Law, political variables, such as centralized authority in labor policy making and legislative bargaining in the Diet, seemed to determine reform outcomes. Although these variables affected the processes of policy deliberation and negotiation, the institutional features of the labor market also shaped the political dynamics of reform. Under the conditions of employment protection for the large proportion of the workforce, Japan's employers and policy makers attempted to enhance labor market flexibility through the relaxation of rules and regulations governing working conditions and hours as well as the control of overtime payment, while keeping job security for insiders intact. In addition, a group of employers and insiders (at least in leading export-oriented sectors) made a political concession, conceding to managerial discretion in the flexible allocation of work hours at the firm level, in return for continued employment protection for privileged insiders, which pressured Rengō to accept the revision of the Discretionary Work Hours Rule in the process of labor market reform at the national level.

### EASY HIRING OF OUTSIDERS FROM EXTERNAL LABOR MARKETS

In 1986, the Japanese government legislated the Worker Dispatch Law (Rōdōsha hakenhō) in order to diversify employment contracts and working conditions for a group of highly skilled professionals. According to Takanashi Akira, who led a policy discussion on the Worker Dispatch Law as chair of the Central Employment Stability Deliberative Council, neither business nor labor initially supported this legislation because both parties were concerned about the possibility of the breakdown of Japan's traditional employment practices, represented by strong employment protections for insiders.[49] To address such worries, the MOL stipulated that employers could only hire dispatched workers from thirteen professional occupational categories, such as software engineers and interpreters, in response to new business environments.

Although the Japanese business community was reluctant to introduce the Worker Dispatch Law in the mid-1980s because of the possibility of the negative consequences of the legislation on labor-management practices, it shifted its position toward the liberalization of the labor market, especially for dispatched workers. In the deepening crisis of the Japanese economy during the 1990s, Nik-keiren proposed to liberalize the rules governing employment and working conditions for outsiders in order to enable firms to adjust to economic downturns and fluctuations of the business cycle (*Nikkeiren Times,* various years). Accepting policy requests made by the business community, in late 1995 the Deregulation Subcommittee recommended that the MOL completely liberalize all occupational categories for the hiring of dispatched workers as well as deregulate fee-paying private employment service agencies (*Asahi Shimbun* December 6, 1995; Miura 2002b, 206). The MOL submitted a labor reform bill to the Diet in March 1996 based on the Deregulation Subcommittee's policy recommendation, but it added only twelve more occupational categories, as opposed to the full-scale liberalization of hiring dispatched workers suggested by the Deregulation Subcommittee (*Asahi Shimbun,* December 8, 1995; *Nikkeiren Times,* January 1, 1996). As illustrated in the previous section, despite the top-down pattern of the agenda setting led by the Deregulation Subcommittee, the MOL preferred to reduce the possibility of any political confrontations with Rengō at the labor deliberative council and the possibility of policy disagreement within the ruling coalition government of the LDP, the JSP, and Sakigake.

Amid a wave of deregulation policies intended to resuscitate Japan's faltering economy, the Obuchi cabinet introduced a "negative system" that would lift all legal restrictions on the hiring of dispatched workers through a major revision of the Worker Dispatch Law in 1999. This revision was one of the most contested labor reforms because it would undermine the principle of Japan's permanent employment practices by allowing employers to resort to external labor markets. Pressed by the imperatives of labor market reform to cope with economic distress, Rengō, representing the interests of insiders in large firms, agreed to liberalize the external labor market in exchange for a prohibition on hiring dispatched workers in the manufacturing sector, in which most of Japan's unionized workers were employed (Imai 2006; Miura 2002b). Rengō decided to shield its unionized members from the pressure of change by consenting to the extensive labor market liberalization for dispatched workers. As a result, the 1999 revision of the Worker Dispatch Law allowed employers to hire dispatched workers from all occupational categories, except for those designated by the MOL (dock work, construction, security, nursing and other social services, and manufacturing). The restrictions on these occupational categories were further liberalized during the Koizumi cabinet.

The 1999 revision of the Worker Dispatch Law was a political compromise between organized labor representing the interests of insiders, business, and the government under the institutional constraints of employment protection for insiders as a majority of the workforce. The business community and the government promoted reform for outsiders without proposing any reform agendas for the weakening of employment protection for insiders. In the face of economic distress and pressure to reform the labor market, organized labor consented to the liberalization of the labor market for dispatched workers in exchange for implicit guarantee of job security for insiders. Yet it was also a crucial departure from the Japanese model of the employment system. Although it did not challenge the high level of employment protection for insiders, the liberalization of the hiring of dispatched workers became a watershed, an important transition toward the rapid expansion of the secondary labor market composed of outsiders, which might lead to the decline of employment protection for insiders in the long run.

## FISCAL STIMULUS PACKAGES AS SOCIAL PROTECTION PROGRAMS

The Obuchi cabinet made extensive use of fiscal stimulus packages to fund public works projects in order to create jobs and boost the economy, instead of developing generous social safety nets to absorb the risk for workers. During the period of 1995–2001, the Japanese government spent around 11–18 percent of its general accounts budget on public works, although the Koizumi cabinet slashed a massive number of public works projects through its fiscal and structural reforms (Kasza 2006, 101; G. Park 2011, 217–246). In addition, in 1997, the government created employment subsidy programs for employers in order to prevent layoffs and retain regular workers in the process of corporate restructuring (Genda and Rebick 2000). The programs, which offered financial support packages to help firms (especially SMEs) avoid shedding regular workers in economic downturns, prioritized employment protection for male breadwinners.

Although regular workers (insiders) accepted greater flexibility in the allocation of work hours through labor market reform, which might reduce overtime earnings and deteriorate working conditions, employment protection for regular workers was rarely challenged during the Obuchi cabinet. Given strong employment protection coupled with employers' commitment to job security and public policies in favor of the interests of insiders, enterprise unions and organized insiders lacked any strong incentives to develop generous social protection programs for the unemployed and non-regular workers in precarious employment conditions. Even if they were unemployed, regular workers with longer enterprise tenure years were entitled to receive more-generous benefits (e.g., unemployment insurance benefits or early retirement packages) than were non-regular workers. In such political and economic circumstances, social protection programs in favor of outsiders were not attractive options for policy makers. Such policy preferences for social protection further exacerbated economic disparity between insiders and outsiders in the process of labor market reform in the late 1990s.

## Labor Market Reform under the Koizumi Cabinet

The Koizumi cabinet (April 2001–September 2006) launched far-reaching market-oriented reforms, ranging from the labor market and the financial sector to fiscal reform (Amyx 2006; Mochida 2008; G. Park 2011). While its structural reform brought forth Japan's mild economic recovery in the mid-2000s, it simultaneously contributed to the rapid increase in economic inequality (Tiberghien 2011). The Koizumi cabinet further liberalized the labor market for outsiders, resulting in the rapid expansion of the hiring of these workers, especially in the manufacturing sector, but employment protection for insiders was rarely challenged by his structural reform. Meanwhile, Prime Minister Koizumi cut back a massive number of public works projects through fiscal reform during his term, projects that had played a key role in providing social protections for SME workers as well as rural areas during economic downturn. Japan's social protection programs in favor of the interests of insiders further reinforced labor market inequality and dualism in the process of labor market reform.

### FURTHER LIBERALIZATION FOR OUTSIDERS

In 2003, the Koizumi cabinet undertook another round of revision of the Worker Dispatch Law that would eliminate all legal restrictions on hiring dispatched workers even in the manufacturing sector and extend the period of employment contract terms of dispatched workers from one year or less to three years in order to allow employers more leverage in long-term business projects (Araki 2004 and 2005; Matsubuchi 2005). Rengō did not explicitly oppose the complete liberalization of the labor market for dispatched workers in 2003, though it expressed its regret over the revision of the legislation.[50] Some scholars argue that given the common practice of illegally hiring dispatched workers in the manufacturing sector, Rengō might have believed that the further revision of the Worker Dispatch Law would not substantially change labor practices at the workplace (Miura 2005). Meanwhile, others point out that Rengō was more concerned about the 2003 revision of the Labor Standards Law, which would modify regulatory frameworks on the conditions of dismissing regular workers for managerial reasons, workers with whom Rengō's organizational interests were closely tied (Yun 2009).

The 2003 revision of the Worker Dispatch Law liberalized all rules and regulations on the hiring conditions of dispatched workers, allowing employers to hire dispatched workers in manufacturing production lines with an extension of employment contract terms.[51] Since the enactment of the Worker Dispatch Law in 1986, female clerical workers had accounted for the largest proportion of dispatched workers in the Japanese labor market, but the 2003 revision of the Worker Dispatch Law was attributed to the rapid expansion of male dispatched workers, especially in the manufacturing sector. This trend showed a new type of employment practice since blue-collar male workers in the manufacturing sector had always been the core sector of the regular workforce in the Japanese labor market.[52] According to the General Survey on Dispatched Workers (2008) by the MOHLW, 41.6 percent of dispatched workers were employed in manufacturing sectors, the highest percentage, followed by 14.1 percent of dispatched workers employed in the wholesale and retail industries.[53] The expansion of the hiring of dispatched workers driven by labor market reform laid the grounds for later widespread layoffs of these workers (*haken giri*) under the global financial crisis of 2008.

In addition, the 2003 revision of the Labor Standards Law accelerated the trend of liberalizing the labor market for fixed-term contract workers by relaxing the upper limit of employment contract terms from one year to three years (five years for highly skilled workers or workers over sixty years old) (Matsubuchi 2005). Like the 2003 revision of the Worker Dispatch Law, it enabled employers to rely more on the hiring of outsiders in order to flexibly respond to the fluctuations of the business cycle and to control labor costs by hiring cheap outsiders. All these reforms for outsiders proceeded in a less confrontational manner. Japan's labor market liberalization for outsiders was regarded as a political compromise to balance between employment protection for middle-aged male breadwinners and labor market flexibility for secondary income-earners, such as young, elderly, and female non-regular workers.

## PERSISTENT PROTECTION FOR INSIDERS

In contrast to labor market liberalization for outsiders, the Koizumi cabinet retained extensive employment protection for insiders by strengthening procedures for layoffs of these workers. When the government revised the Commercial Code to facilitate corporate restructuring and business reorganization in the late 1990s and early 2000s, it passed the Labor Contract Succession Law in 2000, which stipulated the protection of regular workers' labor contracts in cases of corporate divisions (Noble 2011).[54] Even if Japan's employers and policy makers prioritized corporate restructuring in order to resuscitate the country's faltering economy, they did not propose any regulatory reforms to alleviate firms' financial burden on retaining regular workers in the process of reorganizing and streamlining inefficient business organizations. By ensuring job security, policy makers aimed to minimize the possibility of job loss for the regular workforce in corporate restructuring, workers who made up the majority of the Japanese workforce.

The 2003 revision of the Labor Standards Law incorporating a clause on abusive dismissals reinforced employment protection for regular workers. Although Japan's Civil Code stipulated the principle of employment at will, it was extremely difficult for employers to dismiss regular workers for managerial reasons because of strong case laws against layoffs. In the midst of the first oil crisis, the Supreme Court of Japan established a precedent limiting an employer's right to lay off regular workers for managerial reasons. In 1979, the Tokyo High Court further specified four prerequisites with which employers must comply in order to lay off workers for managerial reasons: the absolute necessity of firing workers, the lack of alternative tools to avoid firing workers, the existence of a fair procedure to decide who will be fired, and an agreement with the representatives of workers. Such case laws fortified employment protection for the regular workforce, especially in SMEs with no enterprise unions during economic downturn.

Political debates on the levels of employment protection for the regular workforce came to the fore when the Regulatory Reform Committee, into which the Deregulation Subcommittee was reorganized, submitted its policy recommendations on the legalization of laying off regular workers for economic reasons to the prime minister in December 2000 (*Nihon Keizai Shimbun*, January 13, 2001). Japanese firms had rarely employed the dismissal of regular workers even in times of economic distress, deterred not only by legal protections but also social norms and practices (Ahmadjian and Robinson 2001; Dore 1986; Vogel 2006). Nevertheless, Japan's protracted recession and the rise of corporate bankruptcies increased the number of labor disputes over dismissals. Thus, the business community demanded that the government clarify legal guidelines on dismissing workers in order to prevent or quickly resolve disputes associated with dismissals whose conditions were only specified in case laws (Nakagubo 2004, 13–18). Not surprisingly, since employment protection was the most critical issue for labor unions and insiders, Rengō was very serious about blocking any revision that would undermine employment protection for insiders, arguing that the government should include much stricter legal clauses to prevent arbitrary layoffs by employers.

Despite conflicts over the specific wording and expressions of the legal clause, business, labor, and government agreed to stipulate a doctrine of abusive dismissal to prevent dismissals inappropriate in general social terms and lacking objectively reasonable grounds (according to Article 18-2 in the Labor Standards Law).[55] In the case of the 2003 revision of the Worker Dispatch Law, the

LDP-led ruling coalition, which controlled both chambers in the Diet as the legislative majority, refused to amend the legislation. Yet it agreed to incorporate the demands of the opposition camp (e.g., the DPJ and the Liberal Party) by amending the bill to remove the explicit stipulation of employers' rights to lay off workers under conditions of financial distress in the legal clause. Nagase Jinen, LDP's prominent labor policy expert (*rōdō zoku*) and a member of the House of Representatives, also emphasized the reinforcement of employment protection for the regular workforce in the legislative bargaining involved in the 2003 revision of the Labor Standards Law.[56] Considering Japan's employment protection system covering a majority of the workforce in the labor market, its policy makers were very reluctant to advance comprehensive reform for regular workers under the privileges of internal labor markets.[57] Without any further relaxation of the conditions under which employers could lay off regular workers, the previous case laws were added to the Labor Standards Law in 2003. Although the 2003 revision of the Labor Standards Law codified the doctrine of abusive dismissal, as opposed to inserting new protective measures for job security for regular workers, it was largely interpreted as providing strict restrictions on employers' rights to lay off these workers for managerial reasons (Hanami 2004). In addition, the revisions of the Elderly Employment Stabilization Law in 2004 and the Labor Contract Law in 2007 enhanced the levels of employment protection for regular workers, especially elderly workers, by raising the mandatory retirement age from sixty to sixty-five in response to a raise in the pensionable age and by stipulating that dismissals would be null and void if proper procedures were not taken by the employer, respectively (H. Suzuki 2010). By doing so, Japan's policy makers attempted to further secure the levels of employment protection for insiders, while increasing labor market flexibility for outsiders.

By explaining the persistence of employment protection for insiders, an MOHLW bureaucrat has pointed out that it was not essential to further relax the level of employment protection for insiders, since Japanese firms have employed diverse labor adjustment strategies to increase intra-firm (or functional) labor market flexibility, such as work transfer or the expansion of temporary and part-time workers, without resorting to layoffs to increase inter-firm (or numerical) labor market flexibility for insiders.[58] It is quite the opposite position to what Korea's policy makers proposed in the process of labor market reform: easy hiring and firing of insiders for greater flexibility. Additionally, the former chair of the labor deliberative council claims that the Japanese government has always prioritized employment protection for insiders (especially, middle-aged male breadwinners) to prevent the collapse of the Japanese family structure and the consequent problems of social dislocation, which emphasizes the interdependence of a wide range of political, economic, and social institutions centered on employment protection systems in the Japanese labor market.[59] These political and social considerations of employment protection for insiders have been further strengthened amid the politics of labor market reform in Japan, leading to the further liberalization of the labor market for outsiders.

## SOCIAL PROTECTION REFORMS BIASED IN FAVOR OF INSIDERS

Contrary to the Obuchi cabinet's focus on massive public works projects to boost Japan's faltering economy, the Koizumi cabinet drastically reduced its budget allocation for public works projects (G. Park 2011; Tiberghien 2011). In addition, it promoted social protection reforms, such as the Employment Insurance Program and the National Pension Program, in order to solve the problems of the fiscal stability of social welfare programs and insufficient coverage of welfare benefits for outsiders under the pressure of economic distress and demographic changes.

Japan's steady economic growth and low unemployment rates meant that there was no serious alarm about unemployment and the sustainability of the Employment Insurance Program, which had been established in 1974 after the first oil crisis.[60] Yet the financial deficits of the Employment Insurance Program (especially in Fiscal Year 1994) started to raise concerns about the fiscal stability of the program and, simultaneously, the rise of the non-regular workforce provoked policy debates on the extension of the program's coverage to these workers exposed to a much higher risk of unemployment in economic downturns. To restore financial stability to the program, the government has increased insurance contribution premiums from 0.8 percent to 1.5 percent since the late 1990s and modified the duration of unemployment insurance benefits according to the reason for unemployment (Japan Institute for Labor Policy and Training 2010). The most noticeable change in the Employment Insurance Program was that Japan's policy makers revised this program in 2000 to favor regular workers with longer enterprise tenure years.[61] For the voluntarily unemployed (e.g., job-hoppers), the duration of insurance benefits was significantly shortened from 90–300 days to 90–180 days, whereas the period of eligibility for laid-off workers (when those layoffs resulted from corporate bankruptcy or industrial restructuring) was extended from 90–300 days to 90–330 days (Matsubuchi 2005, 90–91). By differentiating the levels of insurance benefits, policy makers aimed to prevent an increase in voluntary unemployment and to save limited financial resources for those forced to leave their jobs in economic downturns, especially middle-aged male breadwinners.[62] By doing so, they endeavored to provide more generous insurance benefits for insiders, although the levels of unemployment benefits were still meager compared with those in other CMEs.

Demographic changes (e.g., an aging society) and economic downturns exerted severe pressure on the retrenchment of the public pension program in Japan as well. The 1985 pension reform was the first retrenchment of pension benefits since the establishment of the universal public pension program in 1961, despite strong opposition to the reduction of benefits from the general public as well as LDP politicians. Japan's public pension system was fragmented into three institutional pillars divided by occupation. First, the National People's Pension (Kokumin Nenkin) covered the self-employed, farmers, and workers in firms with less than five employees. Second, the Employees' Pension Insurance (Kosei Nenkin Hoken) was for private-sector workers in firms with more than five employees. Lastly, the Mutual Aid Association Scheme was for public-sector workers, private-school employees, and rural cooperative employees. Under these institutional arrangements of the public pension program, the government increased contribution premiums of the Employees' Pension Insurance for private-sector workers from 10.6 percent to 12.4 percent in order to handle the financial instability of the pension system resulting from an aging society. In addition, it introduced the Basic Pension (Kiso Nenkin), partially financed by tax revenues, which would integrate the risk pool of the program into one flat-rate insurance scheme across occupations (Estévez-Abe 2008, 216–221; Shinkawa 2003). The 1985 pension reform was not aimed to alleviate insider-outsider differences, but it resulted in the sharing of risk between workers in very small firms (with less than five employees) and other workers, by increasing the premiums of the Employees' Pension Insurance and introducing the Basic Pension.

Economic distress and rising concerns about the aging society and declining fertility rates have provoked more controversial policy debates on Japan's public pension system over the past two decades. During the 1990s and 2000s, several rounds of public pension reform reduced earning-related benefits by 5 percent, raised contribution premiums for the Employees' Pension Insurance, and gradually began to shift the minimum age for pension insurance benefits from sixty to sixty-five years old. To persuade labor unions and workers who opposed the increase in the minimum age for pension benefits, the government promised to gradually extend the coverage of the Employment Insurance Program to workers over sixty years old and change the mandatory retirement age from sixty to sixty-five. However, such compensation annoyed the business community since it meant additional labor costs for older workers under seniority-based wages, leading to firms' introduction of "the wage peak system" intended to restrain annual wage increases for older workers.

In particular, the pension reform of 2004 was relevant to new challenges in the labor market. The rapid rise of the non-regular workforce in Japan has been one of the most noticeable changes during the 1990s and 2000s. The proportion of part-time workers reached approximately 25 percent of the labor force by the early 2000s, more than two-thirds of the non-regular workforce.[63] To cope with these recent changes in the labor market, the government attempted to extend the coverage of the Employees' Pension Insurance to include part-time workers. First, it aimed to improve social protections for part-time workers, most of whom were located in the blind spots of the public pension system. Second, the extension of the coverage entailed the additional contribution of premiums to help the government restore the financial stability of the pension program.

Both business and organized labor strongly opposed the government's reform proposal to extend the Employees' Pension Insurance to part-time workers (Osawa 2007; Sakamoto 2005). Employers, especially those in the service industry, the sector hiring a majority of part-time workers, refused to pay new premiums because of the pressures of rising labor costs (Osawa 2007). Meanwhile, organized labor had to coordinate complicated economic interests within its own group. Young and single part-time workers might support the extension of the Employees' Pension Insurance since employers would pay half of the pension insurance premiums for them. However, a majority of part-time workers—middle-aged females who were secondary income earners in their families—opposed the extension of the program coverage. They preferred to keep the amount of take-home pay as it stood without paying additional contributions for benefits, since most female part-time workers were already covered by their husbands' public pension programs, most of the husbands being employed as regular workers.[64] In addition, enterprise unions and regular workers, most of whom had been protected by public pension programs, were not much interested in expanding social protection programs for non-regular workers. As a result, Japan's organized labor, representing the interests of insiders and their dependent family members, took a stance against the expansion of the public pension to part-time workers by forming political coalitions with business in reform politics. Despite the government's proposal to alleviate insider-outsider differences, political coalitions of employers, male regular workers, and their part-time female spouses consolidated the dualistic welfare system in Japan. Employment status, gender, and family structure reinforced the already fragmented public pension program, protecting the privileges of regular workers and leaving non-regular workers (especially part-time workers) unprotected.

## The LDP's Labor Market Reform after Koizumi

To cope with the pressing problem of dualism and inequality in labor market reform, all political parties, regardless of their place on the ideological spectrum, have focused increasingly on the improvement of employment protection and working conditions for non-regular workers since the mid-2000s. In 2007, the LDP-led coalition government revised the Part-Time Work Law to ensure wage equality between part-time workers and regular workers. In contrast to the original legislation of the Part-Time Work Law (enacted in 1993), which relied on employers' voluntary efforts rather than legal obligations, the 2007 revision stipulated that employers provide equal payment to part-time workers under the principle of equal pay for equal work if their tasks and responsibilities were the same as those of regular workers. The extent to which the revision of the Part-Time Work Law will improve employment conditions and the wages of part-time workers is still unclear because of difficulties in measuring job tasks and responsibilities (J. Song 2010).

The 2008 revision of the Labor Standards Law on overtime payment demonstrated the important political influence of the New Kōmeitō (as the LDP's coalition member) and the pro-labor, opposition DPJ on labor market reform for regular workers. To solve the problem of a declining Japanese birth rate, the Abe cabinet (September 2006–September 2007) advocated a policy platform of "work and life balance" to alleviate the burden of child bearing and child rearing. By proposing increasing overtime payments, policy makers intended to encourage firms to reduce long work hours and workers to spend more time on child care. In the fall of 2006, the Council on Economic and Fiscal Policy (Keizai Zaisei Simon Kaigi) proposed the "Labor Big Bang" to enhance diversity and flexibility in employment as well as working conditions and hours.[65] Among these reform agendas, one of the most controversial was the system of "white-collar exemption" from overtime payment because of disagreement within the ruling coalition bloc (*Japan Times,* April 5, 2007; Tsuru 2008). The Abe cabinet proposed excluding overtime payment for most white-collar workers so that firms could control labor costs, despite regulatory changes. Meanwhile, the New Kōmeitō, the LDP's small but critical coalition partner, fiercely opposed the "white-collar exemption" system, worrying that it would not reduce the burden of child bearing and child rearing on workers and that such a policy platform would fundamentally undermine its core policy platform on social welfare policies for the lower-middle working class. Also, the New Kōmeitō was very concerned about political backlash against the legislation in the Upper House election scheduled for July 2007. The strong opposition of its coalition partner pressured the Abe cabinet to back off from the original policy proposals of the "Labor Big Bang," and the MOL-submitted reform bill finally excluded the "white-collar exemption" clause.

After the LDP's defeat in the 2007 Upper House election, the LDP-led coalition government had to confront the opposition-controlled Upper House, which

allowed the opposition parties to exert much stronger power over legislative bargaining in the Diet. The original bill submitted before the 2007 Upper House
election proposed that premiums for overtime wages be increased from 25 percent to 50 percent only when total overtime exceeded eighty hours a month.
However, the opposition camp forced the LDP to amend the bill to reduce the
threshold for increased overtime payment from eighty to sixty hours a month,
a substantial improvement for workers (Weathers and North 2009, 635). In
addition, in the Lower House, the DJP-led opposition camp, taking advantage
of its control of the Upper House, forced the LDP-New Kōmeitō ruling coalition
to amend the minimum wage law that was designed to deal with the problems
of "the working poor" (*Asahi Shimbun,* November 28, 2007). Confronting the
divided Diet after the July 2007 Upper House election, the Fukuda cabinet (September 2007–September 2008) decided not to submit another labor reform bill
to further deregulate employment and working conditions for hiring dispatched
workers (*Asahi Shimbun,* November 30, 2007). The rise of the pro-labor opposition camp in the Upper House blocked the further liberalization of the labor
market for outsiders in Japan.

## Labor Market Reform under the DPJ

The DPJ finally came to power after the general election in September 2009.
Although the party itself is composed of politicians in a wide range of ideological
spectrums, it has always taken more labor-friendly policy positions than the LDP.
In early 2009, a group of laid-off dispatched workers, most of whom had been
dismissed as a consequence of the global financial crisis of 2008, organized several demonstrations demanding better social safety nets for the unemployed and
non-regular workers with precarious employment conditions.[66]

In response to the massive layoffs of non-regular workers, especially in the
manufacturing sector, in March 2010, the DPJ-led government (September
2009–December 2012) submitted a draft revision of the Worker Dispatch Law
to re-regulate the labor market by prohibiting employers from hiring dispatched
workers in the manufacturing sector and imposing stricter regulations on the
hiring of dispatched workers for other occupational categories.[67] After two years
of deliberation in the Diet, the revision of the Worker Dispatch Law was passed
in March 2012, which would prohibit the hiring of dispatched workers on a
daily basis (with employment contract terms less than thirty days) and improve
working conditions for dispatched workers. Nevertheless, the revised legislation
did not eliminate the clauses regarding the hiring of dispatched workers in
the manufacturing sector and the registration-type dispatch system, which did

not completely reverse a direction of labor market liberalization for outsiders.[68] The DPJ government also shortened the enrollment period of the Employment Insurance Program for dispatched workers from six months to one month in April 2010 in order to allow these workers, who faced far more intense job insecurity, to benefit from unemployment insurance.[69]

The DPJ has attempted to alleviate widening economic gaps between insiders and outsiders by improving protections for the latter, while preserving the high levels of employment and social protections for the former. Contrary to its predecessor, the conservative LDP, the DPJ has focused more on the expansion of social protections for outsiders, most of whom have had to bear the costs of labor adjustments over the past two decades. Despite these policy efforts, the DPJ government has been unable to avoid the deepening of labor market inequality and the segmentation of dualism, especially along the dimension of employment status, because of the institutional constraints of the labor market in favor of the interests of insiders.

* * *

This chapter presents the political processes and outcomes of Japan's labor market reform over the past two decades. During this time Japan has adopted more market-oriented principles in the labor market than before, such as the increase of labor market flexibility and the diversification of employment and working conditions, but it did not conform to the neoliberal model of the labor market, represented by easy hiring and firing practices in response to the fluctuations of the business cycle. The institutional arrangements of employment protection systems and decentralized industrial relations affected the trajectory of Japan's reform by shaping the incentives and strategies of employers, workers, and policy makers and leading to the formation of a political coalition in support of reform for outsiders while retaining insider-favored social protections. Institutional protections for the interests of insiders, entrenched in these arrangements of the labor market, further ensured their job security, high wages, and generous social protections. Such institutional configurations transferred the costs of labor adjustments to an increasing number of outsiders, exacerbating inequality and dualism in the Japanese labor market.

Japan's labor market reform has responded to political and economic challenges incrementally, while maintaining the key tenets of the institutional foundations of the Japanese labor market model. Nevertheless, Japan's labor market has also experienced a rapid decline of the proportion of insiders, which had been tightly protected by a wide range of social, economic, and political institutions. The shrinkage of proportion of insiders might serve as the driving force of institutional change by shifting the incentives and strategies of employers as well as policy makers in the long term. Considering the fact that a majority of young workers have not been able to join internal labor markets, the future institutional stability of the Japanese labor market is not very promising (Hamaaki et al. 2010). The remaining question is whether or not the shrinking size of insiders over the past two decades can continue to ensure the stability of Japan's labor market institutions in the future.

# KOREA: LIBERALIZATION FOR ALL, EXCEPT FOR CHAEBŎL WORKERS

In the wake of the 1987 democratic transition and the 1997 Asian financial crisis, Korea promoted a series of labor market reforms in order to transform its rigid labor market institutions into more flexible ones.[1] Unlike Japan and other CMEs that focused on liberalization of the labor market for outsiders, Korea prioritized comprehensive reform for all workers. Ironically, this comprehensive reform furthered labor market inequality and the segmentation of the dualistic labor market, as opposed to encouraging a narrowing of the economic gap between insiders and outsiders. Why did Korea adopt comprehensive labor market reform for all workers in response to economic challenges? And why, notwithstanding across-the-board labor reform, did it result in a great degree of labor market inequality and dualism? This chapter analyzes the ways in which the small proportion of the workforce covered by employment protection, as well as decentralized industrial relations based on large chaebŏl unions, have shaped the political dynamics of Korea's labor market reform over the past two decades.

The first section below illustrates how recent political and economic challenges placed a severe strain on the institutional arrangements of the Korean labor market, which were established during the period of authoritarian rule. The second section outlines the diverging policy positions of business and labor on labor market reform and labor adjustment strategies in the face of changing political and economic environments. This section examines the ways in which large chaebŏl employers developed policy preferences for reform for regular workers (insiders), while regular workers (especially those in chaebŏl firms), empowered by the strength of large enterprise unions after democratization, attempted to consolidate internal labor markets, represented by job security, high wages, and generous welfare benefits. The third section analyzes a series of reform attempts led by policy makers during the period of 1987–1997, all of which resulted in intense political confrontations between business and labor. The fourth section examines the political dynamics of labor market reform after the Asian financial crisis. It explains how center-left policy makers under pro-labor presidents pursued comprehensive reform for all workers, and how such reform reinforced inequality and dualism between chaebŏl workers (as "core" insiders) and the others in the Korean labor market. A summarization follows, providing broader empirical and theoretical implications for the politics of Korea's labor market reform and its labor market institutions.

# New Political and Economic Challenges for the Labor Market

The institutional arrangements of the Korean model of capitalism, identified as a coordinated market economy (CME) with group-based strategic coordination, were under intense pressure to change after democratization in 1987. Contrary to the institutional development of the Japanese model of capitalism, a set of market institutions in the Korean economy were constructed under the auspices of the authoritarian Park regime (1961–1979). The regime implicitly and explicitly offered employment protection for workers, but only in exchange for wage restraints unilaterally imposed by the state, and its repressive labor control policy forced workers and labor unions to accept industrial peace at the workplace over any distributional conflicts. The following Chun regime (1980–1987), which came to power with another military coup in 1979, further consolidated far more decentralized industrial relations by outlawing industry unions and legalizing only enterprise unions at the workplace in order to strictly confine the locus of unions' activities to the firm level.

During the period of authoritarian rule, chaebŏl (i.e., family-owned and -managed large business conglomerates) did not need to worry about the strict legal clause on employment protection for workers, since state repression against labor movements, which had been utilized extensively to sustain Korea's export-oriented growth, effectively dismantled any resistance from workers and unions (Jang-jip Choi 1997; Koo 2001; Y. Lee 2009). Given the state-imposed wage guidelines on behalf of business, chaebŏl lacked political and economic incentives to establish wage-bargaining institutions that would encompass firms and industries. Even if chaebŏl emulated the labor management practices of large Japanese firms, it was not possible to build up the institutional pillars of the labor market without the role of state control and intervention in the labor market in Korea.

The authoritarian regime left Korea with a heavily regulated labor market in terms of conditions for dismissing workers combined with the underdevelopment of wage-bargaining institutions.[2] Yet democratization and the growing power of the chaebŏl and labor unions caused the drastic decline of state control over the labor market and industrial relations as well as the institutionalization of the dualistic labor market in Korea (E. M. Kim 1997; Lim 2003). First, policy makers were no longer able to force chaebŏl employers and workers to abide by the state-dictated wage-bargaining guidelines. Although policy makers attempted to moderate excessive wage increases driven by chaebŏl unions, their political efforts were futile. The state threatened chaebŏl by wielding its authority over the state-controlled financial resource allocation, which had always been one of the most crucial tools to discipline chaebŏl. However, chaebŏl already had more leeway in accessing financial resources in the 1980s and 1990s, such as chaebŏl-affiliated non-banking financial institutions (B-K. Kim 2003, 62–64). In addition, chaebŏl became very reluctant to comply with the state's intervention in wage bargaining because of militant chaebŏl unions' strong demand for wage increases, which had great disruptive potential in industrial relations. Meanwhile, chaebŏl unions, empowered by democratization, exerted their organizational capacities in collective bargaining by threatening or actually unleashing intense labor strikes.

Second, democratization began to consolidate internal labor markets for blue-collar production workers in the chaebŏl sector, most of whom had been excluded from employment protection coverage during the authoritarian regime. Korea's permanent employment practices did not extend beyond white-collar clerical workers in large firms and the public sector until the 1980s. During the period of the 1960s and 1970s, low-skilled blue-collar production workers frequently changed workplaces across firms and industries, looking for high-paying jobs and taking advantage of a labor shortage. Seniority-based wage systems and corporation-provided employee benefits, two of the primary mechanisms to institutionalize internal labor markets by stabilizing high labor mobility, did not expand to include low-skilled blue-collar production workers either (H-K. Song 1991, 107–136). It was only after the 1987 democratic transition that chaebŏl employers gradually agreed to guarantee job security for blue-collar production workers, pressured by the surge of militant chaebŏl unions (Hwang 2006; E. Jung and Cheon 2006).[3]

Last, labor market inequality and dualism between insiders (e.g., chaebŏl workers) and outsiders (e.g., SME workers and non-regular workers) increased dramatically in conjunction with democratization; this trend was further exacerbated after the financial crisis. The segmentation of the dualistic labor market, between workers in large chaebŏl firms and those in SMEs, was already entrenched in the Korean labor market because of its large firm-centered economic structures combined with decentralized industrial relations.[4] Yet the consequences of labor market inequality and dualism, such as job security and wage differentials across firm size, were prevented by the authoritarian government's intervention in the labor market (see chapter 3). As already shown in figures 1.5 and 1.6 in chapter 1, after democratization it became noticeable that workers in firms with more than five hundred workers (roughly equivalent to chaebŏl workers) were privileged with much higher levels of employment protection and wages than other workers.

Despite institutional similarities in the Japanese and Korean labor markets, Korean employers' commitment to job security for workers was much weaker than that of its Japanese counterparts since they heavily relied on the state's control of the labor market during the authoritarian rule.[5] In addition, no public policy programs supported the institutional pillar of employment protection for the workforce in the Korean labor market. It was the power of large chaebŏl unions that secured the high level of employment protection and wages for their unionized members at the firm level. Unlike Japan, Korea never developed a mechanism of wage coordination across firms and industries, even after democratization and the financial crisis, which has contributed to rapidly rising wage differentials along the dimensions of employment status and firm size over the past two decades. The following section examines the policy positions of business and labor on labor market reform and labor adjustment strategies after democratization, which have been derived from the institutional features of the labor market.

## Positions of Business and Labor on Labor Market Reform and Labor Adjustment

Democratization dramatically changed the rules of the game in the Korean labor market. The business community, especially chaebŏl, which had always resorted to state force to repress autonomous and democratic labor movements and to control wage increases, had to find their own ways of managing the dual challenges of sharp wage hikes driven by militant chaebŏl unions and intensified global market competition. Meanwhile, chaebŏl workers and unions, whose political and organizational capacities were strengthened by democratization, insisted on job security and economic compensation (e.g., high wages and generous benefits) for unionized insiders by flexing their muscles through a series of strikes. Korea needed to establish a new labor market model to adjust to political and economic challenges, but neither business nor labor was willing to make concessions that might undermine their political and economic interests. This section elaborates the positions of large business and organized labor on labor market reform and labor adjustment strategies over the past two decades.

## The Business Community's Positions on Labor Market Reform and Labor Adjustment

After democratization, the most pressing concern for the Korean business community was how to respond to the strong demand for job security and wage increases pushed by militant labor unions, given the drastic decline of state control over the labor market and industrial relations. Korea's real wage increase rates surpassed labor productivity growth rates between 1987 and 1989, a period during which unprecedented numbers of strikes broke out (see figure 5.1).[6] The economic boom of 1986–1989, having greatly benefited from favorable global economic conditions, the so-called "three lows" (low interest rates, low oil prices, and low yen-to-dollar rate), could only temporarily solve the problems of drastic wage hikes and job security.[7] The end of the double-digit economic growth in the early 1990s started to impose a heavy burden on corporate finance due to rapidly increasing labor costs and labor market rigidities. Only a few large chaebŏl with monopolizing market power were able to shift soaring labor costs to SME subcontractors and consumers and to make a swift transition toward high-end product markets by selling out labor-intensive production lines.

A combination of the declining capacity of state control over the labor market and the surging power of well-organized chaebŏl unions gave rise to labor market inequality and dualism between chaebŏl and SMEs, which the authoritarian regime had tightly controlled through policy intervention (see chapter 3 for details). Since large chaebŏl employers were only interested in minimizing the risk of work stoppage and interruption in their own firms, they made concessions to militant chaebŏl unions in wage bargaining. Chaebŏl frequently defected from the implicit consensus on wage increases among the business community by paying workers' wages during strikes and buying off industrial peace through even higher wages and more-generous benefits at the firm level. Such behavior increased chaebŏls' distrust of one another over the labor market and industrial relations. In Japan, the business community developed an intra- and inter-industry wage-bargaining mechanism, *shuntō*, notwithstanding its decentralized industrial relations based on large enterprise unions. The far more fragmented Korean business community did not even attempt to build a wage-bargaining institution across firms and industries. Korea's two prominent business associations—the Federation of Korean Industries (FKI), composed of large chaebŏl, and the Korean Employers' Federation (KEF), comprising large chaebŏl as well as SMEs—did not possess any political or organizational capacity to coordinate their member firms over wage bargaining.[8] The lack of a wage-coordination mechanism over the Korean economy contributed to a huge increase in wage differentials across firm size in particular (see figure 1.6 in chapter 1).

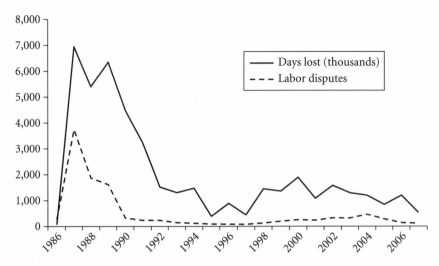

**FIGURE 5.1**   Number of labor disputes and workdays lost in Korea, 1986–2007
*Source:* Korean National Statistical Office, http://kostat.go.kr.

As shown in figure 5.2, Korea's exponentially rising labor costs during the late 1980s and mid-1990s raised serious concerns over the price competitiveness of its export goods in the international market and placed a strain on corporate finance (for SMEs in particular). Thus, during the 1990s, its conservative policy makers prioritized labor market reform for wage restraints with the explicit policy goal of the sustainability of high-speed economic growth. Yet the government-led reform attempts failed to moderate wage increases (as will be elaborated in the following section). At the same time, chaebŏl had to cope with strong demand for employment protection for blue-collar production workers at the firm level. Although chaebŏl emulated the Japanese model of labor management practices, ranging from permanent employment practices and seniority-based wages to generous benefits during the period of industrialization, the privileges of internal labor markets were mostly applicable to white-collar clerical workers, excluding blue-collar production workers (Hwang 2006; E. Jung and Cheon 2006; H-K. Song 1991). After democratization, well-organized chaebŏl unions began to demand a much higher degree of job security for their members.[9]

At first, as large Japanese employers had done, chaebŏl employers attempted to increase intra-firm (or functional) labor market flexibility through managerial discretion over labor management in order to respond quickly to new business conditions, but they did not bear fruit in the increase of intra-firm labor market flexibility because of the strong opposition of labor unions. During the early 1990s, chaebŏl employers endeavored to introduce a broad range of new labor

**FIGURE 5.2**   Unit labor cost in Japan and Korea manufacturing, 1970–2009
*Source:* US Department of Labor, International Labor Comparisons, Section
of Productivity and Unit Labor Cost, table 10, http://www.bls.gov/fls/home.
htm#productivity, accessed June 23, 2011.
*Note:* Unit Labor Cost is calculated by real wage index divided by productivity
index; ULC, Indexes 2002=100, National currency basis.

management practices, emulating Japan's production movements to increase
productivity and upgrade skills in the 1950s and 1960s. They expected that skill
upgrading and multi-skill training for blue-collar production workers would
enable their firms to respond more flexibly to business cycle fluctuations, in
exchange for providing economic incentives (e.g., promotions and high wages)
for these workers to invest in skills training at the firm level. These attempts
turned out to be unsuccessful, however. Chaebŏl unions blocked the institutionalization of skill upgrading and multi-skill training systems because they
worried that such selective economic incentives and competition among union
members, driven by the introduction of the new labor management system,
would severely undermine their organizational solidarity (Hyung-je Cho 2005,
109–115; D-O. Kim and Bae 2004, 77). For the union leadership that had to
confront intense electoral competition every two years, short-term economic
benefits—wage increases and employee benefits—were far more attractive as
well as important agendas to negotiate with employers in collective bargaining.[10]
Chaebŏl employers' futile efforts to shift the system of Fordist mass production
to diversified quality production (like in Germany and Japan) by bringing in
new labor management practices at the firm level resulted in the acceleration of

standardized production for the purpose of minimizing firms' dependence on human skills in the Korean labor market (Hyung-je Cho 2005).[11]

After all these failures in establishing wage coordination and introducing new labor management practices, the Korean business community advocated shedding regular workers in the process of labor market reform. To some extent, chaebŏl employers might prefer to institutionalize internal labor markets composed of blue-collar production workers in order to secure the skilled workforce like their Japanese counterparts. However, the degree of chaebŏl employers' commitment to job security for these workers was not as strong as their Japanese counterparts. Chaebŏl employers considered employment protection for blue-collar production workers burdensome.[12] In addition, employers had little to lose since they did not have a high stake in the employment protection system, which had been very recently institutionalized for blue-collar production workers even in the chaebŏl sector. The business community preferred to eliminate legal restrictions on layoffs of the regular workforce, given the strength of militant unions blocking the implementation of labor adjustment methods at the firm level.

The business community framed labor market flexibility as an essential condition to improve Korean firms' competitiveness and profitability in the international market (Mo 1999). It argued that comprehensive labor market reform, represented by easy hiring and firing of regular workers, would bring forth huge economic benefits not only for the business community but also for the overall Korean economy, since such reform would yield a quick economic turnaround and allow firms to generate more jobs without worrying about the difficulty of dismissing redundant workers during economic downturns. In particular, chaebŏl employers considered the regular workforce in the chaebŏl sector with the privileges of internal labor markets to be the core problem of labor market rigidity, blocking firms' swift adjustment to economic challenges. Thus, a primary policy goal of the chaebŏl for labor market reform was unilateral management authority over decisions on the hiring and firing of insiders. Liberalization of hiring rules and procedures for outsiders (non-regular workers) was only a secondary issue for the chaebŏl.

## Organized Labor's Positions on Labor Market Reform and Labor Adjustment

Immediately after President Chun Doo-hwan's handpicked successor, Roh Tae-woo, pledged a direct presidential election on June 29, 1987, more than three thousand industrial disputes broke out (see figure 5.1). Led by chaebŏl unions and workers in heavy and chemical industries whose organizational capacities had been tightly suppressed by the authoritarian state, these spread to other industrial sectors. Even without the political leadership of the Federation of Korean Trade Unions (FKTU, or Hanguknochong), the only official national labor federation, chaebŏl workers organized autonomous and democratic enterprise unions and wielded their organizational power by taking advantage of the geographically concentrated industrial complex along the southern shore, where the Park regime (1961–1979) had strategically located heavy and chemical industries. Union organization rates jumped from 13.8 percent to 17.8 percent between 1986 and 1987, and regional federations for SMEs in manufacturing sectors, loose industry federations for white-collar workers, and chaebŏl union councils were organized (Jang-jip Choi 1992; Se-gyun Kim 2002, 122–127).

The 1987 democratic transition altered the political dynamics within Korea's labor movements. The coexistence of well-organized chaebŏl workers and unorganized SME workers hindered coordination across labor unions and the workforce. Opposing the official leadership of the FKTU, which had collaborated with the authoritarian regime to repress autonomous and democratic labor movements, dissident labor activists organized the National Congress of Trade Unions (NCTU, or Jŏnnohyŏp) in 1990, but the NCTU, which was not legally recognized, immediately lost its organizational capacity. On the one hand, the internal dynamics and political strategies of the NCTU caused the premature failure of a new experiment in the Korean labor movement. NCTU's radical propaganda based on class struggle and its militant political strategy estranged the labor movement not only from the general public but also from enterprise unions and workers. The factionalism within the NCTU between different ideological and political goals of leadership—a radical class-conflict strategy versus a moderate political strategy based on the institutionalized party system—debilitated its political stance toward the state and business. And the organizational foundation of the NCTU—regional federations for SMEs mostly composed of female workers in labor intensive industries—alienated from its inception powerful chaebŏl unions composed of male blue-collar workers in heavy and chemical industries. On the other hand, external factors—such as political repression by the national security agencies (e.g., KCIA) on democratic labor movements and the divide-and-conquer strategy of employers to transform militant unions to pro-company unions—further weakened the institutional stability of the NCTU (Jang-jip Choi 1992; B-K. Kim and Lim 2000; Se-gyun Kim 2002; J. Song 2012c; Bum-sang Yoo 2005). The NCTU finally dissolved after the Korean Confederation of Trade Unions (KCTU, or Minjunochong) was formed in 1995.

The KCTU, a second national labor federation, was initiated by dissident labor union activists and composed of militant chaebŏl unions in heavy and chemical industries, most of whose member unions seceded from the FKTU. Although policy makers refused to recognize its legal status as a national labor federation, the organizational capacity of the KCTU, derived from well-organized chaebŏl unions, secured its political status in the labor market and industrial relations from the beginning. In addition, fractured business associations were conducive to the survival of the KCTU since business associations lacked the political capacity to coordinate the diverse interests across firms and industries for industrial relations, including political strategies toward the KCTU.

This does not mean that the KCTU succeeded in coordinating interests within labor and centralizing the rank and file of large enterprise unions, however. Contrary to the FKTU's coherent organizational structures and strong union leadership, the labor movement groups making up the KCTU, all of which opposed the docile FKTU, encompassed a wide ideological and political spectrum, and its leaders incessantly struggled to aggregate the various political positions. The very structure of the KCTU—its members comprising well-organized and militant chaebŏl unions—contributed to the destabilization of its organizational capacity. chaebŏl unions, which defrayed a large portion of union dues to the KCTU and mobilized union members in labor movements, always swayed the already fragmented KCTU leadership. Their lack of interest in equalizing the disparity of wages and working conditions across firms and industries frustrated the KCTU's political attempts to build more encompassing labor organizations beyond the dominant structure of enterprise unions.

After the KCTU was formed, the FKTU had to compete with it to maintain its own dominant position in labor politics. FKTU-affiliated unions were mostly concentrated in SMEs lacking financial and organizational resources, whereas KCTU-affiliated unions were centered on large chaebŏl firms.[13] Thus, for the FKTU, the organizational survival of its affiliated unions became a more important concern in the process of labor market reform, compared with the KCTU, and the FKTU leadership took more cooperative approaches toward business and government in return for its leadership roles in industrial relations and the persistence of protective measures for SME unions. Meanwhile, KCTU-affiliated labor unions with abundant organizational resources were more prone to striking than their FKTU counterparts, and the KCTU leadership took more radical and militant political strategies than the FKTU.[14]

As in Japan, employment protection for workers was the primary concern for labor unions in Korea, but Korea's organized labor was under great disadvantages. First, contrary to Japan's Rengō, neither the cooperative FKTU nor the militant KCTU had institutionalized channels through which to access labor policy making. Although organized labor was invited to the bargaining table of labor market reform in the late 1990s and 2000s, neither large employers nor political parties forged an alliance with organized labor, leaving labor with no political allies.[15] In fact, some scholars point to a weak union-party linkage as one of the primary reasons why Korea's organized labor failed to prevent comprehensive labor market reform for insiders as well as outsiders at the national level (Y. Lee 2009). Second, the institutional features of Korea's employment protection—the less-institutionalized practices of employment protection covering a small proportion of the workforce—incentivized employers and policy makers to adopt sweeping labor market reform for all workers in times of crisis, as opposed to maintaining protection for insiders. Korea's employers and policy makers did not have any political and economic incentives to forge a coalition with insiders, given the small proportion of the workforce covered by employment protection. While some chaebŏl unions were capable of defending the interests of their members against employers' labor restructuring at the firm level, job security for insiders became far more vulnerable to the forces for change in Korea during the past two decades.

## Political Confrontations between Business and Labor

The Korean business community and organized labor were unable to reach an agreement over labor market reform and labor adjustment strategies. In the face of democratization and financial crisis, employers, afflicted with the problems of large wage increases, intense labor strikes, and a workforce surplus, advocated the increase of labor market flexibility for all workers. In particular, a heavily regulated labor market with strict legal regulations on dismissing regular workers was considered a serious roadblock for employers conducting labor restructuring in response to crisis. By contrast, organized labor pressured the government to further restrict the conditions for dismissing regular workers for managerial reasons. In Korea, industrial variations of organized labor (e.g., export-oriented sector versus sheltered sector) were not salient in the policy positions on reform. Most chaebŏl unions and workers advocated job security for insiders and tried to maximize short-term economic benefits, as opposed to long-term firm competitiveness and profitability, since they rarely trusted employers' commitment to employment protection, even for insiders. These institutional features of employment protection shaped diverging economic incentives and political strategies of business and labor for labor market reform. Thus, it is not surprising to see intense class conflict between large chaebŏl employers and their unions and workers in the process of Korea's labor market reform during the 1990s and 2000s.

# The Politics of Labor Market Reform after Democratization

Immediately after the 1987 democratic transition, the labor market became one of the most contested economic institutions for business, labor, and government in Korea. Korea's conservative policy makers prioritized the stabilization of confrontational industrial relations and the moderation of rapid wage increases as the policy goals of labor market reform. Yet several failed reform attempts shifted the policy toward the increase of labor market flexibility through the weakening of employment protection for workers. As illustrated in table 5.1, Korea's labor market reform focused more on labor market flexibility for regular workers (especially chaebŏl workers) after the late 1990s, in conjunction with the improvement of collective labor rights and the expansion of social protections as compensation policies. This section examines the ways in which Korea's policy makers advanced reform in searching for a new labor market model between 1987 and 1997, confronting the strength of militant unions and intense global competition, and it discusses how and why these reform attempts turned out to be rather unsuccessful in promoting labor market reform based on political consensus between business, labor, and government.

## Pro-Business Reform during the Roh Tae-woo Era

The Roh Tae-woo government (1988–1992), democratically elected but staffed by the authoritarian ruling elite, frequently stepped into industrial disputes in order to tame militant chaebŏl unions and quash democratic labor movements dominated by radical labor activists (Mo 1999). But democratization no longer allowed the Roh government to employ labor control policies using the coercive measures of national security agencies. In addition, the Ministry of Labor (MOL), which had taken only a secondary role in administering repressive labor control polices, strove to transform itself into an impartial mediator between business and labor after democratization. Neither military leaders nor other national security personnel were appointed as labor ministers in the Roh Tae-woo government, which signaled an important shift in the characteristics of the MOL in labor policy making (see figure 3.2). Nonetheless, the role of business associations and organized labor was rather limited in the process of labor policy making since there was no institutionalized channel that societal interest groups could use, except for lobbying politicians, political parties, and bureaucrats, or protesting with massive street demonstrations. Thus, it was policy makers who dominated the political process of labor market reform during the Roh government.

### DEMOCRATIZATION, ELECTIONS, AND THE OPPOSITION-LED REFORM

Democratization imposed intensified electoral competition on politicians and political parties in Korea. In the 1988 National Assembly election, the first legislative election after democratization, the ruling Democratic Justice Party (DJP)

**TABLE 5.1**  Korea's labor market and social protection reform since the late 1980s

| REFORM MEASURE | REFORM OUTCOME |
| --- | --- |
| Revision of the Industrial Relations Law (1989) | Direction and target: improving collective labor rights for all workers |
| | Content: legalization of the third-party intervention; vetoed by President Roh Tae-woo in 1989 |
| Revision of the Labor Union Law (1989) | Direction and target: improving collective labor rights for all workers |
| | Content: relaxation of the administrative and legal procedures to establish unions; vetoed by President Roh Tae-woo in 1989 |
| Revision of the Labor Standards Law (1989) | Direction and target: improving working conditions for all workers |
| | Content: reduction of the standard workweek from forty-six hours to forty-four hours |
| Revision of the Labor Standards Law (on collective dismissal) (1997) | Direction and target: increasing labor market flexibility for insiders (especially chaebŏl workers) |
| | Content: legal recognition of employers' rights to dismiss regular workers under "urgent" economic distress; very difficult to implement in the face of the opposition by organized labor |
| Revision of the Labor Union Law (1997) | Direction and target: improving collective labor rights for all workers (especially unions in the chaebŏl sector) |
| | Content: legalization of multiple unions at the national level with delay in legalizing multiple unions at the firm level |
| Revision of the Labor Standards Law (on collective dismissal) (1998) | Direction and target: increasing labor market flexibility for insiders (especially chaebŏl workers) |
| | Content: further relaxation of the conditions to lay off regular workers for managerial reasons (including mergers and acquisitions) |
| Revision of the Labor Standards Law (on work hours) (1998) | Direction and target: increasing labor market flexibility for insiders |
| | Content: flexible allocation of work hours for insiders in response to business conditions |
| Revision of the Labor Union and Industrial Relations Law (1998) | Direction and target: improving collective labor rights for all workers |
| | Content: lifting of the legal ban on unions' political participation |

*(Continued)*

**TABLE 5.1** *(Continued)*

| REFORM MEASURE | REFORM OUTCOME |
| --- | --- |
| Expansion of the Employment Insurance Program (1998) | Direction and target: enhancing social protections for insiders |
| | Content: rapid expansion of the Employment Insurance Program to regular workers in small- and medium-sized firms (by October 1998); outsiders excluded from the coverage of the program until 2004 |
| Expansion of the Pension Program (1999) | Direction and target: enhancing social protections for all the population |
| | Content: rapid expansion of the pension program to regular workers in small- and medium-sized firms and the urban self-employed |
| Non-Regular Worker Protection Law (2006) | Direction and target: increasing labor market flexibility and improving employment protection for outsiders |
| | Content: extension of employment contract terms from one to two years in exchange for changing the employment status of non-regular workers to that of regular workers after a two-year initial employment contract |
| Revision of the Labor Standards Law (on collective dismissal) (2006) | Direction and target: increasing labor market flexibility for insiders |
| | Content: further reduction of prior-notice period from sixty to fifty days in the case of collective dismissal for managerial reasons |
| Revision of the Labor Union and Industrial Relations Law (on the hiring of temporary workers during strikes) (2006) | Direction and target: weakening collective labor rights (especially for insiders) |
| | Content: legalization of the hiring of temporary workers during strikes in the public utility sector |
| Pension Reform (2007) | Direction and target: insider-favored social protections |
| | Content: exclusion of outsiders from the category of "waged workers" in the pension program |
| Revision of the Labor Standards Law (on collective dismissal) (2010) | Direction and target: increasing labor market flexibility for insiders |
| | Content: further reduction of prior-notice period from fifty to thirty days in the case of collective dismissal for managerial reasons |
| Revision of the Labor Union and Industrial Relations Law (on multiple unions) (2010) | Direction and target: improving collective labor rights for all workers |
| | Content: legalization of multiple labor unions at the firm level |

| REFORM MEASURE | REFORM OUTCOME |
| --- | --- |
| Revision of the Labor Union and Industrial Relations Law (on the "time-off system") (2010) | Direction and target: no conclusive reform direction with respect to collective labor rights, but with a high possibility of the negative effects on labor unions in small- and medium-sized firms because of the lack of financial resources<br><br>Content: legal prohibition on payment of union officials' wages from firms' payrolls, in exchange for acknowledging union officials' union-related activities, the so-called "time-off system" |

failed to secure its legislative majority in the Korean National Assembly (under unicameralism), only winning 125 seats out of 299 (41.81 percent).[16] Meanwhile, three major opposition parties—the Peace Democratic Party (PDP) led by Kim Dae-jung, the Unified Democratic Party (UDP) led by Kim Young-sam, and the New Democratic Republican Party (NDRP) led by Kim Jong-pil—won 71, 60, and 35 seats, respectively (55.51 percent of the seats in total), appealing to regionalism.[17]

Encouraged by the eruption of a wave of labor strikes during the summer of 1987, a group of labor activists struggled to mobilize workers along the lines of class in elections, but explosive democratic labor movements did not automatically bring political success to the working class. Two political parties organized by radical labor activists, neither of which was linked to the official national labor federation FKTU, ran for the 1988 National Assembly election. The electoral result did not show a promising political future for labor-based parties in Korea, even after democratization. The People's Party (Minjungdang) was unable to win even a single seat, gathering only 0.33 percent of the vote, while its rival, the Hangyŏre Democratic Party (Hangyŏre Minjudang) won one seat, with 1.28 percent of the vote (B-K. Kim and Lim 2000, 112; Bum-sang Yoo 2005, 251). These parties, which defined themselves as defenders of the interests of the working class, failed dismally to appeal to workers, who identified themselves through their regional ties in the founding election after democratization (B-K. Kim 2000b, 179–183).

Although all three major opposition parties advocated democratic values during electoral campaigns, the opposition camp itself contained a wide spectrum of political ideologies, including the conservative NDRP, the center-right UDP, and the center-left PDP. The three charismatic party leaders in the opposition camp, the so-called "three Kims," had had very different political careers as well. Kim Young-sam and Kim Dae-jung, both of whom were later elected president of Korea, in 1992 and 1997, respectively, had fought for democracy against the authoritarian regime. In contrast, Kim Jong-pil had been one of the top political leaders during the authoritarian Park regime (1961–1979) although his political activities were banned during the authoritarian Chun Doo-hwan regime that followed. Given the ideological differences within the opposition camp and the different political career paths of its leaders, it was not easy for the opposition to forge a coherent coalition. What they had in common, however, was that they wanted to differentiate themselves from the ruling DJP, which inherited the political legacy of the authoritarian Chun regime. Thus, the opposition camp proposed a wide range of democratic reform measures, including public hearings on corruption charges against Chun himself and chaebŏl (as his allies in state-led economic development). Labor market reform for the improvement of workers' basic rights was one of these pro-democratic areas promoted by the opposition.

Taking advantage of the political atmosphere of democratization, labor unions and labor activists pressed political parties to advance reforms for the interests of labor. The FKTU, which had collaborated with the authoritarian regime, utilized its political ties with individual politicians (e.g., former presidents or officials of the FKTU) in the ruling DJP and the conservative opposition NDRP led by Kim Jong-pil. Meanwhile, dissident labor activists adopted a political strategy of mobilizing workers into street protests, so as to display the political and organizational capacities of the working class. The business community reacted furiously to the political initiative of labor market reform in favor of labor, which could empower workers and militant labor unions in industrial relations. Nonetheless, the voice of business against labor market reform was rather muted in the process of legislative debates in the National Assembly as a result of the political calculations of opposition parties to gather more support from workers and labor unions in the context of intensified electoral competition under democracy (Young-gi Choi et al. 2000, 86–89).

In 1989, three opposition parties—the PDP, the UDP, and the NDRP—submitted three bills to improve workers' basic rights and working conditions, which had been strongly requested by labor activists and unions: revisions of the Industrial Relations Law, the Labor Union Law, and the Labor Standards Law.[18] First, the bill revising the Industrial Relations Law aimed at relaxing a legal restriction on third-party intervention in industrial disputes in order to allow upper-level labor federations as well as labor activists to mediate industrial conflicts between business and labor at the firm level on behalf of enterprise unions and workers. It was the authoritarian Chun Doo-hwan regime that imposed the legal ban on third-party intervention, since policy makers believed that third-party intervention by radical labor activists and union officials in industrial disputes intensified conflict between business and labor rather than resolving it.

Labor activists and union officials argued that this legal restriction was intended to cut off enterprise unions at the firm level from labor movements at the national level. Second, the bill on the revision of the Labor Union Law proposed to improve workers' basic legal rights by further relaxing the administrative and legal procedures for union organization, including organization of low-ranking civil officials and workers in the defense industry, whose sectors strictly prohibited workers from organizing labor unions during the authoritarian regime. Last, the bill on the revision of the Labor Standards Law included the reduction of hours in the standard workweek from forty-six to forty-four in order to improve working conditions.[19]

After intense political debates in the National Assembly, the ruling DJP and the opposition camp agreed to the revisions of the Industrial Relations Law and the Labor Standards Law. But the revision of the Labor Union Law was passed by a majority vote in the 145th plenary session of the National Assembly (on March 9, 1989) in the face of the ruling DJP's strong opposition to the legalization of labor unions for civil officials and workers in the defense industry (Korean National Assembly Secretariat [Gukhoe Samuchŏ] 1989). The opposition-led pro-labor reform failed, however, since President Roh Tae-woo vetoed the revisions of the Industrial Relations Law and the Labor Union Law, and these bills (along with two other important ones, the expansion of the national health insurance system and the introduction of local elections) were sent back to the National Assembly.

There is no clear empirical evidence to demonstrate that the business lobby affected the political decision of the presidential veto on the two bills. But opposition politicians expressed doubt about the heavy influence of the large chaebŏl, since the legislation, especially the revision of the Labor Union Law, might further aggravate contentious industrial relations in the chaebŏl sector (Young-gi Choi et al. 2000, 81–82). Unlike their Japanese counterparts, who were invited to participate in labor policy making, neither the Korean business community nor organized labor had an institutional channel through which to access the political process. Their only available political resources to affect labor policy making were the less institutionalized channels of lobbying and street demonstration.

The failed reform attempt in 1989 clearly revealed the policy preferences of the conservative Roh government. Regardless of democratization, Korea's conservative policy makers still significantly favored the interests of business by restricting workers' basic rights. Pro-business labor policies were further accelerated after President Rho Tae-woo and the two opposition leaders, Kim Young-sam and Kim Jong-pil, merged three political parties—the ruling DJP and two opposition parties, the UDP and the NDRP—into the Democratic Liberal Party (DLP) in January 1990.[20] The new ruling conservative DLP, with almost 73 percent of the seats in the National Assembly, empowered the Rho government to tighten its grip on the labor market and industrial relations in the early 1990s.

The judiciary branch, which was rarely independent from the executive branch, also set the precedent that employers could lay off regular workers for urgent managerial reasons, and that minor procedural problems would not invalidate an employer's decision regarding layoffs (e.g., Korean Supreme Court, 91-da-8647 and 91-da-19463).[21] In particular, two precedents of the Korean Supreme Court were crucial in interpreting broadly acknowledged employers' rights to dismiss workers. In 1989, the Supreme Court established a precedent that employers needed to satisfy four conditions before laying off workers: urgent business necessity, significant efforts to avoid firing workers, reasonable criteria to select a list of workers to lay off, and consultation with the representatives of workers (Korean Supreme Court, 87-daka-2132).[22] While these conditions were very similar to what the Tokyo High Court stipulated in 1979, the four conditions were utilized to "justify" employers' rights to lay off workers in Korea, as opposed to the imposing of restrictions on layoffs in Japan. After two years, in 1991, the Korean Supreme Court established another precedent that would extend the justifiable conditions of dismissals to "urgent" business necessity. The MOL's administrative guidelines further expanded the interpretation of the judiciary's precedent by adding technological changes and industrial restructuring into the justifiable conditions for dismissals (Korean Labor Standards Law 32003-9). Under the conservative Roh government, the interests of the business community were well represented in labor policy making, despite the democratic transition.

## LABOR MARKET REFORM UNDER CONSERVATIVE DOMINANCE

It was not a coincidence that the conservative Roh Tae-woo government initiated a series of business-friendly labor market reforms, focusing on the control of rising labor costs and the stabilization of contentious industrial relations, after the three-party merger in January 1990. Since the new ruling DLP controlled the National Assembly as an absolute legislative majority, the executive branch did not need to worry about the possibility that the opposition camp would unilaterally pass labor market reform bills without the support of the ruling party. Distressed by wage hikes in the chaebŏl sector and consequent wage-driven inflation after the end of its high economic growth period in the early 1990s, two competing ministries on labor policies—the MOL and the Ministry of Trade and Industry (MTI)—proposed labor market reform to strengthen firms' competitiveness in the global market and achieve industrial peace, but with different policy solutions.

The MTI, which predominantly represented the interests of the business community, endeavored to solve the problems of conflict-ridden industrial relations and firms' competitiveness by increasing labor market flexibility and imposing restrictive rules on industrial strikes. In April 1990, the MTI pushed forward the revision of the labor law, disregarding the MOL's jurisdiction over labor policy making. In particular, the characteristics of the chaebŏl-centered economic structure, with a majority of SMEs subordinate to the chaebŏl, led the MTI to advance labor market reforms that would minimize the negative consequences on the Korean national economy of chaebŏl unions' intense and prolonged labor strikes. Thus, the MTI's proposal aimed to increase the costs of holding labor strikes by eliminating wage payment during strikes and allowing chaebŏl to hire temporary workers to reduce the economic costs of work stoppage and production interruption. Such a business-friendly proposal angered workers and unions, however, forcing the MTI to finally withdraw it in July 1990.

Meanwhile, the MOL prioritized wage restraints by institutionalizing a mechanism of wage coordination in the labor market. In 1990, the ministry ambitiously announced a single-digit wage increase policy so as to restrain excessive wage increases driven by militant labor unions, considered to be detrimental to the price competitiveness of Korea's export goods in the global market. It designated major public corporations and large chaebŏl as pattern setters in wage bargaining, emulating Japan's *shuntō*, in which a few large export-oriented firms took a leading role in inter- and intra-industry wage bargaining over the Japanese economy. Unlike in Japan, however, it was the government that determined who would play the role of pattern setter in wage bargaining on behalf of business and labor.

The government-led single-digit wage increase policy could not force presumed "followers"—i.e., SMEs and other smaller chaebŏl firms—to comply with the principle. As indicated by the double-digit nominal wage growth rates in 1990 and 1991, 18.8 percent and 17.5 percent respectively, wage increases far exceeded the government's wage ceiling (Korea Labor Institute 2005, 48). Even large chaebŏl, while worrying about losing state-allocated financial resources if they did not conform to the government's guideline, offered militant labor unions more generous employee benefits in order to compensate for wage restraints. In 1990 and 1991 only, firms with more than one thousand workers increased corporation-provided employee benefits by 39.89 percent and 53.73 percent respectively, and these chaebŏl firms' strategies significantly widened the benefit differentials across firm size.[23]

After failing to impose the single-digit wage increase policy on public corporations and large chaebŏl firms, the MOL proposed a "total wage system" in order to prevent public corporations and large chaebŏl firms from subsidizing wages through increasing employee benefits in 1991. However, the total wage system failed to secure political support even from the ruling DLP since the ruling party was unwilling to undertake labor market reform that would undermine the interests of labor unions and workers, in the face of the upcoming National Assembly and presidential elections in 1992. In particular, since wage increases and employee benefits were the two most important concerns for workers and labor unions, the MOL-proposed reform for the total wage system could have provoked intense discontent against the ruling party in the elections. Unlike an incumbent president with a single five-year non-renewable term, electoral politicians as well as presidential candidates (or hopefuls) were wary of policy agendas that might bring forth political backlash by labor unions and workers. In 1992, a year in which National Assembly and presidential elections were held, no labor legislation was passed, indicating that the ruling DLP and its politicians preferred to postpone discussing controversial labor reform until after all major elections were over.[24]

After a series of failed attempts at wage moderation, the MOL, seeking to dominate labor market reform by setting aside the economic bureaucracy (especially the MTI), established the Research Committee on the Revision of the Labor Law (RCRLL) to discuss a full-scale labor market reform, including the increase of labor market flexibility and the improvement of workers' basic rights, which were strongly demanded by business and labor respectively (B-K. Kim 2003, 66). Unlike previous labor market reform attempts, the RCRLL equally represented business and labor and delegated policy authority to public interest representatives—mostly scholars in industrial relations, labor law, and other pertinent fields—in emulation of Japan's labor deliberative councils, composed of the political representatives of business, labor, and public interests.[25] This signaled that the MOL was seeking to redefine its role as the primary and neutral state agency to incorporate diverse societal interests into labor policy making. Nonetheless, the political deadlock between business and labor at the RCRLL as well as the DLP's internal debates over the revision of the labor law impeded the submission of draft bills to the National Assembly.

The conservative Roh government promoted labor market reform focusing on the institutionalization of wage moderation and the stabilization of conflict-prone industrial relations in favor of the interests of business. By doing so, Korean policy makers endeavored to solve the problems of labor market rigidity after democratization. Simultaneously, the government endeavored to reflect changing political conditions by incorporating societal interests into policy-making procedures, even if legacies of authoritarian rule continued to affect the labor market and industrial relations. These political efforts, however, did not bring forth reform that would establish a new rule of the game based on the political consensus of business, labor, and government.

## Compromised Labor Market Reform during the Kim Young-sam Era

Shortly after taking office, President Kim Young-sam (1993–1997), who had been a long-term opposition leader against the authoritarian regime but ran as presidential candidate of the ruling conservative DLP after the three-party merger in 1990, endeavored to distinguish himself from his predecessor, Roh Tae-woo, who had inherited the legacy of authoritarian rule as one of the former military coup leaders. The Kim government formulated various reformist measures, such as the "real name financial transaction system" and the "breakup of the elite clique (*hanahoe*) within the military," in order to improve economic transparency and consolidate Kim's political legitimacy. In the realm of labor politics, the Kim government restricted the political intervention of national security agencies in industrial disputes—especially the KCIA, which had played a pivotal role in implementing repressive labor control—and incorporated the voices of under-represented organized labor into labor policy making to some degree (*Hangyoreh Shinmun,* March 31, 1993; *Donga Ilbo,* April 29, 1993).

Rhee In-je, the first labor minister of the Kim government, ambitiously promulgated progressive labor policies for the improvement of workers' basic rights and bargaining power in industrial relations (e.g., the principle of "no work, but basic wage payment during strikes" and unions' rights to negotiate for managerial discretion in collective bargaining). But the intense industrial conflicts of the Hyundai Group in June 1993 severely undermined the political position of Rhee within the government, and his pro-labor reform proposals were thwarted by the economic bureaucracy that sided with the interests of the large chaebŏl. Thereafter, the Kim government, which became far more concerned with work stoppage and interruption at production sites, prioritized the stabilization of industrial relations over the improvement of workers' basic rights and unions' bargaining power in the labor market.

Beginning in 1994, the Kim government proposed "globalization" as one of the key policy agendas, a concept that was understood as the improvement of the competitiveness and efficiency of the Korean political economy. Policy makers believed that the strong leadership of the government, as opposed to market forces, would enhance the competitiveness and efficiency of the national economy (J-Y. Jung 2006). In particular, labor market reform for greater flexibility was interpreted as one of the most important policy tools to achieve the goal of globalization by allowing large chaebŏl to streamline inefficient business organizations and to swiftly adjust to intensified global market competition. After the Kim government's failed attempt to build another mechanism of wage coordination (e.g., the tripartite system based on the National Council on the Korean

Economy and Society [Kukmin Gyŏngje Sahoe Hyŏp'ŭihoe]), policy makers finally gave up their efforts to moderate wage increases in the labor market. After that, the government began to focus on labor market reform for greater flexibility by weakening the level of employment protection, which covered a small proportion of the workforce (mostly in large chaebŏl firms) (Dae-whan Kim, Choi, and Yun 2010, 86–87).

A new round of labor market reform came with the establishment of the Presidential Commission on Industrial Relations Reform (PCIRR) in May 1996, led by Park Se-il, senior secretary to the president on social welfare, who envisioned a comprehensive reform on the basis of consensus between business and labor for labor market flexibility and workers' basic rights.[26] The PCIRR, composed of five representatives each from business and labor, ten academic scholars, and ten representatives of public interests, aimed to build new institutional foundations for the Korean labor market and industrial relations.[27]

Most of all, the PCIRR adopted two novel approaches. First, the PCIRR-led labor market reform was the first attempt to propose a trade-off between *samje* (three systems) and *samkŭm* (three prohibitions), both of which were symbols of the political conflicts between business and labor over labor market flexibility and workers' basic rights. The Korean business community demanded the introduction of *samje* (three systems)—the rights of management to lay off regular workers for managerial reasons, to flexibly allocate work hours for regular workers, and to hire non-regular workers on a temporary basis—all of which stood for labor market flexibility (B-K. Kim and Lim 2000). In contrast, *samkŭm* (three prohibitions) represented old repressive labor control under the authoritarian rule: the legal prohibitions on labor unions' political activities, on third-party intervention in industrial disputes at the firm level, and on multiple labor unions at the workplace. Not surprisingly, organized labor pressured the government to abolish these legal bans on labor movements. Second, it invited not only the FKTU, the only official labor federation, but also the KCTU—the de facto second national federation, not legally recognized—into the political processes of labor market reform.[28] Despite its presence in labor politics since 1995, government and business had refused to acknowledge the KCTU as a bargaining partner in labor policy making, but the PCIRR decided to accept KCTU's participation for the first time.

In policy debates on a trade-off between *samje* and *samkŭm*, conflicts were most contentious with respect to the legalization of multiple labor unions and the recognition of employers' right to lay off regular workers for managerial reasons. Two major business associations, the FKI (representing large chaebŏl) and the KEF (encompassing large chaebŏl firms as well as SMEs), claimed that managerial discretion in hiring and firing workers should be legally guaranteed so that firms could adjust to rapidly changing business environments and maintain market competitiveness. As discussed in the previous section, Korean employers (especially in the chaebŏl sector) believed that strong employment protection for regular workers was too burdensome to maintain under intensified global market competition. They complained that they were unable to implement any labor adjustment strategies, such as work transfer or the flexible allocation of work hours, and that employment protection for regular workers, backed by well-organized unions, was too rigid. In contrast, two competing labor federations, the FKTU and the KCTU, requested the insertion of much stricter legal clauses to limit the implementation of layoffs for managerial reasons so as to further consolidate employment protection for regular workers at the national level (Korea Presidential Commission on Industrial Relations Reform 1996).[29]

Although labor activists called for the immediate removal of *samkŭm* (three prohibitions), the FKTU and the KCTU were unable to reach an agreement regarding the legal ban on multiple labor unions. The FKTU, whose organization was dominated by SME unions, proposed to legalize multiple labor unions at all levels in order to check the KCTU, which was based on well-organized large chaebŏl unions by facilitating intense union competition at the firm level. Meanwhile, the KCTU leadership, which had already obtained a secure footing in the chaebŏl sector, preferred to permit multiple labor unions at the national level only, since it was more interested in gaining legal recognition as the political representative of organized labor (Korea Presidential Commission on Industrial Relations Reform 1996).

However, union officials at the national level and rank-and-file members at the firm level had very different policy preferences for labor market reform. At the firm level, regular workers and their enterprise unions were more concerned about the risk of losing jobs after labor market reform, given the few alternatives for equal payment and working conditions in case of unemployment. Meanwhile, union officials at the national labor federations (both the FKTU and the KCTU) paid more attention to the elimination of the legal restrictions on labor movements since these issues were more tightly linked to their organizational survival.[30]

More complicated was that the legalization of multiple labor unions triggered another political confrontation between management and labor at the PCIRR. As a precondition for allowing multiple labor unions at the firm level, the KEF demanded a legal prohibition on payment of union officials' wages from firms' payrolls since it believed that such labor management practices, which had been institutionalized in order to co-opt union officials during the authoritarian regime, encouraged the use of the strike more readily than if there was no such system (B-K. Kim and Lim 2000; Bum-sang You 2005).[31] Thus, the KEF intended to preempt frequent industrial strikes by stipulating the legal ban on employer-paid union official wages, in exchange for the legalization of multiple labor unions.

The political deadlock over *samje* and *samkŭm* frustrated the PCIRR's attempt to draw up a draft bill based upon consensus. Both business and labor deliberately took more hawkish approaches to a trade-off between *samje* and *samkŭm* as a bargaining strategy because they were well aware that the reform group at the PCIRR sought unanimous political agreement over policy recommendations (Se-il Park 2000, 73). As an advisory body, advising the president but with no legal authority, the PCIRR could not force any political decisions on the state bureaucracy and societal interest groups. A more fundamental problem was that the backup provided by the top political leadership was too unstable to compete with the bureaucracy.

Since the summer of 1996, large chaebŏl and the economic bureaucracy had framed Korea's economic slowdown as a "crisis" and further pushed pro-business labor market reform for greater flexibility (Mo 1999). The labor minister himself, with a career background as an economic bureaucrat, focused more on labor market flexibility and industrial peace than on the improvement of workers' basic rights.[32] Neither employers nor policy makers were willing to form a coalition in support of employment protection for insiders, given the less institutionalized practices of employment protection covering a small proportion of the workforce (mostly chaebŏl workers).

After the failure of the PCIRR to achieve consensus between business and labor, an inter-ministerial committee, composed of fourteen ministers, undertook the reform initiative in November 1996. The final version drafted by the MOL represented the policy position favored by businesses, incorporating all their demands: the right of employers to lay off regular workers for managerial reasons, to flexibly allocate workers' work hours, and to hire non-regular workers during strikes on a temporary basis (B-K. Kim and Lim 2000; Byung-hoon Lee and You 2001; Mo 1999 and 2001; Se-il Park 2000).[33] Once again, the economic bureaucracy, which represented the interests of the large chaebŏl, defeated progressive social welfare policy makers in the process of labor market reform, which indicated the triumph of the business community over organized labor (W. Lee 1997, 47).

Two opposition leaders, Kim Dae-jung and Kim Jong-pil, protracted the enactment of labor reform bills, employing a sit-in at the National Assembly. They claimed that the Kim Young-sam government should postpone labor market reform until after the scheduled presidential election in December 1997. President Kim and the ruling party leadership, however, unilaterally passed the bills at a plenary session in late December 1996.[34] Introducing the government-submitted bills with the authorization of the Speaker of the National Assembly, the ruling conservative New Korea Party bypassed the Environment and Labor Standing Committee and secretly called a plenary session without notifying opposition parties.[35] Even worse, a small group of top leaders—a few top party leaders, the senior secretary on economic policy, the senior secretary for political affairs, and the labor minister—arbitrarily inserted two additional conditions into the draft bills. The first additional condition was that the legalization of multiple labor unions at the national level be postponed until 2000, which broke the government's implicit political promise to the KCTU in return for the participation in the PCIRR. The second additional condition was that mergers and acquisitions also be included as a justified condition for employers to lay off redundant regular (Bum-sang You 1999, 120, 126, 178). These versions of the reform bills predominantly favored the business community by lowering employment protection for regular workers while maintaining strict legal restrictions on workers' basic rights.

Only after facing a one-month-long general strike initiated by the FKTU and the KCTU did the ruling and opposition parties, neither of which had actively participated in the process of drafting the bills, agree to revise the legislation in January 1997 (Y. C. Kim 1998; Koo 2000). The political timing of additional labor market reform could not have been worse. Since President Kim Young-sam was already in his last year of a five-year non-renewable term in 1997, his government had lost the political momentum necessary for arduous reform. More seriously, the bankruptcy of Hanbo Steel on January 23, 1997, which triggered the collapse of the fourteenth largest chaebŏl, Hanbo Group, unveiled a huge corruption scandal, entangling President Kim's son as well as a significant number of powerful politicians in both the ruling and opposition parties.

Neither the ruling New Korea Party nor the opposition, the National Congress for New Politics and the United Liberal Democrats were willing to undertake the intense bargaining and negotiation necessary to draft a comprehensive new reform bill. The revised bills recognized employers' right to lay off regular workers for managerial reasons, but only in the case of urgent business conditions and with a two-year grace period, making the practical implementation of this clause extremely difficult. Multiple labor unions at the national level would be immediately legalized, but those at the firm level would encounter a three-year delay.[36] The 1997 labor market reform protected the core interests of the KCTU and its affiliated chaebŏl unions since the reform legislation prevented chaebŏl firms, which had to downsize unprofitable corporate structures during economic downturns, from implementing labor restructuring for insiders. The only substantial policy change brought forth was the legalization of multiple labor unions at the national level.

The Kim Young-sam government sought to incorporate the logic of consensus-based labor policy making, allowing societal interest groups to participate in policy debates and deliberations. However, the diverging policy preferences of business and labor for reform, deriving from the institutional features of employment protection, undermined the political authority of the PCIRR and reform-minded policy makers in decision making, and the contested politics of reform further intensified conflicts and distrust between business and labor. Unlike their Japanese counterparts, large chaebŏl employers and their regular workers were involved in intense political conflicts over labor market reform, turning reform into a zero-sum game of distributive politics at the firm and national levels. Given the less-institutionalized practices of the employment protection system covering a small segment of the workforce, Korea's employers had much stronger policy demands for labor market liberalization for insiders, and its conservative policy makers tended to advance far-reaching reform for all workers.

The conservative Kim government aimed to bring forth more comprehensive labor market reform in exchange for the improvement of workers' basic rights. Neither the increase of labor market flexibility nor the improvement of workers' basic rights was fully achieved through the 1997 labor market reform. In early 1997, Korea's economy already showed signs of a serious recession. Even chaebŏl, often believed to be "too big to fail," fell under serious financial distress and were forced to streamline their business organization. However, the 1997 reform did not enable the chaebŏl to carry out rapid and extensive corporate restructuring, limiting the option of labor restructuring for redundant insiders. Further labor market reform would have to wait until after the presidential election in December 1997, when new political leadership would undertake the initiative.

# Labor Market Reform after the Asian Financial Crisis

The 1997 Asian financial crisis was a critical turning point for Korea toward a more flexible labor market. Taking advantage of the exigency of the crisis, policy makers pressured societal interest groups—especially organized labor—to accept comprehensive labor market reform that would weaken the level of employment protection for insiders. After a decade of comprehensive labor market reform, however, Korea further deepened labor market inequality and dualism, contrary to policy makers' anticipation of a declining gap between insiders and outsiders. A shrinking number of chaebŏl workers (as "core" insiders) continued to enjoy the privileges of even stronger internal labor markets (e.g., job security, high wages, and generous social protections) despite across-the-board liberalization of the labor market, whereas a majority of workers in much smaller and less profitable chaebŏl firms and SMEs as well as non-regular workers were directly exposed to the vagaries of market forces. This section analyzes how the institutional features of the employment protection system facilitated far-reaching labor market reform for insiders as well as outsiders during the financial crisis, and how decentralized industrial relations based on large chaebŏl unions further reinforced labor market inequality and dualism between chaebŏl workers and the others in the Korean labor market.

## Labor Market Reform, Inequality, and Dualism during the Kim Dae-jung Era

Amid the economic upheaval of the financial crisis, Kim Dae-jung embarked on comprehensive labor market reform to relax the level of employment protection for regular workers in order to facilitate corporate restructuring and to quickly resuscitate the Korean economy, even prior to his inauguration as president in February 1998. In fact, Kim, as center-left opposition party candidate in a very tight presidential race, firmly pledged to guarantee employment protection for workers, despite the conditions for labor market reform that the International Monetary Fund (IMF) had attached to its $57 billion financial rescue package for Korea. Soon after winning the election by a narrow 1.5 percent margin in late December 1997, Kim reneged on his electoral promise and prioritized the relaxation of employment protection for regular workers in order to streamline inefficient business organizations under the pressure of severe financial distress.[37]

The financial crisis served as an important window of opportunity for President-elect Kim to catalyze prompt and sweeping policy responses by utilizing the logic of two-level games.[38] He dexterously exploited the severity of the crisis and external pressure from the IMF and the US government to drive labor market reform, targeting regular workers in the chaebŏl sector, and to simultaneously avoid political blame for shifting his policy stance. There was no doubt that the Asian financial crisis and international actors, exemplified by the IMF and the United States, played a pivotal role in shaping Korea's labor market reform, in exchange for offering financial rescue packages. What is missing in this analytical framework is who determined the specific contents of the reform. It was President-elect Kim who interpreted labor market reform as the increase of flexibility through the legalization of employers' right to dismiss regular workers for managerial reasons (e.g., corporate restructuring) (H-K. Lee et al. 2007, 241–243). Given the predominance of the chaebŏl in the Korean economy, labor market reform for greater flexibility in employment contracts and working conditions for regular workers, which would allow chaebŏl firms to shed regular workers in corporate restructuring, was regarded as an imperative for its rapid economic turnaround. In particular, Kim considered regular workers in large chaebŏl firms, who were covered by tight employment protection, an obstacle for firms' swift and flexible adjustment to the crisis.

President-elect Kim carried out his comprehensive labor market reform by establishing the Tripartite Commission, modeled on social pacts in western European countries. Appointing Han Kwang-ok, a national assemblyman and one of Kim's longtime political followers (*gashin*), as chairman of the commission in January 1998 before his inauguration, Kim placed great political emphasis on labor market reform. Despite the principle of consensus-based labor market reform at the Tripartite Commission, key reform agendas—e.g., the immediate implementation of employers' right to lay off regular workers under urgent economic distress—were already hand-picked by Kim himself.[39] In Chairman Han's interview with Korean journalists, he explicitly stated that the primary goal of the Tripartite Commission would be to persuade organized labor to accept the legalization of the layoff clause in corporate restructuring (*Chosun Ilbo,* January 7, 1998). Ironically, most reform plans discussed at the Tripartite Commission were replicas of the Kim Young-sam government's failed labor market reform bills—bills that Kim Dae-jung himself had fiercely refused to pass as an opposition leader in late 1996. President-elect Kim simply required a form of consensus-based policy making at the Tripartite Commission to preempt the political resistance of organized labor, one of his political constituencies in the presidential election, as well as to bind societal interest groups, especially labor unions, to abide by new rules and regulations in the labor market.[40] In the midst of the crisis, the Tripartite Commission was limited to being a perfunctory labor policy-making institution to facilitate the government-led comprehensive labor market reform.

Why, then, did President-elect Kim seek to establish a new institutional mechanism for labor market reform (namely the Tripartite Commission), even though Korea lacked any political and ideological legacy of social pacts? Korea's presidential system, with a single five-year non-renewable term that is usually further weakened by the staggered electoral cycle of the National Assembly, allows an incumbent president to enjoy only a very short period of stable and strong political authority over policy making, in contrast to the common perception of the "imperial presidency" in Korea. Therefore, the president usually prefers to advance all tough policy changes early in the five-year term in order to avoid the problem of a lame-duck presidency. Moreover, Kim Dae-jung was the first opposition leader to win a presidential election since the 1987 democratic transition. The pre-electoral coalition between the National Congress for New Politics (NCNP) and the United Liberal Democrats (ULD) could not control the legislative branch until they later poached several opposition Grand National

Party (GNP) members to secure a legislative majority in the National Assembly. Thus, President-elect Kim embraced the idea of social pacts—materialized as the Tripartite Commission—as a strategy to overcome his own political problems in policy making.[41]

With Kim Dae-jung's strong reform drive, members of business associations and labor federations, as well as the ruling and opposition parties, were brought together to discuss labor market reform at the Tripartite Commission.[42] The exigencies of the financial crisis facilitated comprehensive labor market reform by suppressing political resistance of organized labor (representing the interests of insiders) at the bargaining table. Equally important was that the institutional features of the employment protection system contributed to Korea's comprehensive reform. The business community always wanted to lower the levels of employment protection for the regular workforce to increase labor market flexibility, even before the financial crisis. It considered employment protection systems, pressured by the power of militant labor unions, detrimental to firms' production and investment strategies in intensified global market competition. Korea's employers calculated that costs of retaining redundant workers in times of economic distress would be much higher than the future returns of keeping them within firms. In addition, given the small proportion of the workforce covered by employment protection, center-left policy makers calculated that a quick economic turnaround driven by comprehensive reform for all workers would be a far more effective mechanism to appeal to the general public, as well as to enhance political accountability and competitiveness in elections, than advocating for the interests of the small segment of the workforce in large chaebŏl firms. Meanwhile, insiders were unable to find any political allies in support of their continued employment protection.

Less than a month after the Tripartite Commission first convened in January 1998, political representatives of the FKTU and the KCTU grudgingly accepted the immediate implementation of employers' right to lay off regular workers for managerial reasons, including in cases of mergers and acquisitions, and their right to hire non-regular workers on a temporary basis through the enactment of the Worker Dispatch Law.[43] Both issues had been intensely debated between business, labor, and government throughout the 1990s. In return for the political concession, the Tripartite Commission promised to improve workers' basic rights and social protections for the unemployed. It agreed to lift the legal ban on labor unions' political participation, to legalize teachers' labor unions, and to expand the state-funded public welfare programs for the unemployed (e.g., the rapid expansion of the Employment Insurance Program).[44] Meanwhile, the commission deferred until the end of 2001 the final decision on whether to allow workers to be represented by multiple unions at the firm level and whether to keep union officials on the company's payroll, since the business community worried that multiple labor unions at the firm level would further complicate conflict-ridden industrial relations, and organized labor (especially unions in SMEs) was more concerned over stable financial resources for union activities.[45]

The Kim Dae-jung government's comprehensive labor market reform in the midst of the Asian financial crisis resulted in mixed policy outcomes. First of all, compromise among a few political elites could not force societal interest groups to abide by the reform. In particular, the KCTU, composed of large chaebŏl unions, could not even make a credible commitment to labor market reform because of its internal factional conflicts between hard-liners (especially from chaebŏl unions) and soft-liners. Just a few days after the announcement of the "Social Pact for Labor Market Reform" in February 1998, the rank-and-file union members of the KCTU used a non-confidence vote to throw out its union leadership, which had consented to the immediate recognition of employers' right to lay off regular workers for managerial reasons.[46] The KCTU, which had continuously threatened to withdraw from participation in the Tripartite Commission, finally pulled out in January 1999, leaving the more externally docile and internally cohesive FKTU as the only representative of the working class (D. Park 2001).

Second, despite comprehensive labor market reform led by the Tripartite Commission, the commission was troubled from the beginning because of its organizational structure and lack of support from political parties. As a presidential advisory body, the commission was devoid of the legal authority to force societal interest groups and the bureaucracy to abide by the political compromise made at the commission. For instance, the MOL, which President Kim Dae-jung had put aside in his labor market reform, did not respect the policy recommendations suggested by the commission. High-ranking MOL bureaucrats downgraded the effectiveness of consensus-based labor policy making and refused to consult the commission because of its lack of legal power to impose any policy decisions on the ministry (Dae-whan Kim, Choi, and Yun 2010, 270–290; Y. Lee 2009, 61; Roh 1999, 302).

The Tripartite Commission became more enfeebled by weak support from political parties and politicians. Pushed by President-elect Kim Dae-jung, politicians from both the ruling coalition of the NCNP and the ULD and the majority-opposition GNP joined to discuss labor reform at the commission. Except for a few political leaders of the NCNP, personally delegated by Kim Dae-jung, the ruling coalition was not very enthusiastic about labor market reform since this controversial policy was unlikely to mobilize votes or other forms of political support. The GNP acquiesced to the labor reform proposed by the commission in order to avoid any blame during the severe financial crisis, but it eventually withdrew from the commission, criticizing it for having made too many concessions to organized labor *(Chosun Ilbo,* February 6, 1998). After the second half of 1998, neither the ruling nor the opposition parties attended the Tripartite Commission. After the legalization of employers' right to lay off regular workers for managerial reasons, the Kim Dae-jung government itself did not put much faith in the commission either (Roh 1999, 257–265).

Lastly, the consensus-based labor policy-making mechanism of the Tripartite Commission was dysfunctional under the conditions of the zero-sum class conflict between business and labor. In times of severe economic distress employers preferred to advance further liberalization for insiders, focusing on the weakening of the level of employment protection stipulated by the Labor Standards Law, whereas insiders and their unions were eager to defend job security under the attack of employers at the firm and national levels. To make matters worse, Korean business associations attempted to bypass the Tripartite Commission after the legislation of employers' right to lay off regular workers for managerial reasons. Large chaebŏl firms, in particular, did not take any further interest in other labor market reform agendas, except for the increase of labor market flexibility for insiders, and they distrusted that the incompetent KCTU leadership could discipline militant chaebŏl unions to abide by social pacts at the firm level (Bum-sang You 2000, 394). Based on these calculations, business associations became indifferent to the Tripartite Commission, which finally resulted in the withdrawal of the FKI—composed of large chaebŏl—from the commission in 2005.

The opportunity for further labor market reform was too transient for the Kim Dae-jung government. The ULD left the ruling coalition government in 2001, which left the president's party as a legislative minority in the National Assembly and brought on early lame-duck status for President Kim.[47] The Tripartite Commission became more marginalized after the FKTU and the KCTU decided to walk out.[48] Neither societal interest groups nor the government had the will to make this institution function to produce mutually positive outcomes.

Contrary to policy makers' *ex-ante* predictions, the Kim Dae-jung government's comprehensive labor market reform reinforced labor market inequality and dualism between chaebŏl workers and the others, which had already been exacerbated since the 1987 democratic transition. Decentralized industrial relations based on large chaebŏl unions complicated the implementation of comprehensive labor market reform at the firm level as well as the expansion of social protection programs for those affected by reform (mostly SME workers and nonregular workers). The implementation of the reform was rather limited since well-organized chaebŏl unions, which comprised only 5.8 percent of labor unions but more than 70 percent of union members, exerted their organizational capacities in collective bargaining and industrial disputes to block labor restructuring for their union members at the firm level (Korean Ministry of Labor 2005).[49] By contrast, after comprehensive labor market reform, not only non-regular workers but also regular workers in SMEs without the strength of well-organized labor unions were forced to accept labor restructuring for managerial reasons.

At the firm level, large chaebŏl employers failed to implement employers' right to lay off regular workers for managerial reasons in the face of the resistance of chaebŏl unions against labor adjustment. An intense political confrontation at Hyundai Motor Company in 1998 was a case in point. In May 1998, Hyundai, which dominated Korea's automobile industry with more than 40 percent of the domestic market, undertook massive corporate restructuring programs in order to respond to the drastic decline in domestic sales, interest hikes, and loan recalls in the wake of the Asian financial crisis (Sung-jae Cho et al. 2004, 25–26). The management, entangled in complicated cross shareholding and cross loan guarantees with other affiliate Hyundai firms and suffering from a 490 percent debt-to-equity ratio as of 1997, announced its decision to lay off 8,189 regular workers, comprising 18 percent of its total workforce (Joo 2002).[50] Since it was the first large-scale attempt to implement employers' right to lay off regular workers for managerial reasons, it was considered a watershed for labor restructuring in the chaebŏl sector, where well-organized unions were capable of obstructing it.

The dispute was finally resolved after three months with the political intervention of the ruling NCNP's top leaders, dispatched by President Kim Dae-jung, including Roh Moo-hyun—then vice-chairman of the NCNP and the next president of Korea—who strove to arbitrate between management and the Hyundai union. However, neither national business associations nor national labor federations were interested in mediating. The KCTU, the national federation affiliated with the Hyundai union, further complicated political negotiations between management and the union by threatening to raise a general strike to block the layoffs at Hyundai. National business associations (e.g., the FKI and the KEF) also did not make any efforts to bargain with labor on behalf of the business community.

Management and the labor union finally agreed to the layoff of 277 workers, including 144 women working in the company cafeteria, and the implementation of an unpaid vacation program for 1,961 workers in August 1998 (*Hangyoreh Shinmun,* August 18, 1998).[51] Symbolically, the Hyundai management could lay off the regular workforce for managerial reasons, but it could not conduct the large-scale labor adjustment programs that it had originally proposed. The political turmoil over labor restructuring deepened distrust between management and the union. In June 2000, the Hyundai union, haunted by fears of massive layoffs, urged management to sign a contract called the "Agreement to Job Security" in order to assure employment protection for its members. It also asked at the collective bargaining table in 2003 that management notify and consult with the union in advance regarding any corporate strategies pertinent to labor adjustments, such as moving production sites abroad, introducing new car models, divesting its business organization, and subcontracting production lines. Management consented to all these conditions (Sung-jae Cho et al. 2004, 81).

For management, the expansion of the hiring of non-regular workers in the external labor market was the only solution for increasing labor market flexibility while avoiding any potential conflicts with its militant union. Unsurprisingly, non-regular workers hired on a temporary basis and employed by SME in-house subcontractors became an important buffer for regular workers in subsequent corporate restructuring at Hyundai. In exchange for job security for its rank and file, the labor union agreed to an increase of 16.9 percent in the hiring rate of non-regular workers. As a result, the number of non-regular workers rose from 1,808 in 1999 to 3,517 in 2000. However, the management froze new hires of regular workers in production lines after 1998 (Joo 2002, 84–87).[52]

Witnessing the limitations of implementing the lay-off clause in labor restructuring as a result of the fierce opposition of well-organized unions, a majority of chaebŏl firms decided to avoid the costly option of laying off regular workers. They instead opted for labor restructuring through the expanded hiring of non-regular workers and the increased usage of in-house subcontracting and outsourcing of production lines to SMEs (E. Jung 1999, 16). This would help them control labor costs and sustain economic efficiency and market competitiveness. In particular, the system of subcontracting functioned as a primary mechanism for the increase of labor market flexibility by streamlining business organizations and preempting chaebŏl workers' and unions' resistance against firms' production strategies. As a result, the very bottom tier of SME subcontractors locked in the system had to put up with the pressure of cost reductions from higher-tier SME subcontractors. In the case of the automobile sector, based on several tiers of the subcontracting system, the wage levels of regular workers in SME subcontractors were even lower than those of non-regular workers in large chaebŏl firms, indicating the severe cost-cutting pressure on SME subcontractors in the production system (Sung-jae Cho et al. 2004, 180–189).

A small fraction of the workforce under the protection of chaebŏl labor unions was relatively shielded from any political and economic pressure of labor market changes and further consolidated their levels of employment protection even more than before. In the context of labor restructuring, Korean employers adopted similar adjustment methods to those developed by their Japanese counterparts. Decentralized industrial relations based on large enterprise unions ensured the privileges of insiders, regardless of the different patterns of labor market reform. Yet the political mechanism underlying these labor adjustment strategies was quite different in the two countries: political alliance between large employers and insiders in Japan versus the strength of chaebŏl labor unions in Korea.

The rapid expansion of social protection programs during the Kim Dae-jung government did not solve the problems of widening economic disparity between insiders and outsiders. To offer a social safety net for the unemployed during the financial crisis, the government rapidly extended the coverage of the Employment Insurance Program, which had been initially introduced for firms with more than thirty workers in 1995 in order to facilitate corporate restructuring, to firms with more than one worker, and with a much longer period of benefits in early 1999 (H-K. Song 2003; Korean Ministry of Labor 2008b). Nevertheless, a large number of SME workers and non-regular workers were still excluded from the Employment Insurance Program because of the problems of legal enforcement and policy loopholes (as shown in table 1.7). More importantly, large employers and insiders opted for "segmentalist" approaches to the expansion of social protections for those in precarious employment conditions or unemployed, since a social policy regime—an occupationally segmented and work-based one—already offered more generous social protections for insiders (especially those in large firms).

The Kim government also expanded the coverage of the National Pension Program (Kukmin Yŏnkŭm), which had been launched in 1988 for firms with more than ten workers, to include the urban self-employed by 1999.[53] Except for a few occupational categories (e.g., civil servants, military personnel, and teachers), the National Pension Program—composed of a workplace-based system for waged workers and a region-based system for the self-employed and farmers—integrated all citizens into one pension scheme from its beginning, a system designed to pool the risk over the entire population under the principle of egalitarianism. Still, it did not alleviate the immediate problem of unemployment since the National Pension Program offered at best very meager benefits for early retirement (at fifty-five or over), in contrast to its continental European counterparts.

Although its crisis-stricken economy experienced a rapid turnaround, Korea confronted severe problems of labor market inequality and dualism along the dimensions of employment status and firm size. The center-left Kim Dae-jung government promoted comprehensive labor market reform for all workers and simultaneously expanded employment and social protections for outsiders. Nevertheless, Korea's decentralized industrial relations based on large chaebŏl unions further exacerbated the deepening of labor market inequality and dualism, regardless of policy changes and social protections. Such institutional features of the labor market continued to protect regular workers in large chaebŏl firms from job insecurity, low wages, and meager social welfare benefits, while

SME workers and non-regular workers were left directly exposed to the vagaries of the market. Comprehensive labor market reform, ironically, generated
the reinforcement of inequality and dualism between insiders and outsiders, as
opposed to reducing the economic gap, because of the effects of decentralized
industrial relations on the implementation of reform and the development of
social protections.

## Labor Market Reform, Inequality, and Dualism during the Roh Moo-hyun Era

During his presidential race in 2002, Roh Moo-hyun, a center-left candidate of
the ruling NCNP and former labor lawyer, promised to prioritize the alleviation
of inequality and dualism in the labor market, which had been exacerbated after
the financial crisis.[54] His presidential transitional committee underscored a wide
range of labor market and social protection reforms as their top policy agendas
(Seung-jun Park and Lee 2004, 78–81). Yet the Roh government was not able to
reverse the trajectory of increasing labor market inequality and dualism despite
the appointment of pro-labor policy intellectuals and labor activists to key labor
policy-making positions (Roh 2006).

Immediately after his inauguration in February 2003, President Roh and his
top officials proposed a new round of labor market reform by emulating the
Dutch model of social partnership (*Chosun Ilbo*, June 30, 2003, July 2, 2003, July
5, 2003; *Hangyoreh Shinmun*, July 4, 2003). Lee Joung-woo, policy chief of the
Office of the President and in charge of the labor market reform, claimed that
the Dutch model, based on political consensus between business, labor, and government, would solve Korea's problems of contentious industrial conflicts and
increasing labor market inequality and dualism between insiders and outsiders.[55]
As a leftist policy intellectual who was very skeptical of the neoliberal model of
capitalism as an alternative for the Korean market economy, Lee argued that a
political compromise between wage restraints and unions' participation in management would stabilize conflict-ridden industrial relations. Such stability was
regarded as a crucial precondition for sustainable economic growth in Korea.

Neither the business community nor organized labor supported the notion
of a social partnership. chaebŏl employers furiously rejected the idea of unions'
participation in management because they were afraid that "myopic" chaebŏl
unions, obsessed with short-term economic interests (e.g., high wages and generous benefits) without worrying about long-term competitiveness and profitability of firms, would interrupt their business strategies as well as further fortify
the already high levels of employment protection for workers.[56] Meanwhile, the
FKTU and the KCTU doubted the possibility of implementing the Dutch model

of social partnership because of chaebŏl employers' hostility to unions. They also suspected that the government's proposal was only a disguise for a political strategy to further increase labor market flexibility for workers and impose wage restraints on them. This new political attempt at labor market reform faded when Lee stepped down as policy chief in December 2003.[57]

President Roh began to distance himself from organized labor after a series of intense labor disputes in the spring of 2003 (including those led by the Transportation and Delivery Industry Union, the Korean Railway Union, and Hyundai Motor Company union) (*Hangyoreh Shinmun,* July 1, 2003, July 2, 2003, July 29, 2003). Criticizing chaebŏl unions and workers for pursuing their own short-term economic interests, President Roh contended that chaebŏl unions and their members should make political concessions on employment protection and wages so that employers could improve conditions for SME workers and non-regular workers. He considered the chaebŏl workforce—"core" insiders under the privileges of strong internal labor markets—the driving force for increasing labor market inequality and dualism. Large chaebŏl added fuel to the intense debates on the deepening of labor market inequality and dualism. The KEF even announced that if chaebŏl workers and unions agreed to freeze wage increases in collective bargaining, employers would promise to spend the portion of wage increases designated for the regular workforce on improving employment and working conditions for the non-regular workforce, most of whom were underpaid and under-protected (*Chosun Ilbo,* March 31, 2005; Korean Employers' Federation 2006, 7). Ironically, the center-left Roh government and large chaebŏl employers took the same position, siding with the weakening of the privileges of chaebŏl workers (namely "core" insiders), especially job security and high wages. In the face of the zero-sum logic of distributional conflicts between insiders and outsiders in the context of rising labor market inequality and dualism, the political position of chaebŏl unions and workers—a small proportion of the workforce in the Korean labor market—was drastically marginalized and alienated.

The problems of interest aggregation in labor policy making further complicated the Roh government's labor market reform. Although the establishment of the Tripartite Commission provided business associations and labor federations with the institutionalized channel to participate in labor policy making after the financial crisis, it became more difficult for societal interest groups to agree over contentious reform agendas since business and labor were neither able to coordinate with each other nor to orchestrate diverging interests within each group.[58] In 2005, the FKI, composed of the large chaebŏl, finally decided to withdraw from the Tripartite Commission, and in its place, the Korean Chamber of Commerce and Industry, comprising SMEs, joined. Large chaebŏl and the FKI's leaders did not feel it necessary to attend the commission since it had been unable to produce any meaningful labor reform for big business. More fundamentally, they did not believe that the labor reform proposals discussed at the commission were directly pertinent to their own problems.[59] Meanwhile, the KEF, composed of both large firms and SMEs, shifted increasingly toward representing the political and economic interests of SMEs, which alienated large firms and led to the withdrawal of some large chaebŏl firms from the organization (e.g., Hyundai Motor Company).[60]

Political competition between the FKTU and the KCTU and the internal conflicts within the KCTU did not promote the representation of organized labor in policy making either. The Green Social Democratic Party, which the FKTU established in 2002, could not win even a single seat in the 2004 National Assembly election, whereas the Democratic Labor Party, loosely affiliated with the KCTU, won ten seats, two from single-member districts (SMD) and eight from proportional representation (PR) systems, due to the introduction of the new electoral system.[61] After its dismal electoral defeat, the FKTU took more cooperative approaches toward the business community and the government in order to be recognized as a more reliable bargaining partner in labor policy making. Although the KCTU adopted more confrontational policy positions, its leadership was always challenged by the many factional conflicts within its organization. A few chaebŏl unions (e.g., Hyundai Heavy Industries union and GS-Caltex Oil Corporation union) even withdrew from the KCTU, refusing to follow its militant political and organizational strategies. A series of corruption scandals in 2005 that entangled chaebŏl unions and top union officials seriously tarnished the moral reputation of chaebŏl unions as well as the labor movement in general.

Frustrated by the negative political feedback from business and labor on the Dutch model of social partnership, in April 2003 the Roh government proposed another labor market reform, this time based on the concept of "flexicurity" (flexibility plus security) in order to increase labor market flexibility for insiders (especially in large chaebŏl firms) and improve protection for outsiders. In July 2003, the Subcommittee on Policy for Non-Regular Workers under the Tripartite Commission submitted its policy recommendations to the government (Korea Development Institute 2006, 109). But the policy deliberation and negotiation did not proceed smoothly. The FKTU and the KCTU argued that the reform bills were pro-business because they eliminated restrictive conditions on hiring non-regular workers, whereas business claimed that the reform bills significantly favored the interests of labor because of strict requirements on discrimination against non-regular workers.

During the Roh government, the political authority of the Tripartite Commission was continuously challenged by the MOL, which attempted to initiate a top-down pattern of labor market reform, as opposed to the consensus-based decision-making at the commission. Putting aside the commission, the MOL launched the Committee on the Advancement of Industrial Relations in

2003 in order to discuss the revision of labor laws and the stabilization of industrial relations. After three years of intense policy debates, the ruling Uri Party (as a legislative minority) and the major conservative opposition, GNP, passed the MOL-submitted reform legislations in December 2006. The Non-Regular Worker Protection Law, enacted in 2006, stipulated that employers could extend employment contract terms for non-regular workers from one to two years provided they change the employment status of non-regular workers to that of regular workers after a two-year initial employment contract.[62] The Labor Standards Law was simultaneously revised in order to increase labor market flexibility for regular workers and stabilize contentious industrial relations. Three legal clauses of the Labor Standards Law were particularly important for employment protection and industrial relations: (1) the further relaxation of the conditions for laying off regular workers for managerial reasons by reducing the prior-notice period from sixty to fifty days; (2) the legalization of hiring temporary workers during industrial strikes in the public utility sector; and (3) the delay in allowing multiple unions at the firm level until the end of 2009.[63] While the introduction of the Non-Regular Worker Protection Law was intended to improve employment protection for outsiders, the revision of the Labor Standards Law aimed to further increase labor market flexibility by easing the process of laying off regular workers for managerial reasons as well as discouraging strikes in the public utility sector. The legalization of multiple labor unions at the firm level was postponed again as a political compromise between the FKTU, business, and government.

Among organized labor, only the FKTU agreed to the MOL-proposed reform bills, in return for delaying the legal prohibition of payment to union officials' wages from the firm payroll. Since the FKTU was mostly composed of SME labor unions lacking financial resources, its organizational interests led the FKTU leadership to consent to the government-led reform, even including the increase of labor market flexibility for insiders. Meanwhile, the KCTU fiercely refused to participate in the bargaining on "flexicurity," demanding much stronger employment protection for outsiders but without the sacrifice of job security for insiders. The official policy of the KCTU was to block any deregulatory measures intended to increase labor market flexibility targeting non-regular workers if there were no protective measures on employment and working conditions for those workers. Yet its core rank-and-file workers in the chaebŏl sector were rather indifferent to labor market reform for non-regular workers unless the interests of the chaebŏl workforce were seriously threatened by these policy changes. To some extent, the shortening of the prior-notice period from sixty to fifty days could further weaken the level of employment protection for insiders, but nevertheless, for chaebŏl workers and unions with great disruptive potential in industrial relations, the consequences of such legal changes would not be huge. Although the

Democratic Labor Party opposed the legislation, the party was too small and weak to block a grand policy coalition of the ruling Uri Party and the GNP. After the National Assembly passed the laws, the KCTU went on strike in an effort to have them repealed, but its efforts were ineffective.

Despite comprehensive labor market reform for all workers, combined with the improvement of protection for non-regular workers, Korea could not avoid deepening labor market inequality and an increasingly dualistic labor market over the following decade. In particular, employment protection for regular workers in the chaebŏl sector became even stronger. The average number of enterprise tenure years for workers in firms with more than five hundred workers, an indicator of stable employment within enterprise, increased from 5 to 9.2 between 1992 and 2007, whereas average enterprise tenure years for the entire workforce in the Korean labor market rose from 4 to 6 years during the same period (see figure 2.3).[64] As elaborated in the previous section, Korea's comprehensive labor market reform, aiming at greater labor market flexibility for all workers, did not greatly affect chaebŏl workers because of the power of chaebŏl unions at the firm level to defend job security for their members during labor restructuring.

Decentralized industrial relations based on large chaebŏl unions further enlarged wage differentials along the lines of employment status and firm size. While a few large competitive chaebŏl were still capable of offering high wages to their unionized regular workers, smaller chaebŏl and SMEs struggled to survive. Rarely covered by collective bargaining, the majority of non-regular workers were exposed to the fluctuations of the business cycle. As of 2004, non-regular workers received 65 percent of the wages of regular workers in the Korean labor market.[65] To overcome the limitations of firm-centered collective bargaining, a few industrial sectors (e.g., the financial and metal industries) set up federations and attempted to lead industry-wide wage bargaining in the early 2000s. Enterprise unions in large competitive chaebŏl firms, however, refused to respect the principle of solidarity wage bargaining at the industry level and opted for more decentralized collective bargaining at the firm level (J. Song 2012c).

In the realm of social protection, the Roh government implemented a wide range of active labor market policies for the unemployed and for workers with precarious employment conditions. It also endeavored to create more jobs in the social service sector to provide more stable employment opportunities for low-income workers (Korea Development Institute 2006). As illustrated in the case of the pension reform during the Roh government, however, a majority of social protection programs still targeted regular workers in large firms, leaving SME and non-regular workers unprotected.

Korea was unable to avoid the problem of financial instability despite the relatively short history of the National Pension Program. The financial structure of generous benefits with low contribution premiums as well as rising concerns over an aging society motivated policy debates on pension reform as early as the late 1990s. After the first round of pension reforms in 1998 during the Kim Dae-jung government, which had retrenched insurance benefits, raised insurance premiums, and increased the age of pension eligibility, the Roh government proposed another pension reform in 2003. While all parties concerned—from business, labor, and government, to the general public—agreed that pension reform would ensure the financial stability of the program, they could not form a consensus on how to achieve such a difficult policy goal. After a four-year-long debate, in 2007 the ruling and opposition parties finally consented to reduce the level-of-replacement ratio from 60 percent to 40 percent, but they decided not to increase contribution premiums in order to preempt resistance to the reform by business, labor, and the public.

However, the pension reform of 2007 failed to alleviate insider-outsider gaps in social protection. Under the National Pension Program, non-regular workers were not qualified as "waged workers" who could join the workplace-based system, because of high labor turnover rates deriving from the precarious employment conditions of these workers. Since employers were not required to pay half of the premiums for these workers, non-regular workers had to pay the entire premium to join the region-based system, which substantially discouraged them from enrolling in the National Pension Program (J. Cho, Kim, and Kwon 2008, 409). Given the fact that almost half of those in the workforce were employed as non-regular workers (see figure 1.3), the business community, especially SMEs with scarce financial resources, opposed recognition of the non-regular workforce as "waged workers" in order to control their social welfare contributions. Although organized labor representing the interests of insiders did not explicitly express a policy stance on the issue, the exclusion of non-regular workers from the status of "waged workers" favored the interests of insiders because it ensured the financial stability of the National Pension Program by discouraging or even blocking non-regular workers with higher risks from enrolling. At best, insiders under decentralized industrial relations were indifferent to the extension of the work-based pension eligibility to outsiders.

Economic distress and intensified market competition imposed enormous pressure on both organized insiders and unorganized outsiders in Korea. Nevertheless, the costs of labor adjustments in terms of employment protection, wages, and social protection were disproportionately transferred to the latter, who were excluded from the protection of enterprise unions. At the beginning of Roh's presidential term, his government was expected to reverse the increasing inequality and dualism in the Korean labor market. Contrary to Rueda's prediction (2007), the left-center Roh government advocated the relaxation of "overprotection" for chaebŏl workers (equivalent to "core" insiders), who comprised less than 10 percent of the workforce.[66] In addition, the enactment of the Non-Regular Worker Protection Law in 2006 was designed to improve employment protection and working conditions for outsiders, with the aim of reducing labor market inequality and dualism. Nevertheless, the Roh government was not able to achieve its policy goal since decentralized industrial relations based on large enterprise unions contributed to the widening economic disparity between insiders and outsiders by safeguarding the interests of insiders and blocking social protections to encompass the entire workforce. Like the previous administrations, the Roh government endeavored to search for a new Korean labor market model to satisfy business, labor, and government, but its labor market reforms all led to the reinforcement of insider-outsider differences, aggravating contentious industrial relations between business and labor as well as between insiders and outsiders.

## Labor Market Reform during the Lee Myung-bak Era

After ten years of rule by the two center-left governments, the conservative Lee Myung-bak government assumed office in 2008. The former CEO of a chaebŏl firm (Hyundai Construction), Lee and his GNP administration prioritized the interests of the business community over labor in policy making. Although the FKTU announced its official support for Lee, his presidential transition committee rarely focused on any labor-related policy, which finally resulted in the end of the alliance between the FKTU and the GNP in February 2011 (*Hangyoreh Shinmun*, January 8, 2008, February 25, 2011). In addition, the role of the Tripartite Commission as a presidential advisory council (renamed the Economic and Social Development Commission) was far more marginalized. The Lee government, adopting MOL-led pro-business labor policy making, weakened the political authority of the consensus-based commission (*Hangyoreh Shinmun*, January 15, 2008, March 14, 2008). Lee's pro-business stance irritated organized labor and intensified the political conflict between business, labor, and government during his administration.

The Lee government further advanced labor market liberalization to shrink the size of the regular workforce. The MOL shortened the advance notice period of collective dismissal for regular workers from fifty to thirty days (as of June 4, 2010) through a presidential decree, which enabled the ministry to avoid potential political confrontations in the process of legislative bargaining in the National Assembly.[67] In the context of industrial relations, the Lee government finalized two controversial labor reform proposals that had been debated for more than a decade. First, the government submitted a draft reform bill that would prohibit employers from paying union officials' wages from companies' payrolls, in exchange for acknowledging union officials' union-related activities, the so-called "time-off system," which was implemented in July 2010. In the case of the time-off system, a large number of SME unions were concerned about the weakening of union power because of the lack of financial resources. In contrast, large chaebŏl unions were less affected by it since they had relatively abundant financial resources to fund union officials' activities and were able to ask their employers to make concessions to union officials' activities at the firm level. As the political representatives of business and labor, the KEF and the FKTU participated in the process of policy deliberation and negotiation. The FKTU, which had always opposed the legal prohibition on using companies' payroll systems to provide union officials' wages, agreed to the reform bill in exchange for the delay of the implementation of multiple labor unions for the next two and a half years, which was strongly demanded by its core member, the Longshore and Warehouse Union (*Hangyoreh Shinmun*, December 5, 2009). However, the KCTU refused to consent to the reform bill, demanding the complete elimination of the legal prohibition clause from the Industrial Relations Law.

Second, after four delays to its implementation, multiple labor unions at the firm level (under the condition of a unified bargaining channel between management and labor unions) were finally legalized in 2010. Since this legalization was recent (effective as of July 1, 2011), it is too early to examine the consequences of multiple unions on the labor market and industrial relations. Nevertheless, several anecdotal cases have demonstrated intensified competition among enterprise unions at the firm level, which may ultimately lead to industrial peace in the Korean labor market as Japan's second enterprise unions (*daini kumiai*) established cooperative industrial relations with management through competition against militant enterprise unions in the 1950s and 1960s.

In the face of the National Assembly and presidential elections scheduled for 2012, the conservative Lee government announced the improvement of employment and working conditions, especially for non-regular workers, in conjunction with the expansion of social safety nets for lower-income workers. However, such proposals were mere electoral campaign promises and did not materialize as concrete policy. These ambitious labor market and social protection proposals were unlikely to reduce the degree of labor market inequality and dualism unless the problems of decentralized industrial relations based on large enterprise unions were fixed in the labor market.

* * *

Korea has undergone significant institutional changes in the labor market over the past two decades. Authoritarian control over industrial relations and the labor market started to break down after the democratic transition, and the division of the labor market into privileged insiders and underpaid and under-protected outsiders was further intensified after the financial crisis. In the face of these political and economic challenges, all Korean policy makers sought a new labor market model, proposing labor market reform for greater flexibility, stable industrial relations, and the expansion of social safety nets. While Korea had emulated the Japanese model since it had undertaken industrialization projects in the 1960s, the different degrees and coverage of the employment protection system caused the political paths of reform in the two countries to diverge. Under the conditions of less institutional practices of employment protection covering a small segment of the workforce, Korea's employers and policy makers, regard-less of the political partisanship of the government, promoted comprehensive labor market reform for all workers in times of economic crisis, contrary to their Japanese counterparts. Meanwhile, insiders endeavored to secure their high level of employment protection in the face of labor market reform, but with no politi-cal allies to support them.

Korea's comprehensive labor market reform resulted in the reinforcement of inequality and dualism between insiders (e.g., chaebŏl workers) and outsiders (e.g., SME workers and non-regular workers). Even after comprehensive reform, chaebŏl workers continued to benefit from the privileges of job security, high wages, and generous social protection at the firm level with the secure protection of chaebŏl unions, whereas a majority of SME workers and non-regular workers confronted a much higher risk of job insecurity, low wages, and lack of social protections. Decentralized industrial relations based on large chaebŏl unions contributed to the institutional trajectories of increasing inequality and dualism in the Korean labor market.

Korea's chaebŏl employers and insiders could have consented to compromise between employment security and managerial discretion (ranging from skills training systems and work transfer to the introduction of new technology) imme-diately after democratization, which would have resulted in policy trajectories identical to those of Japan's labor market reform. With such a small proportion of the workforce under employment protection as well as decentralized indus-trial relations based on militant chaebŏl unions, the politics of Korea's reform turned out to be far more turbulent and confrontational, rapidly widening the economic disparity between insiders and outsiders over the past two decades. Considering that employment protection for insiders has been supported by the power of large enterprise unions, the institutional stability of employment pro-tection for insiders may weaken, depending on changes in the strength of large enterprise unions, which might trigger yet another round of reform and institu-tional changes in the Korean labor market.

# CONCLUSION

During the past few decades, labor market reform has been one of the most controversial political agendas in advanced industrialized countries afflicted with economic downturns, high unemployment rates, intense market competition, and de-industrialization. Policy makers have considered labor market reform—represented by deregulation and liberalization of rules and regulations on employment contracts and working conditions and hours—crucial to bring forth a quick economic turnaround and to create more jobs.

Despite similar trajectories in the increase of labor market flexibility, the patterns of reform have diverged remarkably across countries. Some have adopted labor market liberalization for employing outsiders (e.g., part-time, temporary, and fixed-term contract workers) with continued protection for insiders (full-time permanent workers), whereas others have pursued far-reaching reform that also aims at improving businesses' flexibility for employment of insiders, who had been under the privileges of job security, high wages, and generous social protections. In addition, some countries have reinforced labor market inequality and dualism between insiders and outsiders in the wake of labor market reform, while others have maintained a high level of economic equality by expanding social protections for those affected. Why did these countries choose different political responses to the similar pressures to change? Why did some fail to alleviate widening economic disparity between insiders and outsiders, whereas others were able to effectively cope with social and economic dislocations driven by labor market reform? This concluding chapter draws out the significance of my study's findings for the analysis of the politics of labor market reform in Japan and Korea and considers broader theoretical and empirical implications for institutional changes in the labor market and social protections.

# The Institutional Arrangements of the Labor Market

This book has analyzed the political processes and outcomes of labor market reform in Japan and Korea over the past two decades, two countries which have been identified as primary examples of a coordinated market economy confronting a stronger pressure to reform its "rigid" labor market institutions in an era of globalization than a liberal market economy would face. Under political and economic pressure, Japan and Korea promoted a series of labor market reforms in order to solve the problems of economic distress and intensified market competition, although each adopted a different method.

Despite its protracted recession since the early 1990s, Japan opted for labor market reform that primarily liberalized rules and regulations on employment contracts and working conditions for outsiders. The key institutional tenets of employment protection regimes for insiders (regular workers) remained relatively intact. Japan's labor market reform focusing on outsiders, with continued protection for insiders, led to the deepening of inequality and dualism along the two dimensions of employment status (e.g., regular workers versus non-regular workers) and firm size (e.g., large firms versus SMEs). A rapidly increasing number of non-regular workers had to bear the costs of labor adjustments in response to economic challenges and business cycle fluctuations. Various functionally equivalent programs (e.g., social and economic regulations and public works projects), which served as important alternatives to state-funded social protections for workers (insiders as well as outsiders), have been substantially weakened over the past two decades, contributing to the widening economic disparity in the Japanese labor market.

By contrast, Korea adopted comprehensive labor market reform, targeting regular workers in the chaebŏl sector (namely "core" insiders), and its reform path was far more complicated and politically contentious than its Japanese counterpart. Although policy makers anticipated that lowering the level of employment protection for insiders would reduce the insider-outsider differences, if not equalize employment and working conditions between them, well-organized chaebŏl unions representing the interests of insiders blocked the implementation of labor market reform through intense industrial disputes at the firm level. Thus, although Korea's reform substantially weakened the level of employment protection for regular workers in SMEs, and certainly for non-regular workers, it strengthened, ironically, the privileges of internal labor markets for regular workers in large chaebŏl firms. In the wake of labor market reform, Korea has confronted a sharp rise in labor market inequality and dualism between insiders and outsiders, a reform outcome similar to what Japan has experienced for the past two decades.

The main findings of this book reveal the importance of the institutional arrangements of the labor market in explaining the process and outcomes of labor market reform—the diverging patterns of reform and the convergence to the increase of labor market inequality and dualism. Despite many similar institutional configurations of the political economy in Japan and Korea, the institutional discrepancies in the characteristics of the employment protection system determine the different patterns of labor market reform by shaping the interests and strategies of employers, workers, and policy makers. Japan's institutionalized practices of employment protection were extended to cover a majority of the workforce in the labor market, which imposed an institutional constraint on employers as well as policy makers and limited a range of reform options.

Meanwhile, in the Korean labor market, employment protection for insiders was under far more intense pressure to change. Despite the strict regulations on employment protection for regular workers imposed by the authoritarian regime, Korea's employment protection system was far less institutionalized, with limited coverage of the workforce, than Japan's. It was well-organized chaebŏl unions that pressured chaebŏl employers to guarantee a high level of employment protection for their union members (i.e., "core" insiders) after the 1987 democratic transition, by wielding their organizational power. During the late 1980s and 1990s, Korea was in the process of establishing internal labor markets for blue-collar production workers, most of whom had been excluded from the coverage of employment protection during the period of high-speed growth. However, as illustrated in chapter 5, chaebŏl employers were reluctant to make a firm commitment to job security even for insiders since they regarded employment protection as burdensome, believing it would prohibit firms from adopting flexible labor adjustment strategies in response to business cycle fluctuations. Thus, when its national political economy showed signs of recession, Korean employers pressured the government to advance comprehensive labor market reform that would relax employment protection and working conditions for all workers. Its policy makers also considered that comprehensive labor market reform would be imperative in times of crisis, given the weak institutional strength of employment protection covering a small segment of the workforce.

While variations in the institutional characteristics of employment protection lead to different patterns of reform in the two countries, the similarity in decentralized industrial relations based on large enterprise unions exacerbated labor market inequality and the segmentation of the dualistic labor market along the dimensions of employment status and firm size. In Japan, the inter-action of labor market reform for outsiders and decentralized industrial rela-tions further reinforced the widening economic disparity between privileged insiders and under-protected and underpaid outsiders. In Korea, comprehen-sive labor market reform resulted in uneven consequences of policy changes on the workforce, constrained by decentralized industrial relations based on large chaebŏl unions. A shrinking percentage of the workforce in the chaebŏl sector has continued to benefit from the privileges of job security, high wages, and social protections, whereas a majority of SME workers and non-regular workers have been exposed to a much higher risk of job insecurity, low wages, and meager benefits. Korea's decentralized industrial relations based on large chaebŏl unions overruled the original intention of the state—the reduction of the widening gap between insiders and outsiders—and led to the further deep-ening of inequality and dualism.

## Labor Market Reform in Other Settings

While this book develops its analytical framework based upon the two empirical cases of Japan and Korea, its central claim of the importance of the institutional characteristics of the labor market can be applied to explaining the political dynamics of labor market reform in other settings. This section examines the politics of labor market reform in Germany and the United Kingdom to elaborate how the institutional arrangements of the labor market determined the trajectories of reform in these two countries. The German case shows many important similarities with the Japanese case in terms of the pat-tern of reform and the degree of labor market inequality and dualism: selec-tive labor market reform and widening economic disparity between insiders and outsiders. Among other variables, the politics of the German labor market reform can be explained by the interaction of the institutional arrangements of the labor market and the characteristics of industrial relations. Under the institutionalized practices of employment protection for insiders (e.g., skilled regular workers) as a majority of the workforce in the labor market, Germany adopted selective labor market reform to increase employers' flexibility for hiring outsiders, shielding insiders from the pressure of reform. Yet the decen-tralization of the German industrial relations system based on the sectoral interests contributed to the underdevelopment of social protections for those affected by reform (mostly labor market outsiders) over the entire economy, leading to the widening economic gap between insiders and outsiders.[1]

Despite many differences in the politics of labor market reform (e.g., the political relationship between organized labor and political parties), Britain and Korea had crucial similarities with respect to the pattern of reform and the degree of labor market inequality and dualism, whose features were shaped by the institutional arrangements of the labor market. Like Korea, Britain developed weak institutional arrangements of employment protection for workers, which became vulnerable to the pressure to change in economic downturns. In addition, Britain's decentralized industrial relations did not facilitate the rapid expansion of social protections for those affected by labor market reform during the 1980s, which resulted in increasing labor market inequality. Although other political variables (e.g., the political partisanship of the government, neoliberal ideology, and centralized or decentralized policy-making authority) affected the political pathways of reform in Germany and the United Kingdom, the institutional features of the labor market—employment protection systems and industrial relations—also shaped the political process and outcomes of labor market reform in these two countries.

Beginning in the late 1970s and early 1980s, the British Conservative government embarked on drastic labor market reform, ranging from the weakening of public-sector unions by imposing strict regulations on union activities, the liberalization of hiring and firing restrictions, and the decentralization of wage bargaining, to the reduction of the duration of unemployment benefits (Coe and Snower 1997, 6–8). In the period after World War II, Britain established the institutional configurations of quasi-corporatist wage bargaining supported by the state, especially the Labor government, which had close ties to unions. Despite the institutional features of quasi-corporatism at the national level, neither British employers nor unionized insiders developed a set of labor market structures at the firm level, which would have undergirded and stabilized quasi-corporatist wage bargaining at the national level. In addition, British industrial relations were seriously troubled by a series of intense strikes in the 1960s and 1970s, in conjunction with the improvement of the collective labor rights of unions (Brown, Deakin, and Ryan 1997). In the context of human capital investment, British employers were rarely interested in investing in specific skills training systems for insiders, which led to the underdevelopment of internal labor markets and a low-skill institutional equilibrium, as opposed to the high-skill institutional equilibrium in Germany and Japan (Finegold and Soskice 1988; Martin and Swank 2004; Michie and Sheeham 2003). Under these institutional conditions of the labor market, the Conservative government that came into power in 1979 aimed to transform the British labor market into a more market-oriented one with further decentralized industrial relations in order to tame its contentious industrial relations and increase labor market flexibility, which resulted in the breakdown of the postwar model of the British labor market (Howell 2005; King and Wood 1999; Soskice 1999; Wood 2001).

When the Thatcher government assumed power in 1979, it advanced a wide range of labor market reforms to weaken the political power of labor unions (especially public-sector unions) and to liberalize rules and regulations on employment contracts for insiders (Freeman and Pelletier 1989). Around the mid-1980s the postwar quasi-corporatist labor policy-making system finally fell apart in the United Kingdom, and its wage-setting institutions became further decentralized and uncoordinated (Howell 2005; OECD 2004, 151). The institutional mismatch between quasi-corporatist wage bargaining at the national level and the absence of supporting institutions at the firm level (e.g., skills formation systems and employment protections) destabilized the postwar British labor model, shaping more comprehensive labor market reform. It was not the uncoordinated British employers but the Conservative governments, with the centralized authority of policy making, that took the initiative for comprehensive labor market and social protection reform (Wood 2001). Nevertheless, the institutional mismatch between quasi-corporatism at the national level and the underdevelopment of any form of labor coordination for employment protection at the firm level was the driving force of comprehensive labor market reform in times of economic distress. Unlike many continental European countries, the United Kingdom has not experienced the increased segmentation of the dualistic labor market because the privileges of insiders have simultaneously declined in the wake of labor market reform over the past few decades. But Britain did confront an increase of labor market inequality driven by the rise of low-end employment positions as well as decentralized collective bargaining coupled with low union organization rates (Clasen and Clegg 2003).

By contrast, the politics of German labor market reform followed a different pattern. During the early 1980s, Helmut Kohl's government, a coalition led by the Christian Democratic Party (CDU), advanced several policies intended to weaken the political rights of unions and increase labor market flexibility. But large German employers, who were more concerned with the preservation of the institutional arrangements of collective bargaining and vocational training systems, were reluctant to accept state-led labor reform for insiders (Soskice 1999; Wood 2001). During the 1990s and 2000s, Germany confronted a strong trend toward the decentralization of collective bargaining and the weakening of industry-based vocational training systems, since a large number of SMEs as well as firms in eastern Germany opted to defect from coordination, coordination that was led by large employers and labor unions at the industry level (Martin and Thelen 2007; Streeck and Hassel 2003). Under changing political and economic conditions (e.g., the 1990 German reunification, the rising burden of social security contribution for employers, intense global competition, and soaring unemployment rates), employers, insiders, and policy makers developed incremental labor market reform by liberalizing rules and regulations governing the employment contracts, working conditions, and social welfare benefits for peripheral non-regular workers (outsiders). Large employers preferred to take advantage of peaceful industrial relations and vocational training systems based on institutionalized cooperation between business and labor in order to maintain international competitiveness. German policy makers prioritized labor market reform focusing on outsiders (e.g., female and young workers) for greater flexibility in response to economic challenges, while maintaining protection for insiders.

As in Japan, labor market inequality and segmentation of the dualistic labor market between insiders and outsiders (especially along the dimension of firm size) were embedded in the German political economy composed of large firms and SMEs. Yet until the mid-1990s, the rise of labor market inequality and dualism was relatively restrained by solidarism (or collectivism) under the leadership of the business and labor associations at the industry level. Compared with Japan and Korea, Germany had a higher rate of union organization, with extensive collective bargaining at the industry level. Nevertheless, Germany has experienced de facto decentralization of industrial relations over the past two decades, which has allowed individual firms to maintain local autonomy in wage settlement, working conditions, and labor adjustments for flexibility (Martin and Thelen 2007; Palier and Thelen 2010; Streeck and Hassel 2003; Thelen 2012; Thelen and Busemeyer 2008). This trend of decentralization in industrial relations has accelerated the degree of labor market dualism along the dimensions of employment status and firm size.

The institutional features of the labor market might not be the only factor to account for the politics of labor market reform in Germany and the United Kingdom. As pointed out by many scholars who work on institutional changes in the labor market and social welfare system in the context of western Europe, the institutional characteristics of welfare regimes might also affect the patterns of inequality and dualism in the process of labor market reform (Häusermann and Schwander 2010; Levy 1999). But since the structures of welfare regimes tend to develop in interaction with the features of the labor market and industrial relations, the characteristics of the labor market—employment protection systems and industrial relations—still provide an important dimension to explain the variations in the politics of labor market reform. Although a more systematical comparative analysis is required to evaluate the validity of my theoretical framework beyond Japan and Korea, the empirical evidence drawn from the United Kingdom and Germany supports the central proposition of my study: that the effects of the institutional features of the labor market determine the process and outcome of labor market reform. By examining two additional cases of labor market reform with the analytical framework of the institutional features of the labor market, this study presents more general implications for the politics of labor market reform beyond Japan and Korea.

## Implications for the Politics of Labor Market Reform

This book has presented several implications for the politics of labor market reform. First, it has developed an integrated theoretical framework to explain the politics of labor market reform, ranging from the policy preferences of employers and workers and policy deliberation and negotiations at the national level to the implementation of labor market reform at the firm level. Most existing literature on the politics of labor market reform, in particular in East Asia, centers on either industrial relations at the firm level or labor policy making at the national level. Few studies have systematically explored how the various interests of reform actors are represented and incorporated into the different stages of labor market reform. By analyzing the political interactions among reform actors at the firm and national levels, this book has provided a more comprehensive picture of institutional changes and developments in employment protection, industrial relations and wage bargaining, and social protections in reform politics.

Second, this study has focused on a set of labor market institutions as the key determinant of the patterns of reform. Despite similar institutional arrangements of the market economy in Japan and Korea, subtle but crucial differences in the two labor markets—e.g., the different characteristics of the employment protection system—caused the diverging political pathways of labor market reform under similar pressure for changes. In particular, in Korea, the less institutionalized practices of the employment protection system covering a small segment of the workforce incentivized employers and policy makers to adopt comprehensive labor market reform for all workers, when its political economy faced severe economic distress and intensified global competition. Meanwhile, in the case of Japan, under the institutional configurations of the employment protection system extended to the large proportion of the workforce, its employers and policy makers prioritized the liberalization of the labor market by focusing on non-regular workers, while maintaining protection for regular workers as institutionalized insiders intact.

Third, this study has enhanced our understanding of labor market inequality and dualism beyond western Europe. While an increasing number of studies in the field of comparative political economy focus on the rapid increase of labor market inequality and dualism, little has been known about recent institutional changes and developments in the labor market and social protection systems in settings outside western Europe. This study adds important empirical findings based on Japan and Korea to the existing literature. In addition, although the theoretical framework is developed based on empirical findings of two cases of labor market reform, it can explain the political dynamics of labor market reform in other contexts. As discussed in the previous section, the analytical framework centered on the institutional structures of the labor market accounts for the trend of the rise of inequality and dualism not only in Japan and Korea but also in other coordinated market economies (e.g., Germany).

# Future Prospects

While the institutional arrangements of the labor market account for the essence of the politics of labor market reform in Japan and Korea over the past two decades, we have to consider the medium- and long-term effects of key structural changes in their political economies on the labor market and social protections: an aging society, the changing composition of the workforce, and globalization. First, one of the crucial structural variables that this book has not sufficiently taken into account is the effect of the ongoing process of the aging of society on the labor market and social protections in the two countries. As of 2010, the proportion of the elderly population (over sixty-five) in Japan was 23.1 percent, and its Korean counterpart was 11 percent.[2] Compared with other advanced industrialized countries, Japan and Korea have experienced a much faster aging of the population. For example, it took 24 years for Japan to make a transition from an aging society (with more than 7 percent of the population considered elderly, sixty-five or older) to an aged society (with more than 14 percent of the population considered elderly), whereas it took 61 years in Italy, 85 years in Sweden, and 115 years in France.[3]

In particular, Japan, which has already entered the stage of super-aged society (where more than 20 percent of the population is over sixty-five), has more imperative tasks in terms of the shrinking of the population of working age— people who care for and pay for the elderly—and the heavy financial burden on its social welfare programs.[4] Scholars of Japanese political economy have already pointed to the intense strain of the aging society on the sustainability of the Japanese labor market model and social protections.[5] The institutional pillars of the Japanese labor market and social protections, characterized by permanent employment practices, seniority-based wages, and work-based social protections, are centered on the underlying assumptions of sustainable economic growth and the stable supply of a young workforce that would compensate for the high costs of maintaining employment and social protections. Despite Japan's mild economic recovery since the mid-2000s, its sluggish growth rates have not yet offered any sign of sustainable economic development, and a majority of large Japanese firms have frozen almost all hiring of new and young regular workers, in return for ensured job security for middle-aged male regular workers. Meanwhile, Japan's baby-boom generation (*dankai sedai*) has just started to retire, imposing the increasing financial burden of social welfare costs on the government, which has already been troubled with the very highest level of public debt among advanced industrialized countries (199.2 percent of the GDP as of 2010) (Japanese Ministry of Finance 2010, 13).

The aging of Japanese society may exert two contradictory consequences on the labor market. On the one hand, large Japanese firms might want to take a wait-and-see strategy until the baby-boom generation—most of which has been under the protection of job security, high wages, and generous social protections—has retired. By doing so, they would attempt to avoid any political and social conflicts with insiders and policy makers in the process of labor adjustments. In turn, firms would fill the vacancy left by retirees with cheap part-time and temporary workers, those already excluded from the privileges of internal labor markets. If that is the case, the present model of the Japanese labor market and social protections would not persist in the long term since such labor adjustment strategies would ultimately undermine the institutional arrangements of the labor market, ranging from employment protection systems and skills formation systems to public policies on the basis of the regular workforce. Once the shrinking of the portion of the workforce under the privileges of internal labor markets, driven partly by the retirement of the baby-boom generation, reaches a "tipping point," Japanese employers, who incur the costs of maintaining insiders during economic downturns, may abandon their prior commitments to protection for the rapidly shrinking number of insiders. Under such changing conditions of the labor market, Japanese policy makers, who were concerned about the possibility of political and economic costs of reform for insiders, may also adopt comprehensive labor market reform in order to allow firms to have more leeway in making labor adjustments for a rapid economic turnaround.

On the other hand, we may see the aging of Japanese society reinforce the present labor market model because of the increasing burden of social welfare costs. The retirement of the baby-boom generation will lead to a rapidly growing number of pensioners, and the increasing costs of health care caused by the aging society will put an intense strain on the Japanese government to maintain the sound financial structure of social welfare programs, if not improve it. The majority of Japan's non-regular workers are excluded from social protections coverage, and they do not pay social welfare contributions, which alarms policy makers in the face of financial pressures driven by the retirement of the baby-boom generation, the aging society, and the decline of social security contributions. Under these circumstances, Japan's policy makers may propose labor market reform to improve job security and social protections for outsiders with the continued employment protection for insiders as one of the most feasible options to solve multiple problems associated with the aging society. Nevertheless, considering the opposition of the Japanese business community to increasing labor costs (e.g., the strengthening of protection for outsiders and social welfare benefits for outsiders), such a reform proposal is less likely to be promoted.

Although Korea is a younger society than Japan, it cannot avoid similar pressures from an aging society. In particular, its policy makers have become concerned with economic insecurity for the aging workforce and the pressure of the aging of society on the financial stability of social protection programs for retirees. Faced with the upcoming presidential election of December 2012, political parties—regardless of their position on the ideological spectrum—and presidential hopefuls competitively announced their promises of improved job security and social protections for workers. One of the most noticeable policy agendas regarding the labor market and social protections was the stipulation for the extension of the compulsory retirement age for regular workers from the late fifties (currently between fifty-five and fifty-seven years old, depending on firms and occupations) to sixty.[6] By making such promises, political parties and presidential hopefuls acknowledged the need for more stable sources of income for workers facing retirement as well as the need to solve the problem of mismatch between the retirement age and the pensionable age (sixty years old as of 2012), although the latter will be extended by one year every five years (*Hankyung Magazine*, March 19, 2012). The business community had a lukewarm response to this agenda, expressing its willingness to consider it only if workers and labor unions would agree to restrain wage increases after a certain age in order to curb the pressures from labor costs linked to seniority-based wages. Labor unions and workers were also rather skeptical since they regarded the stipulation for the extension of the compulsory retirement age as unrealistic, with no job security (or, at best, weak security) even for insiders, those who were already in the labor market and between their late forties and early fifties.

In order to solve the problems of the fiscal structure of social protections, Korea's policy makers have discussed expanding the funding source of social security contributions by extending the coverage of social protections to outsiders. Like other advanced industrialized countries, Korea has also gradually increased the pensionable age to mitigate the fiscal burdens on the old-age pension program. Considering the rapidity of the aging of the population as well as the large size of the non-regular workforce, it is not clear whether such piecemeal policy responses will lessen the consequences of the aging society on Korea's labor market and social protections.

The aging society will also have an important impact on the decline of union organization rates, since union members will retire, and young workers increasingly tend not to join unions, not only in Japan and Korea but also in other advanced industrialized countries, partly because of the diversity of categories of employment contracts as well as de-industrialization. Thus, the aging of the population will create a new task for national labor federations—to incorporate a new group of unorganized workers, mostly outsiders, into their organizations—whereas enterprise unions and insiders might still prefer to consolidate their own privileges. It is not clear what kinds of political coalitions may emerge and lead to policy transformations for outsiders in the context of an aging society. Nevertheless, these socio-demographic variables may serve as the major driving force of changes in the labor market and social protection systems in the long term.

Second, in addition to the challenge of an aging society, it is worth taking into account the socioeconomic consequences of the changing composition of the workforce—the rise of female and young workers as outsiders—on the labor market and social protections in Japan and Korea. Departing from the male-breadwinner model based on full-time permanent jobs, Japan and Korea have experienced steady growth in female employment rates as well as a mounting number of young workers facing precarious employment conditions. In the case of Japan, female employment rates began to increase after the first oil crisis in the mid-1970s, a period during which its economy faced the end of high-speed growth and its firms sought to create an inexpensive labor force through the hiring of non-regular workers (mostly female) (Hara and Seiyama 2005, 122). Over the past three decades, during 1980–2010, Japan's female employment rate (among the age group of fifteen to sixty-four) increased from 52.5 percent to 63.2 percent.[7] Similarly, Korea also experienced a rise in female employment rate during the process of industrialization in the 1960s and 1970s. Between 1980 and 2010, its female employment rate climbed from 46.4 percent to 54.5 percent.[8] Despite the increased hiring of female workers, a majority of Japanese and Korean female workers have not been entitled to receive the privileges of internal labor markets, since most of them are hired as underpaid and under-protected non-regular workers (such as part-time, temporary, and fixed-term contract workers).

Simultaneously, a large proportion of the young workforce in the Japanese and Korean labor markets has had difficulties in finding employment opportunities with job security, decent wages, and social protections, particularly over the past two decades, and some of the youth have experienced long-term unemployment

(Brinton 2011; OECD 2007c). Youth unemployment rates are always much higher than average unemployment rates in most advanced industrialized countries.[9] Nevertheless, the young generation in Japan and Korea (and perhaps that of several continental European countries) has been caught in a vicious cycle of precarious employment positions, job insecurity, low wages, and a lack of social protections, with little possibility of obtaining full-time permanent jobs in internal labor markets. In the case of Japan, the proportion of involuntary part-time workers as a percentage of part-time employment in the age group of fifteen to twenty-four increased from 10.8 percent to 28.8 percent between 2000 and 2010, a larger proportion than that of involuntary part-time workers for all age groups (8.3 percent of part-time employment in 2000 and 22.1 percent of part-time employment in 2010, respectively).[10] In Japan and Korea, the young workforce—regardless of gender—has been far less protected in the labor market and more underpaid than the prior generation, which might intensify generational conflicts in the labor market and social protections by widening economic gaps between the old and the young.

In economic hard times, all workers, regardless of employment status, firm size, gender, and age, confront a much higher risk of job insecurity, wage restraints, and benefits retrenchment. Yet the female and young workforce have always been the primary victims of labor adjustments in the Japanese and Korean labor markets during economic downturns, voluntarily or involuntarily, given the cultural and social assumption of the male-breadwinner system with dependent family members and secondary-income earners. As long as job security and social protections for male breadwinners are ensured, leading to economic security for female and young non-regular workers as household members, albeit not as individuals, the female and young workforce might be satisfied with underpaid and under-protected employment conditions. This male-breadwinner model of the labor market has been destabilized, if not completely demolished. The proportion of the Japanese and Korean workforce covered by internal labor markets has been shrinking, driven not only by socio-demographic changes (e.g., the retirement of the aging workforce) but also by a series of labor market reforms and firms' labor management strategies. A majority of the young male workforce, who are supposed to serve as breadwinners, have not been able to access internal labor markets in times of economic distress, which undermines the model.

Faced with the increasing number of female and young workers in precarious employment conditions, Japanese and Korean policy makers have endeavored to represent the interests of these workers and to improve protection for outsiders through various policy measures, such as the 2012 revision of the Worker Dispatch Law in Japan and the 2006 Non-Regular Worker Protection Law in Korea. In addition, they have proposed the concept of "flexicurity"—flexibility for insiders and security for outsiders—in order to fix the problems of insider-outsider differences in the labor market and social protections. The key assumption of "flexicurity" is a weak boundary between internal and external labor markets in terms of job security, wages, and social protections, indicating the reduction of the insider-outsider differences. Yet it is unlikely that workers would support such a trajectory of change. In particular, considering that the presumption of "flexicurity" is centered on the weakening of insider privileges in the labor market and social protections, insiders and enterprise unions are likely to oppose such policy changes. The question is whether or not the privileges of insiders (e.g., middle-aged male regular workers in large firms) would be sustained in the long term in the context of the declining proportion of labor market insiders. Since insiders are better organized and represented than outsiders, regardless of the decline in numbers, the interests of insiders will be prioritized over those of female and young workers as outsiders. Unless outsiders are mobilized along the lines of employment status, gender, and/or age group in elections or via other forms of political representation, politicians and political parties will not be willing to listen seriously to their voices despite their rising numbers.

Last, but not least, regional and global economic integration may bring forth changes in the institutional features of the labor market by providing a wide array of new labor adjustment options for firms in the context of intensified global market competition and new business environments (Armstrong 2009; Hill and Athukorala 1998; S. J. Kang and Lee 2007; E. M. Kim and Mah 2006; C. Lee and Beamish 1995; Urata 2002; Zhou, Delios, and Yang 2002). Over the past two decades, leading export-oriented firms and industries have extensively increased overseas production, even surpassing the volume of domestic production in Japan and Korea (Lansbury, Suh, and Kwon 2007; Schoppa 2006, 103–105). In the case of Japan, the volume of overseas production in two leading export-oriented sectors—the automobile and electronics industries (as of 2006 and 2005, respectively)—is almost equivalent to the volume of domestic production.[11] These two industrial sectors comprised 41 percent of Japan's outward foreign direct investment (FDI) as of 2004, reaching the amount of 6 trillion Japanese yen (JPY).[12] As a consequence of global outsourcing, an increasing number of SMEs have closed down domestic production sites or moved production facilities overseas (or both), although high value–added production sites are still located in Japan, despite the option of offshore production.[13]

Like their Japanese counterparts, an increasing number of Korean firms have moved their production sites to overseas locations, such as China, Southeast Asian countries, and United States, in order to control increasing labor costs and access new markets. The amount of Korea's outward FDI drastically increased from US$61 million to US$800 million between 1991 and 2010, growing by a factor of more than thirteen.[14] Labor-intensive industries (e.g., garment, textile, and food processing industries) took a large share of the outward FDI in the late 1980s and early 1990s in order to take advantage of cheap labor costs in developing countries. During 1991–2010, however, the electronics and transportation industries, which were capital- and skill-intensive sectors, increased the share of the outward FDI from 25.19 percent to 34.39 percent and diversified production sites, including not only in developing countries but also in advanced industrial countries in western Europe and North America. Such a trend indicates that outward FDI has become Korean firms' new global business strategy, as opposed to being a simple method to save labor and production costs.[15]

Focusing on the increase in overseas production, Schoppa (2006) argues that the slowness of Japan's regulatory changes can be attributed to the lack of political pressure from these leading firms and sectors since they have already utilized exit options out of the rigid Japanese labor market, such as offshore production and global outsourcing. Japan's increasing overseas production has not yet led to massive layoffs of regular workers, but it has contributed to the shrinkage of the regular workforce by closing down production facilities and reducing domestic production, especially in the case of SMEs.[16] Nevertheless, Japan's labor unions and workers have not been responsive to the problems of hollowing out (*sangyō kudōka*), a trend that has accelerated over the past two decades of economic recession, since they have not yet considered the consequences of hollowing out as their own problems under the conditions of firms' commitments to employment and social protections for insiders (Schoppa 2006, 109).

In an era of economic globalization, Korea confronts a problem similar to that of Japan. As an increasing number of large Korean firms have moved their production sites overseas and expanded global outsourcing, labor unions and insiders have been very worried about the possibility of the closing down of domestic production sites and consequent labor restructuring (as in many cases in the US manufacturing sector). In particular, given the lack of employers' prior commitments to job security even for insiders (in contrast to their Japanese counterparts), the strategy of moving production overseas has become a primary reason for industrial conflict between employers and workers at the firm level. Some powerful chaebŏl unions have demanded that management sign an agreement to discuss with unions any business strategies that might affect job security for insiders, such as the transition to overseas production. Unlike its Japanese counterparts, who have been willing to provide social protections for insiders at least, large Korean firms have already closed down domestic production sites and implemented massive downsizing in conjunction with increasing the amount of outward FDI (as demonstrated in the recent case of Hanjin Heavy Industries, a large shipbuilding company that has moved its major production sites to the

Philippines to save on labor costs). It seems that Korea has confronted far more imminent challenges to its labor market and social protections from economic globalization.

Regional and global economic integration, whose process and outcome cannot be fully controlled by domestic policy makers, is a potential and possible immediate cause of the transformation in the institutional arrangements of the labor market. In Japan and Korea, outward FDI has already surpassed inward FDI, which might accelerate the problems of hollowing out in the labor market and social protections. To deal with these economic challenges, domestic policy makers can expand social protections for workers affected by economic globalization or create more jobs in the domestic labor market (most of which, however, will be concentrated in the service sector, with much lower rates of productivity and job growth). As pointed out by Garret (1998a), globalization does not always lead to "a race to the bottom," but capital seems to be increasingly mobile across borders, whereas labor seems increasingly stuck in the domestic market in the era of economic globalization. Although the effects of globalization on the labor market seem to be rather slow-moving, in the long run they will bring forth more fundamental structural changes in the Japanese and Korean labor markets and social protections.

The three structural changes in the national political economy—the aging of society, the changing composition of the workforce, and globalization—may cause fundamental changes in the labor market and social protections, not only in Japan and Korea, but also in other advanced industrialized countries. This book develops an analytical framework based on the institutional arrangements of the labor market as institutional constraints on actors' incentives and strategies and thus on reform paths and outcomes. Yet these changes may shift the institutional arrangements of the labor market themselves, and thus they may result in new political dynamics of labor market reform in the long term.

Since the labor market is located at the intersection of several different domains of market institutions, institutional changes in the labor market will lead to changes in other domains of the market economy, and vice versa. Labor market reform affects firms' business strategies and countries' economic performance, but more importantly, it influences the quality of workers' lives by shaping the levels of job security, wages, and social protections, as well as social and political stability gained or lost by alleviating or exacerbating public discontent. Thus, the politics of labor market reform need to be understood in the context of a much broader implication for a nation's political economy.

# Notes

## INTRODUCTION

1. Dualistic (or segmented) labor markets depart from neoclassical models of the labor market in terms of their different wage levels and managerial practices for internal labor markets, variation that cannot be attributed to workers' qualifications or job tasks. In this book, "labor market dualism" refers to the division of the workforce into insiders and outsiders along the dimensions of employment status (e.g., regular workers versus non-regular workers) and firm size (e.g., large firms versus small- and medium-sized enterprises). The former enjoy the privileges of strong employment protections, high wages, and generous social welfare benefits, whereas the latter have more precarious forms of employment contracts, with low wages and meager social welfare benefits. For a detailed discussion of labor market dualism, see Berger and Piore (1980), Bourguignon and Morrisson (1998), Dickens and Lang (1985), Doeringer and Piore (1971), and Swenson (2002, 24–29).

2. In most advanced industrial countries, "labor market dualism" refers to widening economic gaps between insiders and outsiders along the lines of employment contract (e.g., regular workers versus part-time, temporary, and contract workers). Meanwhile, as will be further elaborated in the following chapters, in Japan and Korea labor market dualism is salient along the dimensions of employment status and firm size because of the large firm-centered economic structure of their national political economies. Thus, unless it is conceptually important to specify the certain dimension of labor market dualism (e.g., employment status or firm size), I will use the terms "insiders" and "regular workers" interchangeably. Similarly, I will use the terms "outsiders" and "non-regular workers" interchangeably, although regular workers in small- and medium-sized enterprises (SMEs) might be identified as "outsiders" along the dimension of firm size (e.g., large firms versus SMEs).

3. Vogel (1996) argues that deregulation tends to create not only liberalization, but also more regulations, namely "re-regulation," since the state bureaucracy prioritizes the preservation of its regulatory jurisdiction even in the process of deregulation. While this book acknowledges Vogel's point, it will use the terms "deregulation" and "liberalization" interchangeably in order to emphasize reform trajectories of greater diversity and flexibility in the labor market.

4. The varieties of capitalism (VOC) framework points to a self-reinforcing mechanism of institutional equilibrium in explaining institutional changes in market economies. It argues that neither employers nor workers are willing to challenge the institutional foundations of the existing system since they have developed economic and political strategies centered on the existing institutional arrangements of the market economy over an extended period of time, in conjunction with public policies strengthening the status of institutional equilibrium. For details, see Hall and Soskice (2001).

5. Regarding positive feedback and path dependence, see Pierson (2004, 17–53).

6. For the data on the size of the economy, see *New York Times* (August 16, 2010); for the data on GDP per capita, see World Bank, http://data.worldbank.org/, accessed June 11, 2011.

7. A comparative study of Japan and Korea in this book is based on the most similar systems design. Regarding the most similar systems design, see Przeworski and Teune (1982, 31–46).

8. Regarding the state-led development strategy, there have been debates on the role of Japan's colonial rule in Korea's economic development after its liberation. Kohli (1994 and 1997) argues that Japan's colonial rule over Korea (1910–1945) left important institutional legacies of strong state structure and bureaucracy, which contributed to Korea's developmental strategy. In contrast, Haggard, Kang, and Moon (1997) argue against Kohli's claim by pointing out the greater discontinuity between the colonial period and the post-1945 period. In particular, these scholars claim that Korea's economy took off only after the Park Chung Hee regime initiated a strong state-led developmental strategy, emulating the model of Japan's postwar economic development.

9. For the data on Korea's economic growth, see Bank of Korea, Economic Statistics System, http://ecos.bok.or.kr, accessed June 10, 2011.

10. The Gini coefficient measures income inequality on a scale of 0 (the most equal) to 1 (the least equal) by calculating the area between the Lorenz curve and the 45-degree line. In the early 2000s, the Gini coefficients in the United Kingdom and the United States were 0.335 and 0.381, respectively, which were much higher than those in Japan and Korea. For the data on the Gini coefficient for Japan, the United Kingdom, and the United States, see OECD (2008, 358) and Society at a Glance 2009, OECD Social Indicators, Organisation for Economic Co-operation and Development, http://www.oecd.org, accessed September 10, 2009; for the data on the Gini coefficient for Korea, see Korean National Statistical Office, Gagyesuji Donghyang [Household Economy Trend].

11. For the data on the proportion of the regular workforce in the Japanese labor market, see Japanese Ministry of Internal Affairs and Communications, Shūgyō Kōjō Kihon Chōsa [Basic Survey on Employment Structure]. This book identifies the workforce as those participating in the labor market as "employees," encompassing all industrial sectors (agriculture, manufacturing, and service industries), occupational categories (e.g., clerks, technicians, and managers), and employment statuses (e.g., regular and non-regular workers). Yet the category of the self-employed is excluded from the definition of the workforce since this study focuses on waged workers.

12. For the data on the proportion of the regular workforce in the Korean labor market, see Korean National Statistical Office, Goyong Gujo Gibon Josa [Basic Survey on Employment Structure]. Korea shares a very similar conceptual definition of the regular workforce with Japan, although Korea focuses more on the term of employment contract (e.g., regular workers are identified as those with employment contract terms of more than one year). Recently its emphasis on employment contract terms has become problematic in defining the boundary of the regular workforce since Korea extended the term of employment contract for non-regular workers from one year to two years in December 2006. As a result, some non-regular workers with employment contract terms longer than one year might also be categorized as "regular workers" after 2007. However, because of the lack of the specific data, it is difficult to identify the proportion of these non-regular workers with employment contract terms longer than one year in the Korean labor market.

13. A large number of regular workers in SMEs do not enjoy the same levels of employment protection, wages, and social welfare benefits as regular workers in large Japanese and Korean firms. Thus, while regular workers in SMEs are identified as "insiders" in terms of employment status, these workers can be defined as "outsiders" with respect to the size of firm.

14. *Keiretsu* is a loose business grouping in postwar Japan, whose business structure inherited from pre-war family-owned business conglomerates, *zaibatsu*. Chaebŏl are family-owned and -managed large Korean business conglomerates, most of which

were created by the state-led developmental strategy of the Park Chung Hee regime (1961–1979). Regarding Japan's *keiretsu* and Korea's chaeböl, see Gerlach (1992) and E. M. Kim (1997), respectively.

15. The Japanese government strengthened administrative and legal procedures for layoffs of regular workers. For details, see chapter 4.

16. Regarding the problems of collective action in Korea's industrial relations and labor market reform, see Yang (2006).

17. Author's personal communications with former legislative staff members at the Korean National Assembly.

18. Professor Takanashi Akira, who led the legislation of Japan's Worker Dispatch Law as a chair of the Labor Policy Deliberative Council, mentioned that he held interviews with Korean bureaucrats who were in charge of drafting Korea's Worker Dispatch Law. Author's interview with Takanashi Akira, January 26, 2006 (Tokyo).

19. "Back-door" (or "side-door") policy refers to the import of the unskilled foreign workforce under the industrial trainee program, despite the fact that the government "officially" bans the hiring of unskilled foreign workers in the labor market (Yamanaka and Piper 2005). In the case of Korea, the Roh Moo-hyun government (2003–2008) shifted from a back-door policy to a front-door policy by implementing the Employment Permit System in 2004, which allowed unskilled foreign workers to be employed with a "worker" status on a fixed-term basis.

20. Regarding the number of foreign residents in Japan, see Immigration Bureau of Japan, Statistics, http://www.immi-moj.go.jp/index.html, accessed October 26, 2012.

21. Some scholars examine the ways in which the state repressed and excluded labor in the process of industrialization in East Asia, with an emphasis on the political relationship between state and labor (Deyo 1987; Koo 2001). However, they have not fully elaborated the characteristics of the labor market as one of the critical institutional pillars of the market economy.

## CHAPTER 1

1. Scholars argue that "institutional complementarities," which refer to the interdependent characteristics of market institutions, are a primary mechanism of institutional changes and continuities in market economies, in that institutional changes taking place in one domain of the market institution are likely to trigger a series of changes in other domains of the market institution. For details, see Aoki (2001) and Hall and Soskice (2001).

2. Employment protection is defined as the rigidity of formal and informal rules and regulations that affects hiring and firing practices, working conditions, and the allocation of work hours. The degree of employment protection is measured by various indicators, such as the difficulty of dismissing workers for managerial reasons, the number and amount of severance payments, the length of prior-notice periods, the requirement for prior consultation efforts with labor representatives, alternative employment contracts, and the flexibility of the allocation of work hours. Among various measures, the OECD measurement of the overall strictness of employment protection legislation (EPL) is calculated using the average scores of employment protection legislation for regular employment and temporary employment. The EPL strictness for regular employment is the average score of regular procedural inconveniences, difficulty of dismissal, and notice and severance pay for no-fault individual dismissals, while the EPL strictness for temporary employment is the average score of the restrictions on the content of fixed-term contracts and temporary work agencies. For details about descriptions and calculations of indicators, see OECD (2004), Annex 2.A and 2.B.

3. Within the VOC approach, some scholars have paid attention to the mechanism of institutional changes. For details, see Hall and Thelen (2009).

4. In fact, outsiders are quite heterogeneous groups in terms of skills (e.g., high-level professionals versus people in peripheral positions), employment contracts (e.g., direct contracts versus indirect employment through temporary agencies or contractors), and work hours (e.g., part-time versus full time). Yet most of them are on definite employment contracts on an as-needed basis.

5. See OECD (2004) for a detailed description of employment protection regulation and scoring methodology.

6. Despite the presence of a foreign workforce in the labor market, this study focuses on the structure of the dualistic labor market comprising the domestic workforce. For the rationale for the exclusion of the foreign workforce from the analytical framework, see the introduction.

7. In the immediate postwar period, US occupation authorities in Japan lifted legal restrictions on workers' basic rights (e.g., the rights to organize, collectively bargain, and strike), which had been imposed by the pre-war military government (Weathers 2001). Thus, there was no further reform agenda for the improvement of workers' basic rights (or collective labor rights) in the politics of Japan's labor market reform during the 1990s and 2000s.

8. In terms of labor militancy, Korea's organized labor has been much stronger than Japan's. Yet Japan's union organization rate is still higher than its Korean counterpart. As of 2008, Japan's union organization rate was 18.1 percent, whereas Korea's was 10.5 percent (Japan Institute for Labor Policy Training, Labor Statistics, http://www.jil.go.jp; Korea Labor Institute 2008, 19).

9. In the case of the United States, large firms adopted welfare capitalism in order to secure the skilled workforce during the period of industrialization in the early twentieth century (Swenson 2002).

10. Nevertheless, the degrees of the institutionalization of internal labor markets even in large firms differed remarkably in the Japanese and Korean labor markets.

11. Japanese Ministry of Internal Affairs and Communications, Shūgyō Kōjō Kihon Chōsa [Basic Survey on Employment Structure]; Korean National Statistical Office, Goyong Gujo Gibon Josa [Basic Survey on Employment Structure].

12. Japanese Ministry of Internal Affairs and Communications, Shūgyō Kōjō Kihon Chōsa [Basic Survey on Employment Structure].

13. Japanese Ministry of Health, Labor and Welfare, Rōdōryoku Chōsa [Labor Force Survey]; in the case of Japan's service sector, more than 50 percent of workers were employed as non-regular workers as of 2007 (Sommer 2009, 6–7).

14. For the data on the proportion of the non-regular workforce along the lines of gender, see Japanese Ministry of Internal Affairs and Communications, Shōgyō Kōjō Kihon Chōsa [Basic Survey on Employment Structure]; as of 2009, the percentage of part-time workers in the Japanese labor market was 20.3 percent, and two-thirds of these workers were female part-time workers ("Part-Time Employment," Organisation for Economic Co-operation and Development, http://www.oecd-ilibrary.org/employment/part-time-employment_20752342-table7, accessed June 28, 2011).

15. Chuma (2002) examines the pattern of large Japanese firms' labor restructuring during the 1990s in a comparison with labor restructuring during the first oil crisis in the 1970s. He argues that the magnitude of labor restructuring in the 1990s was similar to the scale of labor restructuring during the first oil crisis, pointing out that the effects of the protracted recession on labor adjustments were not as extensive as newspaper and magazine coverage reported.

16. In fact, the Japanese government underscored the one-and-a-half model of earning in the family, composed of male breadwinners as regular workers and female secondary-income earners as non-regular workers (Japanese Ministry of Labor 1998). The logic of

the one-and-a-half model developed in the Netherlands was complementary to wage moderation by allowing female workers to contribute to family income and placing male workers under less pressure to earn breadwinner wages (Levy 1999, 263). In the case of Japan, although the expansion of the secondary labor market composed of female workers has contributed to family income, the Japanese model of one-and-a-half earning has been developed in order to increase labor market flexibility for female non-regular workers in response to the fluctuations of the business cycle, in exchange for job security for male regular workers, the main breadwinners.

17. Korean National Statistical Office, Goyong Gujo Gibon Josa [Basic Survey on Employment Structure].

18. Ibid.

19. This claim is strongly supported by Japanese and Korean newspaper and magazine coverage on the preferences of temporary and part-time workers for the types of employment contract.

20. In the context of western Europe, some scholars point out that non-regular workers may prefer to reduce the economic gap between insiders and outsiders by relaxing employment protection for insiders. See Rueda (2007).

21. It might be misleading to interpret "waged workers" as regular workers in these surveys since they include not only regular workers but also non-regular workers in the workforce. Nevertheless, since this comparison focuses on the segmentation of dualistic labor market along the lines of firm size, it does not further specify the different status of employment in this analysis. In addition, because of the lack of availability of the original survey data, it is not possible to distinguish the workforce along the two dimensions of employment status and firm size at the same time.

22. This argument is a very simplified version of wage bargaining. There are several ongoing debates on the relationship between labor market institutions and economic performances, such as the role of political institution (e.g., central banks) in wage bargaining. However, since this study does not focus on the politics of wage bargaining per se, it will not further delve into the wage bargaining literature.

23. Most CMEs have also confronted a similar pressure to decentralize wage bargaining over the past few decades, although a few countries, like Italy and Spain, have moved toward the recentralization of wage bargaining (Pérez 2000; Pontusson and Swenson 1996; Rhodes and Molina 2005; Thelen 2001). Specifically, employers and workers in export-oriented sectors, those far more sensitive to global market competition than domestically sheltered industries, support the decentralization of wage bargaining in order to allow their firms to flexibly adjust to rapidly changing business environments (Pontusson and Swenson 1996). In addition, a large number of SMEs with relatively weak financial and organizational resources compared with large firms have defected from the determination of wage settlements set by upper level business and labor federations or pattern setters in the economy, which has exacerbated wage differentials between large firms and SMEs (Thelen 2001).

24. Japan's average age of the workforce increased from 36.9 years old to 41 years old between 1981 and 2007, and Korea's average age of the workforce increased from 34.3 years old to 37.7 years old between 1993 and 2007. For the data, see Japanese Ministry of Health, Labor and Welfare, Chingin Kōjō Kihon Chōsa [Basic Survey on Wage Structure] and Korean National Statistical Office, Saŏpche Gicho Tonggye Josa Bogosŏ [Report on Enterprise Statistics].

25. In the context of the US welfare state, Howard (1993) claims that the United States, which is always regarded as a welfare laggard, has developed a much larger welfare state if we consider a wide range of tax benefits as social welfare programs.

26. Regarding the concept of commodification (or de-commodification), see Esping-Andersen (1990).

27. The Employment Insurance Program was introduced in July 1995 for firms with more than thirty workers. Amid the 1997 Asian financial crisis, the coverage of the program was rapidly expanded toward firms with more than ten workers in January 1998 and firms with more than one worker in October 1998. Even despite Korea's rapid economic recovery from the crisis, the Employment Insurance Program continued to expand toward workers in the agriculture, forest, and fishing industries (in January 2003), workers in the construction sector (in January 2004), and self-employed businesses with less than five workers, on a voluntary basis (in January 2006). In addition, eligibility for enrollment was relaxed for part-time workers by reducing the number of working hours from eighty hours per month or eighteen hours per week to sixty hours per month or fifteen hours per week (in January 2004) (Korean Ministry of Labor 2008a, 61–74).

## CHAPTER 2

1. Some of the material in this section also appears in J. Song (2012a and 2012b). The copyright information: J. Song (2012a). Copyright © The East Asia Institute. Used with permission by Lynne Rienner Publishers, Inc. J. Song (2012b). Copyright © 2012 Wiley Periodicals, Inc. Used with permission by Wiley Periodicals, Inc.

2. Related to the diversification of the workforce, Häusermann (2010) argues that socio-structural changes, represented by de-industrialization, have transformed the political constituency and coalitions within the left, leading to welfare reform in continental Europe. The author points out that a combination of not only blue-collar industrial workers but also workers in the service sector and professionals has changed the characteristics of political coalitions based on different calculations of social risk.

3. Although Rueda (2007) argues that the policy preferences of outsiders for job security are not as high as those of insiders, Kalleberg et al. (1997) argue that outsiders (especially temporary agency workers, on-call workers, and day laborers) in the US labor market prefer secure employment protection.

4. In Japan, the Japan Socialist Party (JSP, renamed the Social Democratic Party of Japan) forged a relatively strong political and organizational link with labor unions in the public sector, but it has been marginalized in electoral competition over the course of the 1990s and since then. Although some members of the JSP joined the Democratic Party of Japan (DPJ) and have continued to maintain a link with organized labor (Rengō), the organizational structure of the DPJ—composed of politicians from within a wide range of the ideological spectrum—as well as the Lower House electoral reform undermining the role of interest groups have further weakened the political representation of organized labor in policy making. In Korea, a segment of labor movements (e.g., the Korean Confederation of Trade Unions) has forged a loose political coalition with the Democratic Labor Party, but the very small size of the latter in the National Assembly (6 seats out of 299 as of August 2011), has not allowed the coalition to effectively protect the interests of organized labor.

5. In the cases of Japan and Korea, "corporatist institution" refers to a political mechanism that incorporates diverse societal interests (especially the interests of organized labor) into policy making.

6. For details about *shingikai,* see chapter 4.

7. Pempel and Tsunekawa (1979) argue that Japan has not established corporatist policy-making institutions by excluding labor from decision making, whereas Kume (1998) points out that Japan's organized labor has been incorporated into labor policy making, even if it is a different form of political participation in comparison to the corporatist policy-making institution in Scandinavian countries.

8. Estévez-Abe (2008) emphasizes a slightly different dimension of the electoral system since her work more closely examines two institutional variables of the electoral

system, district magnitude and personal vote, rather than the differences between the single-member district (SMD) and proportional representation (PR) systems.

9. In fact, then-president-elect Kim Dae-jung, who had opposed reform to relax the level of employment protection for workers during his electoral campaign, strongly argued that the legalization of employers' rights to dismiss workers for managerial reasons would be imperative for Korea's rapid economic turnaround by facilitating corporate restructuring. See the interview with Lee Jong-chan, chair of the President's Transitional Committee for the Kim Dae-jung government (H-K. Lee et al. 2007, 241–243).

10. It is difficult to interpret the bursting of the Japanese economic bubble as purely driven by endogenous economic variables, given the intense political pressure of the United States and other advanced industrialized countries on the Japanese macroeconomic policies as well as the domestic product and financial market openings, as demonstrated in the cases of the 1985 Plaza Accord and the Structural Impediments Initiative (SII) between the US and Japanese governments during the late 1980s and early 1990s. For detailed information on the SII, refer to Schoppa (1997).

11. For the data on Japan's unemployment rates, see Cabinet Office, Government of Japan, http://www.esri.cao.go.jp/index.html. Compared with other advanced industrial societies in Europe, Japan's unemployment rate was still moderate during the decade-long economic recession. However, since Japanese unemployment rates doubled during the 1990s, the Japanese government and the general public were seriously concerned about rising unemployment rates.

12. Although some countries may provide a high level of employment protection for the non-regular workforce, these workers are likely to be exposed to more precarious employment conditions and shorter employment contract terms than regular workers, by definition. Thus, this study specifies the regular workforce, as opposed to the workforce in general, to identify a group of workers who have privileged strong employment protections in the labor market.

13. Regarding the OECD EPL Index, see chapter 1.

14. One caveat is that the measurement of enterprise tenure years includes regular workers and a segment of non-regular workers. In Japan and Korea, enterprise tenure years are calculated based on the number of workers whose employment contracts are longer than one year. Since a segment of the non-regular workforce has employment contract terms longer than one year, the number of enterprise tenure years does not represent the length of service within enterprises for the regular workforce only. Nevertheless, considering that the majority of non-regular workers in the Japanese and Korean labor markets have employment contracts of less than one year, the number of enterprise tenure years as an indicator of the level of employment protection for regular workers at the firm level is not seriously problematic.

15. For the data on the proportion of the workforce, see Japanese Ministry of Internal Affairs and Communications, Shūgyō Kōjō Kihon Chōsa [Basic Survey on Employment Structure].

16. There are no data to specify the proportion of the chaebŏl workforce. To calculate an estimate, I divided the number of the workforce in the top thirty chaebŏl groups by the number of the workforce in the Korean labor market. The first figure is from Shin-jun Kang et al. (2005, 30) and the second is based on Saŏpche Gicho Tonggye Josa Bogosŏ [Report on Enterprise Statistics] conducted by the Korean National Statistical Office [from Korea Labor Institute (2005, 31)].

17. For instance, when Pioneer, one of the major Japanese electronics companies, attempted to lay off thirty-five middle-range managers in 1993, the company was harshly attacked by the mass media and the general pubic, in what it was often called "the Pioneer

Shock." Since then, few large Japanese firms have tried to challenge the basic principle of job security for insiders.

18. Japan's policy makers have recently attempted to provide more protections for outsiders because of pressing concerns about rapidly rising inequality (or *kakusa*).

## CHAPTER 3

1. Some of the material in this chapter also appears in J. Song (2012b and 2012c). The copyright information: J. Song (2012b). Copyright © 2012 Wiley Periodicals, Inc. Used with permission by Wiley Periodicals, Inc. J. Song (2012c). Copyright © 2012 by the Board of Trustees of the Leland Stanford Junior University. Used with permission by the Board of Trustees.

2. In Japan, permanent employment practices have no formally defined boundaries. Unlike the formal employment contract system in the US, there are no officially signed employment contracts between employers and workers in Japan. Therefore, Reed (1993, 78–82) describes it as a psychological contract.

3. Although US occupation authorities enhanced workers' basic rights in the immediate postwar period, the authorities reversed their pro-labor policy stance in favor of business. In the face of the heightened ideological confrontation with communism, they purged union leaders and socialists, which was the so-called "Red Purge" of the late 1940s. In addition, in 1949, the Labor Union Law was amended to outlaw financial aid from companies to labor unions and to enforce the automatic extension of labor contracts, which allowed management not to consult labor unions on decisions regarding personnel management (Gao 2001, 129).

4. In this section, the terms "workers" and "regular workers" are used interchangeably to refer to insiders, unless I specify workers as non-regular workers or outsiders. While Japanese firms employed a wide range of non-regular workers (e.g., part-time, temporary, and seasonal workers) in response to the fluctuations of the business cycle, the primary form of employment was based on full-time permanent employment with indefinite contract terms during the 1950s through 1970s.

5. In fact, it was combined with the Quality Control (QC) circles movement promoted by the Japan Productivity Center established in 1955. Regarding the QC circles movement, see Estévez-Abe (2008) and Weathers (2001).

6. Gerschenkron (1966) asserts that the role of state intervention in economic development would be far more extensive in late-developing countries in terms of mobilizing financial resources, investing in technological development, and training skilled workers.

7. Apart from these interpretations, there are a variety of analytical approaches that explain the origins of Japan's permanent employment practices, such as the culturalist approach (Dore 1973; Hazama 1997).

8. In Japan, a significant number of part-time workers work as many hours as full-time workers do.

9. The Japanese government also explicitly announced in 1973 that mandatory retirement age should be extended to the age of sixty (Matsubuchi 2005, 17).

10. The system of mutual commitment between employers and regular workers would soon crumble, as employers revoked the terms of their social contracts with regular workers. To strengthen the credibility of mutual commitment, the government's public policy served an important role in the labor market. For details, see Eichengreen and Iversen (1999).

11. Milly (1999, 8–9) points out the dualistic structure of the Japanese labor market between large firms and SMEs.

12. For a detailed discussion of the early postwar labor movements and industrial conflicts, see Kume (1998) and Weathers (2000).

13. Japanese Ministry of Health, Labor and Welfare, http://www.mhlw.go.jp, accessed May 22, 2010.

14. A. Suzuki (2004) points out that the Japanese government did not officially announce the anti-inflation macroeconomic policy during the mid-1970s. Nonetheless, the Japanese government showed its policy priorities and political commitments to the pro-labor macroeconomic policy through the prime minister's participation in Sanrōkon (Roundtable Conference on Industry and Labor).

15. The influence of Sanrōkon on labor policy-making gradually declined after the late 1970s.

16. The 1955 reform of the Unemployment Insurance Program offered better benefits for core male workers with more enterprise tenure years (Estévez-Abe 2008, 127).

17. Although this book focuses on public works projects as a mechanism of social protections for workers in the labor market, the ruling LDP's calculation that public works projects would earn votes and political support was one of the key determinants of their origins and development in Japan. Regarding the electoral dimension of public works project, see Horiuchi and Saito (2003) and Woodall (1996).

18. The Korean chaebŏl was the creature of Park's industrialization project during the late 1960s and early 1970s. The number of affiliated firms and subsidiary companies in the chaebŏl sector exponentially increased after the early 1980s and 1990s. For details, see E. M. Kim (1997) and Won-keun Song and Lee (2005).

19. For a detailed discussion of the institutional origins and development of the Korean labor market, see J. Song (2012c).

20. Given the underdevelopment of internal labor markets, there was no clear distinction between insiders and outsiders in the Korean labor market during the 1960s and 1970s.

21. For example, the Park regime announced the president's Emergency Decree for Economic Stability on August 2, 1972, in order to bail out Korean firms under severe financial distress because of high interest rates on loans from curb markets. The government froze all curb market loans and enabled firms to postpone their interest payments (E. M. Kim 1997, 147–148).

22. Job creation was not a primary goal of the HCI drive. Nevertheless, this massive industrialization project enabled large firms to expand their investments during the economic recession of the first oil crisis, which led to the prevention of massive unemployment.

23. The FKTU was abolished during the military coup in 1961, but it was soon restored by the Korean Central Intelligence Agency with the political purpose of establishing an acquiescent labor federation (Jang-jip Choi 1997, 45–46).

24. As described in the previous section, in Japan the 1949 revision of the Labor Union Law banned this labor practice.

25. The Ministry of Labor (originally named the Administration of Labor Affairs) did not become a ministry until the Chun Doo-hwan government's reorganization. Its administrative status was 'chŏng' (administration), which is one rank lower than 'bu' (ministry), indicating the low political priority of labor policy in the Park regime.

26. During the Park regime, the Ministry of Home Affairs was in charge of maintaining social order with the use of the National Police Agency. I therefore classify it as a security ministry. Since the Administration of Labor Affairs was raised to the status of the Ministry of Labor in 1981, I have placed commissioners of labor into the category of labor ministers.

27. Regarding the underdevelopment of the link between political parties and labor unions in Korea, see Y. Lee (2009).

28. Wage restraints were partly sustained by a massive inflow of unskilled workers from rural areas. Urbanization and industrialization fostered the rapid migration of the rural population into cities, and such a supply of labor contributed to curtailing wage increases during the 1960s. For details, see H-K. Song (1991, 260–261) and Ji-hong Kim (1991, 260–271).

29. For the data on the wage differential across firm size, see Korean Administration of Labor Affairs, *Maewŏl Nodong Tonggye Josa Bogosŏ [Report on Monthly Labor Statistics]* (various issues).

30. For the data on the wage differential across industries, see Korean Administration of Labor Affairs, *Maewŏl Nodong Tonggye Josa Bogosŏ [Report on Monthly Labor Statistics]* (various issues published in 1979). Regarding the failure of the Park regime's wage guideline, see H-K. Song (1991, 262–266).

31. The FKI, composed of the top chaebŏl, specialized in general economic and industrial policies, while the KEF, composed of both large chaebŏl and SMEs, was in charge of industrial relations. The FKI and KEF were established in 1961 and 1970, respectively, modeled after Keidanren (Japanese Federation of Economic Organizations) and Nikkeiren (Japanese Federation of Employers' Association).

32. This pension program was divided into two separate schemes, one for civil servants and the other for the military in 1963. A decade later, in 1975, the authoritarian government established another pension scheme for private school teachers (Klassen and Yang 2010, 6).

33. The Korean business community also opposed the introduction of the national pension program in the 1970s (Klassen and Yang 2010, 6).

34. The first heath insurance program was introduced in 1966 on a basis of voluntary enrollment, which did not have any meaningful effects on the public (T. Kim and Seong 2000, 381). Occupational accident insurance was introduced in 1963, targeting firms with more than five hundred workers in the mining and manufacturing sectors; this coverage was extremely limited considering that Korea had few firms with more than five hundred workers during the 1960s, but it was gradually extended to firms with ten workers by 1982.

35. Since the retirement allowance program gave one month of wages for every year of service at the rate of average monthly wage over the last three months prior retirement, enterprise tenure years and final salary were critical for Korean workers (Klassen and Yang 2010, 7).

## CHAPTER 4

1. Some of the material in this chapter also appears in J. Song (2010, 2012a, and 2012b). The copyright information: J. Song (2010). Copyright © 2010 by the Regents of the University of California. Originally published in a slightly different form, reprinted from *Asian Survey*, Vol. 50, No. 6, pp.1011–1031, by permission of the Regents. J. Song (2012a). Copyright © The East Asia Institute. Used with permission by Lynne Rienner Publishers, Inc. J. Song (2012b). Copyright © 2012 Wiley Periodicals, Inc. Used with permission by Wiley Periodicals, Inc.

2. Regarding Japan's political changes in the 1990s, see Curtis (1999).

3. In comparative context, economic instability and intensified electoral competition in Japan are not as intense or severe as those in Korea, which underwent a democratic transition as well as financial crisis.

4. It is an ongoing topic of debate whether Japan's recent institutional changes in the national economy are adjustments on the margins or important signs of complete transformation toward liberal market economies like the United Kingdom and the United States.

5. Regarding the origins and development of the cross shareholding system in Japan, see Hiwatari (1999).

6. There are debates on the impact of the revision of the Commercial Code and the accounting standards on corporate governance. Noble (2006) contends that the influence of new policies and institutions has been rather limited because of CEOs' discretion in adopting new regulations. Meanwhile, Schaede (2006) predicts that Japanese firms will adopt new behaviors and market strategies as a result of these regulatory changes.

7. On average, over the past two decades workers at large Japanese firms have recorded 2–3 percent wage increases, whereas those at SMEs have shown 1–2 percent wage increases (Japanese Ministry of Health, Labor and Welfare, Labor Economic Indicators).

8. Author's interview with Nakamura Keisuke, September 7, 2005 (Tokyo).

9. Author's interviews with staff members at Nippon-Keidanren (Japanese Business Federation), September 17, 2005 (Tokyo).

10. The average age for male workers in firms with more than ten regular employees increased from 38.6 years to 41.8 years between 1985 and 2006 (Japanese Ministry of Internal Affairs and Communications 2008).

11. Nevertheless, employment restructuring with use of early retirement programs and layoffs for regular workers has gradually increased in the Japanese labor market, especially since 1998 (Araki 2004, 143).

12. Membership of Nippon-Keidanren comprises 1,280 companies, 127 industrial associations, and 47 regional economic organizations as of May 26, 2011, http://www.keidanren.or.jp, accessed July 14, 2011.

13. Author's interview with a staff member at Nippon-Keidanren, September 17, 2005 (Tokyo).

14. Nikkeiren and Keidanren merged into Nippon-Keidanren in May 2002. The former had been responsible for industrial relations as the political representatives of business, and the latter had been in contact with the government and political parties to discuss general economic policies. Even after the merger into Nippon-Keidanren, the division between the two remained within the organization. Former Nikkeiren staff members have continued to work on labor policy making and industrial relations, whereas former Keidanren staff members have specialized in broad economic policy making.

15. The shrinking size of the regular workforce and the expanded use of non-regular workers have been dominant patterns of labor adjustment in other advanced industrialized countries as well, such as Germany and the Netherlands. Iversen (2005, 257–268) describes this trend as selective and shielded labor market deregulation. For details, see Iversen (2005) and Visser and Hemerijck (1997).

16. Several studies address the strong political influence of SMEs on politicians and the LDP under the pre-1994 electoral rule. For further details, see Noble (1998), Ramyser and Rosenbluth (1997), and Uriu (1996).

17. A large number of Keizai Dōyūkai members were educated and trained at US universities, which might affect the neoliberal position of the organization on Japan's market economy.

18. According to recent surveys, a majority of Japanese employers still preferred to adhere to the high level of job security for insiders despite the problems of Japan's employment protection system (Noble 2011).

19. Davis and Shirato (2007) argue that the different characteristics of industrial technology affect the policy preferences of each industry in trade disputes. Similarly, this section focuses on the effects of the industrial characteristics on the preferences and interests of the business for labor market reform and labor adjustments.

20. Author's interview with a manager of the Toyota Motor Corporation, December 19, 2005 (Tokyo).

21. The Japanese electronics industry experienced a negative 13.1 percent of return on equity (ROE) in 2001, whereas the Japanese metal industry generated a 2.8 percent of

ROE in the same year (Internal documents of Denki Rengō [Japanese Electrical Electronic and Information Union]).

22. When I interviewed a union official at Denki Rengō, I asked whether or not there was any pressure on the part of management for workers to volunteer for the early retirement program. He mentioned that more workers than expected had volunteered for the program because of very generous monetary compensation. The amount of the severance package differed according to several employment conditions, such as years of service as well as the age of the worker. One of the most generous retirement packages promised workers the equivalent of seventy-two months' wages (internal documents of Denki Rengō). Author's interview with a union official at Denki Rengō, December 2, 2005 (Tokyo).

23. Author's interview with a union official at Denki Rengō, December 2, 2005 (Tokyo).

24. The magnitude of downsizing in the steel industry from 1990 to 1996 varied across firms, from 14,000 workers at Nippon Steel Corporation to between 1,500 and 3,300 workers at another four firms (Miyuki 2001, 201).

25. Author's interview with a member of the Labor Policy Deliberative Council, September 20, 2005 (Tokyo).

26. Two other national labor federations, Sōhyō (General Council of Trade Unions of Japan) and Shin Sanbetsu (National Federation of Industrial Organizations), joined Rengō in 1989. Sōhyō, founded in 1950 and dominated by public-sector unions, was the largest national labor federation in Japan before the establishment of Rengō in 1987. As the privatization of public corporations drastically debilitated its organizational capacity during the late 1970s and early 1980s, this labor confederation was finally dissolved and merged into Rengō in 1989.

27. The rest of the 27.2 percent comprises independent labor unions.

28. Japan Institute for Labor Policy and Training, Labor Statistics, http://www.jil.go.jp.

29. As of 2008, 45.3 percent of firms with more than one thousand workers were unionized in Japan, whereas only 1.1 percent of firms with less than ninety-nine workers were unionized (Japan Institute for Labor Policy and Training, Labor Statistics, http://www.jil.go.jp). Also, less than 3.5 percent of part-time workers were organized as of 2004 (Japanese Trade Union Confederation [Rengō] 2006, 47).

30. There is no informal or formal policy coordination among these three national labor federations. Rengō leaders do not adopt any cooperative attitudes toward two other small national federations affiliated with the Japan Communist Party. According to my interview with a Japanese journalist, Rengō leaders even harbored hostile feelings toward communist labor unions and union officials. Author's interview with a journalist at *Asahi Shimbun [Asahi Daily Newspaper]*, February 14, 2006 (Tokyo).

31. Author's interview with a member of the Labor Policy Deliberative Council, September 20, 2005 (Tokyo).

32. For detailed information on a variety of policy proposals and wage bargaining strategies since the early 1980s, refer to Denki Rengō's home page (http://www.jeiu.or.jp) and Jidōsha Sōren's home page (http://www.jaw.or.jp), accessed September 15, 2007.

33. The percentage of non-regular workers has noticeably increased since the mid-1990s, and more than half of female workers (55.26 percent as of 2007) were employed as non-regular workers (mostly part-time workers in the service sector) (Japanese Ministry of Internal Affairs and Communications, Shūgyō Kōjō Kihon Chōsa [Basic Survey on Employment Structure]).

34. This wage-gap data is based upon two surveys, Heisei 13 nendo Chingin Kōjō Kihon Chōsa [Wage Structure on Heisei 13] and Ukeoi Jigyōsha Tokubetu Chōsa [Special Report on the In-House Subcontracting System] conducted by the Japanese Ministry of Health, Labor and Welfare (from Kobayashi [2004, 210]).

35. Hiwatari and Miura (2001, 15) point out that the Japanese construction industry is the largest among G7 countries, employing 10 percent of Japan's workforce and producing

10 percent of the GDP, but a majority of local construction firms are small-sized ones with fewer than three workers, which cannot realize economies of scale.

36. Author's interview with a staff member of the Deregulation Committee, September 9, 2005 (Tokyo); see also Kume (2000, 2–13).

37. There have been debates on the real influence of the Deregulation Committee on economic deregulation. Some scholars are very critical of the function of this agency, since all agendas are picked up or drafted by each ministry (Vogel 1996). In particular, Japanese journalists have pointed out that the Ministry of Economy, Trade and Industry (METI) initiated the establishment of this agency and steered it in the direction of economic deregulation behind the scenes (Author's personal communications with Japanese journalists).

38. A deliberative council (*shingikai*) is a formal means of incorporating societal interests into policy making. Composed of academics, business community members, former bureaucrats, union leaders, and even journalists, a deliberative council consults, negotiates, and drafts policy outlines under the jurisdiction of each ministry. It does not have any formal authority stipulated by the Constitution of Japan, but the Japanese government utilizes this system in order to form political consensus in public policy making. As of 1995, the total number of deliberative councils in Japan was 217 (Schwartz 1998, 51). Scholars still debate the role of deliberative councils. Some argue that the bureaucracy takes advantage of this system to manipulate public opinion and societal interests in order to push them toward a predetermined policy direction. Others emphasize the utility of this system in terms of incorporating diverse societal interests into policy making and legislation, despite the heavy influence of the bureaucracy on agenda setting and the selection of council members. For more details on Japanese deliberative councils, see Schwartz (1998) and Noble (2003).

39. Because of administrative reform, the Ministry of Labor merged with the Ministry of Health and Welfare and was renamed the Ministry of Health, Labor and Welfare (as of January 6, 2001).

40. This agency was renamed the Council for the Promotion of Regulatory Reform (Kisei Kaikaku Kaigi) in January 2007. For further details, see its home page, http://www8. cao.go.jp/kisei-kaikaku/, accessed June 1, 2008.

41. Until the mid-1990s, employment service was dominated by the state agency in Japan.

42. Author's interviews and personal communication with Japanese journalists.

43. Some scholars point out that administrative reforms did not substantially undermine the dominant power of the Japanese bureaucracy since administrative reforms were indeed designed and driven by the bureaucracy itself (Mulgan 2003).

44. The Japanese Ministry of Labor (1998) emphasizes the persistence of long-term employment practices for regular workers and the extension of external labor markets for greater flexibility. In particular, the Japanese Ministry of Labor (1999) points to the necessity of the increase in part-time employment in the service sector, in conjunction with the strong support of long-term employment practices in the Japanese labor market.

45. For details on the flexible work system, see the Japanese Ministry of Health, Labor and Welfare, http://www2.mhlw.go.jp/topics/seido/kijunkyoku/flextime/index.htm, accessed June 16, 2009.

46. The first Deregulation Committee had the right to advise ministers and monitor whether or not each ministry followed the policy recommendations of the Deregulation Committee (Miura 2002b, 132, footnote 21).

47. Press release and position papers published by Denki Rengō and Jidōsha Sōren.

48. Rengō insisted that the Central Labor Standard Deliberative Council should first decide upon strict guidelines before implementation and that it would be essential to

have at least one year of deliberation at the council, in particular to determine regulations for the labor-management council on the discretionary work hours system (Nakamura 2005a, 269–270).

49. Author's interview with Takanashi Akira, January 26, 2006 (Tokyo).

50. See Rengo's press release, http://www.jtuc-rengo.or.jp/news/danwa/2003/2003 0606_1116405909.html, accessed September 10, 2011.

51. As of 2003, 7.8 percent of the workforce was estimated to be other types of non-regular workers (e.g., dispatched workers or contract workers) in the Japanese labor market, whose category is referred to a group of non-regular workers not identified as part-time workers. Dispatched workers who registered at the private personnel agencies (*haken kaisha*) were estimated to be around 0.9 percent of the workforce; however, this proportion increased to 1.6 percent in 2004 after the 2003 revision of the Worker Dispatch Law (Japanese Ministry of Health, Labor and Welfare 2005, 278, table 1.1.10).

52. According to Gottfried (2008, 187), more than 80 percent of female dispatched workers were engaged in clerical jobs, compared to the nearly 70 percent of male dispatched workers who performed professional or technical work.

53. For details, see Japan Institute for Labor Policy and Training, *JILPT Recent Statistical Survey Report August 2009,* http://www.jil.go.jp/english/estatis/esaikin/2009/e200908. htm, accessed August 3, 2010.

54. Although the Labor Contract Succession Law protects workers' employment in the case of corporate restructuring, its application is limited to corporate divisions, excluding mergers and acquisitions and the transfer of undertakings, unlike the protection in the European Union (Araki 2005).

55. The four prerequisites stipulated in the case laws were the absolute necessity of firing workers, the lack of alternative tools to avoid firing workers, the existence of a fair procedure to decide who should be fired, and an agreement with the representatives of workers.

56. Japanese Lower House Parliamentary Debate, 156 Diet Session, 17th minutes of the Health, Labor and Welfare Standing Committee, http://hourei.ndl.go.jp/SearchSys/ viewShingi.do?i=115601077, accessed September 6, 2012.

57. Although the proportion of the regular workforce continued to decline after the mid-1980s, the regular workforce was around 70 percent of the total workforce as of 2003 (Japanese Ministry of Internal Affairs and Communications, Shūgyō Kōjō Kihon Chōsa [Basic Survey on Employment Structure]).

58. Author's interview with a bureaucrat at the Japanese Ministry of Health, Labor and Welfare, December 22, 2005 (Tokyo).

59. Author's interview with a former chair of the Japanese Labor Deliberative Council, January 26, 2006 (Tokyo).

60. In 1947, the Japanese government introduced the Unemployment Insurance Program, focusing on passive labor market programs. However, after the first oil crisis, it was reformed into the Employment Insurance Program. For details, see chapter 3.

61. The Employment Insurance Law was revised during the Mori cabinet (April 2000– April 2001) and it was effective as of April 2001.

62. Author's interview with a former bureaucrat at the Japan Ministry of Health, Labor and Welfare, June 11, 2007 (Tokyo).

63. Japanese Ministry of Internal Affairs and Communications, Shūgyō Kōjō Kihon Chōsa [Basic Survey on Employment Structure].

64. Author's interview with a bureaucrat at the Japanese Ministry of Health, Labor and Welfare, January 6, 2006 (Tokyo).

65. The Council on Economic and Fiscal Policy (Keizai Zaisei Simon Kaigi) has concentrated the political authority of decision making in the prime minister. Chaired by the prime minister and composed of top business leaders and neoliberal economists, it

has largely determined the direction of economic policy making, including labor market reform, with its strong agenda-setting power since its establishment in 2001.

66. While dispatched workers were estimated to be 2.2 percent of the workforce (as of 2008), this declined to 1.7 percent as of 2009, in the wake of the global financial crisis (Japan Institute for Labor Policy and Training 2011, 15).

67. According to the Japanese Ministry of Health, Labor and Welfare, the number of dismissed temporary workers was more than two hundred thousand in the manufacturing sector between October 2008 and September 2009 (*Japan Times,* April 30, 2009).

68. Regarding the parliamentary debates on the revision of the Worker Dispatch Law in 2012, see Nihon Hōurei Sakuin [Index of Japanese Laws], http://hourei.ndl.go.jp/Search-Sys/viewShingi.do?i=117401060, accessed August 2, 2012.

69. Japanese Ministry of Health, Labor and Welfare, http://www.mhlw.go.jp, accessed January 23, 2012.

## CHAPTER 5

1. Some of the material in this chapter also appears in J. Song (2012a, 2012b, and 2012c). The copyright information: J. Song (2012a). Copyright © The East Asia Institute. Used with permission by Lynne Rienner Publishers, Inc. J. Song (2012b). Copyright © 2012 Wiley Periodicals, Inc. Used with permission by Wiley Periodicals, Inc. J. Song (2012c). Copyright © 2012 by the Board of Trustees of the Leland Stanford Junior University. Used with permission by the Board of Trustees.

2. This labor market condition is somewhat similar to that in Spain during the Franco regime. See Pérez-Díaz (1987).

3. Unlike Japan's enterprise unions, which encompass blue-collar workers and low-ranking white-collar workers (below the rank of the division chief) together, Korea's labor unions (especially in the manufacturing sector) are exclusively composed of blue-collar production workers, although low-rank white-collar workers are allowed to join enterprise unions in principle. Therefore, most chaebŏl unions represent the interests of unionized blue-collar production workers at the firm level.

4. During the period of high-speed economic growth, there was no clear distinction between regular workers and non-regular workers in the Korean labor market because of the underdevelopment of internal labor markets for blue-collar production workers.

5. Of course, there are variations in terms of labor management practices in employment protection for insiders across firms as well as industrial sectors. But this study highlights general patterns of labor management practices in the Korean labor market.

6. In 1989, Korea's value-added labor productivity growth rate was 6.5 percent, whereas its real wage growth rate was 18.3 percent. For details about labor productivity and real wage growth rates, see Bank of Korea, Economic Statistics System (http://ecos.bok.or.kr), Korea Labor Institute (2002 and 2005), Korean Productivity Center Labor Productivity Statistics (http://www.kpc.or.kr), and H-K. Song (1993, 81).

7. Because of the Plaza Accord in 1985, the Japanese yen became strong against the US dollar during this period. The strong Japanese yen helped Korean products compete with Japanese products in the US market.

8. Regarding the origins of these two business associations, see chapter 3.

9. As already shown in figure 2.3, the ratios of average enterprise tenure years in firms with more than five hundred workers to those for the entire workforce (composed of a majority of SMEs) started to increase rapidly after the 1987 democratization.

10. Author's interview with a labor sociologist specializing in the Korean automobile industry, July 10, 2006 (Seoul). A former executive director in one of the major Korean automobile assemblers has stated that some union officials agreed to the introduction of

new skill training systems, but they were not able to persuade the rank and file (author's interview, August 11, 2006, Seoul).

11. Author's interviews with a labor scholar, July 21, 2006 (Seoul) and a former Korean automobile industry executive, August 11, 2006 (Seoul).

12. Korean Employers' Federation, *Gyŏngchong Saŏp Bogosŏ [Annual Report of the Korean Employers' Federation]* (various years).

13. As of 2008, the FKTU represented 58.2 percent of the number of unions and 48.5 percent of the number of members, whereas the KCTU represented 19.4 percent of the number of unions and 40.2 percent of the number of members, indicating large chaebŏl unions' affiliation with the KCTU (Korean Ministry of Labor 2008b, 203, table 4.3.1).

14. Almost 80 percent of labor disputes were instigated by KCTU-affiliated labor unions between 1997 and 2007; this percentage has rapidly increased since the early 2000s (Korean Ministry of Labor 2008b, 553).

15. The Democratic Labor Party, which has been loosely affiliated with the KCTU, is an exception. Nevertheless, it has not played a crucial role in the process of labor market reform because of its very small number of political representatives in the National Assembly (6 representatives out of 299 congressmen as of August 2011).

16. Korea adopted a mixed electoral system of single-member districts (SMD) and proportional representation (PR) after democratization. In the case of the 1988 National Assembly election, three-quarters of the legislative seats were assigned to SMD and one-quarter to PR. Although the seat allocation between SMD and PR districts has changed slightly over time, Korea's electoral system has tilted significantly toward a majoritarian system.

17. Korean National Election Commission (www.nec.go.kr, accessed September 6, 2007).

18. The final elements of these submitted bills were closer to the policy positions of the conservative NDRP, as opposed to those of the PDP and the UDP that represented the political positions of organized labor and labor activists on reform (Young-gi Choi et al. 2000, 83).

19. Interestingly, there was no discussion on the number of labor unions in each workplace. This might reflect the fact that neither business associations nor the FKTU wanted to address this issue (C. Lee and You 2000, 38–41).

20. Party mergers and break-ups have constituted one of the most frequent patterns of political realignment in Korea since the 1987 democratization.

21. Supreme Court of Korea, Legal Informal System, http://glaw.scourt.go.kr/jbsonw/jbson.do, accessed September 6, 2012.

22. Ibid.

23. For the data on corporation-provided employee benefits, see Korean Ministry of Labor, Giŏp Nodong Biyong Josa [Survey on Firms' Labor Costs]. During the same period, SMEs also vastly increased employee benefits. For example, firms with thirty to ninety-nine employees augmented worker benefits by 31.3 percent in 1990 and 58.55 percent in 1991. Despite the expansion of employee benefits in SMEs, however, the benefit differentials did not narrow because of the extent of the initial differences. On average, workers at SMEs (firms with thirty to ninety-nine workers) received around 70 percent of the benefits of workers at large firms (with more than one thousand employees) during the late 1980s and early 1990s. But worker benefit differentials by firm size have widened more significantly since the mid-1990s, with benefits for workers at SMEs declining to 40 percent of those at large firms.

24. Immediately following the National Assembly and presidential elections in 1992, the National Assembly passed ten labor laws in 1993 (Korean National Assembly, http://likms.assembly.go.kr/bill/jsp/main.jsp, accessed April 10, 2007).

25. The RCRLL consisted of three business representatives, three labor representatives, and twelve public interest representatives. Because of the predominance of public interest representatives appointed by the MOL, the RCRLL was presented as an administrative agency for the MOL in order to justify its policy changes.

26. Although the Kim Young-sam administration proposed labor market reforms in conjunction with its accession to the Organisation for Economic Co-operation and Development (OECD), Kim's reforms were driven by domestic political factors (author's interview with Park Se-il, August 10, 2006, Seoul).

27. Park Se-il has stated that labor market reform should be driven by "neutral" reform-minded academic scholars, as opposed to self-interested societal interest groups and/or electoral politicians whose only concern is to disseminate "populistic" political propaganda. One of his main goals in initiating labor market reform was to force both employers and workers to abide by rules and regulations in industrial relations (author's interview with Park Se-il, August 10, 2006, Seoul).

28. The KCTU, consisting of chaebŏl unions in heavy and chemical industries, was able to survive, although the state refused to recognize its legal status as a national labor federation. The organizational capacity of the KCTU, derived as it was from chaebŏl unions, consolidated its political status in labor politics even before its legalization in 1999.

29. Some scholars have pointed out that labor federations did not oppose the legislation of employers' rights to lay off redundant regular workers for managerial reasons, but they attempted to include legal conditions to prevent the misuse of such rights in firing workers (Byung-hoon Lee and You 2001; Bum-sang You 2000). However, labor officials argued that the two national federations never consented to the legislation (author's interview with an FKTU union official, July 18, 2006, Seoul).

30. Author's interview with a former union official at the FKTU, July 26, 2006 (Seoul).

31. Unlike the KEF, which was composed of large chaebŏl as well as SMEs, the FKI, whose membership consisted of large chaebŏl, opposed the legalization of multiple labor unions at any level.

32. Japanese ministries fight for bureaucratic turf in cases of overlapping administrative jurisdictions, but there is less interference by other ministries when it comes to their own policy domains. Author's personal communications with Japanese bureaucrats.

33. The MOL draft proposed to partially lift *samkŭm* (three prohibitions), including the abolition of the prohibition on labor unions' political participation, third-party interventions in industrial relations, and the presence of multiple unions at the national level.

34. Prime Minister Lee Hong-gu, Chief of Staff Kim Kwang-il, and Senior Secretary on Social Welfare Park Se-il lacked any prior information about additional revisions or the ruling party's plan to pass the bills in the absence of the opposition parties in the National Assembly (author's interview with Park Se-il, August 10, 2006, Seoul); see also Se-il Park (2000, 67).

35. The Democratic Liberal Party was renamed the New Korea Party after Kim Jong-pil and his followers defected from the Democratic Liberal Party in 1995. After the New Korea Party merged with the Democratic Party in November 1997, the New Korea Party was renamed the Grand National Party (GNP) again.

36. After several delays in its implementation, the legalization of multiple labor unions at the firm level took effect in July 2011.

37. His electoral victory was due to a pre-electoral coalition forged with two charismatic opposition leaders, Kim Jong-pil and Park Tae-jun, in 1997.

38. Regarding the logic of two-level games, see Putnam (1988).

39. On December 3, 1997, the KEF asked the government to allow employers to immediately implement their right to lay off redundant regular workers in corporate restructuring as well as to introduce the Worker Dispatch Law (Bum-sang You 2000, 353). Yet such reform request was only materialized after President-elect Kim Dae-jung established the

Tripartite Commission in order to discuss comprehensive labor market reform in January 1998.

40. The FKTU supported Kim Dae-jung during the presidential election, but because of the prohibition on labor union political activities, it was not able to participate officially in the electoral campaign.

41. As briefly described in the previous section, the Roh Tae-woo and Kim Young-sam governments implemented the components of the tripartite system when they attempted to initiate labor reforms, but all of their efforts failed.

42. According to my interviews, union leaders were "forced" to accept these conditions since they were concerned that they could be accused of spoiling the resuscitation of Korea's economy after the financial crisis. However, the political nuances differed among interviewees. One current union leader at the FKTU stated that organized labor had agreed to implement the layoff clause just one year earlier, indicating that it was not a political defeat for organized labor in bargaining. In contrast, a former FKTU union leader stated that organized labor was more or less forced to accept President-elect Kim's decision at the bargaining table (author's interviews with labor unions leaders, July 18, 2006 and July 26, 2006, Seoul).

43. Companies were allowed to hire dispatched workers on a temporary basis from only twenty-six occupational categories stipulated by Presidential Decree No. 15828 (Korean Ministry of Labor, http://www.molab.go.kr, accessed June 1, 2006).

44. For further detailed information, please refer to Major Agreements at the Tripartite Commission between 1998–2005 (Korean Tripartite Commission 2005) (Korean Tripartite Commission, http://www.lmg.or.kr, accessed May 1, 2006).

45. The legalization of multiple unions at the firm level was finally implemented as of July 1, 2011, and the legal prohibition on keeping union officials on the company's payroll was implemented in July 1, 2010. As of 2000, one-third of the staff members at the FKTU and the KCTU were dispatched by enterprise unions and received wages directly from the companies (Korean Employers' Federation 2000, 37). In other words, the legal prohibition on union officials' wages being paid from the company's payroll would lead to the weakening of labor movements not only at the firm level but also at the national level. In fact, the ruling NCNP leadership promised not to stipulate the prohibition on employers' payment of union officials' wages under the table in order to persuade the FKTU to accept the legalization of the layoff clause at the Tripartite Commission. This clandestine dealing between the NCNP and the FKTU was disclosed by the FKTU leadership when the MOL tried to stipulate this clause in the labor law (*Chosun Ilbo,* December 8, 1999).

46. The main groups dominating the non-confidence vote were the Metal Workers' Union and Hyundai Group labor unions (Roh 1999, 224).

47. Several corruption scandals that entangled President Kim's three sons also seriously paralyzed the Kim Dae-jung government during the last year of his presidency.

48. The FKTU reiterated its political strategies of confrontation against and cooperation toward the government, whereas the KCTU refused to attend all official tripartite meetings.

49. Since there is no specific breakdown between chaebŏl and non-chaebŏl firms in the MOL's statistics, I assume that firms with over five hundred employees are chaebŏl firms. Shin-jun Kang et al. (2005), which includes more detailed data on the thirty largest chaebŏl firms, point out that unions in the thirty largest firms constituted 2.1 percent of Korea's unions as of 2001. Although these two sources do not refer to an identical group of firms, I consider firms with over five hundred employees as approximately equivalent to chaebŏl firms.

50. Some labor scholars and labor activists have argued that Hyundai Motor Company's management intended to weaken its militant labor union by dismissing union

officials who lacked positive performance evaluations. However, the management was more interested in implementing the legalization of the layoff clause than in attacking union officials (Hyung-je Cho 2005, 136; E. Jung 1999, 15).

51. Most male workers on unpaid vacation programs returned to their workplace within a year because of the quick economic recovery of the Korean automobile industry, although female service workers were mostly employed as non-regular workers.

52. According to an interview, one-third of production workers (almost ten thousand, including temporary, part-time, and in-house subcontracting workers) are employed as non-regular workers at Hyundai Motor Company. Interestingly, it is non-regular workers who are posted to more skill-intensive tasks since union members prefer much easier job tasks, contrary to what might be expected (author's interview with a labor scholar, July 10, 2006, Seoul).

53. As briefly explained in chapter 3, the introduction of the national pension program began a debate in the 1970s on accumulating industrial capital for the purpose of development as opposed to social protections. This idea dissipated in the wake of the first oil crisis (T. Kim and Seong 2000, 382).

54. The ruling NCNP's presidential campaign promise included pro-labor socioeconomic policies compared to that of the conservative opposition GNP.

55. In contrast, Kwon Gi-hong, a labor minister, expressed his doubt about the implementation of the Dutch model of social partnership to the Korean labor market (*Chosun Ilbo*, July 24, 2003).

56. Korean Employers' Federation press release (July 5, 2003).

57. As a consequence of the organizational restructuring of the Office of the President, Lee was appointed to the chair of the Policy Planning Committee, the presidential advisory committee, a position without policy coordination authority.

58. Author's interview with a senior managing director at the Korean Employers' Federation, May 29, 2006 (Seoul).

59. Author's interview with a staff member at the Federation of Korean Industries, September 9, 2005 (Tokyo).

60. Author's interview with a senior managing director at the Korean Employers' Federation, May 29, 2006 (Seoul).

61. Beginning in the 2004 National Assembly election, voters cast two ballots, one for the candidate in the SMD district and the other for the political party in the PR list. Although the majority of the legislative seats (more than 75 percent of the seats) were allocated to the SMD district, the introduction of the new electoral system allowed small parties, like the Democratic Labor Party, to gain political support from the PR list.

62. The government stipulated that employers should provide employment protections for non-regular workers if they wanted to extend the employment contracts of these workers after the first two-year contract term. On the ground, however, this clause generated a rather perverse situation. A majority of SME employers began to lay off non-regular workers before the implementation of this legal clause or before the expiration of the two-year employment contract term so as to avoid any potential problems regarding the extension of employment contracts for non-regular workers.

63. Korean National Assembly Parliamentary Debates, http://likms.assembly.go.kr/bill/jsp/main.jsp, accessed May 24, 2010.

64. Japan's internal labor markets in large firms have become much stronger over the past two decades as well. In Japan, the number of average tenure years in the labor market increased from 10.9 to 11.8, whereas the average number of tenure years at firms with more than one thousand workers increased from 13.7 to 14.4. Nevertheless, compared to the internal labor market in Korea, the degree of change is not as drastic as it could be in terms of employment protection (see figure 2.3).

65. The wage gap between regular and non-regular workers increased from 67.1 percent to 63.5 percent between 2002 and 2007 (Eun, Oh, and Yoon 2008, 249–253).

66. Regarding the method and data source for calculating this estimate, see chapter 2.

67. Information on Korean Law, http://www.law.go.kr/DRF/MDRFLawService.jsp?OC=molab&ID=3058, accessed August 10, 2011.

## CONCLUSION

1. Sweden is different from both Britain and Germany with respect to the pattern of reform and the degree of increasing labor market inequality and dualism. In particular, the Swedish case diverged from the German case in terms of the degree of inequality and dualism in the labor market. Like Germany, Sweden adopted a series of labor market reforms for outsiders (e.g., part-time, temporary, and fixed-term contract workers). Yet under the institutional constraints of centralized industrial relations and strong political relationship between organized labor and the Social Democratic Party, the Swedish government has been able to provide generous social protection programs for those affected by labor market reform over the past few decades, which encompassed all the workforce in the labor market beyond the boundary of workplace, firm, and industry. The development of social protection programs as compensating policies alleviated the problems of labor market inequality and dualism in Sweden.

2. For the data on the Japanese aged population, see Japanese Ministry of Internal Affairs and Communications, Statistics Bureau, *The Statistics of Handbook of Japan (2011)*, http://www.stat.go.jp/english/data/handbook/c02cont.htm, accessed March 3, 2012; for the data on the population over sixty-five years old in Korea, see the Government E-Indicator, http://www.index.go.kr/egams/stts/jsp/potal/stts/PO_STTS_IdxMain.jsp?idx_cd=1010&bbs=INDX_001&clas_div=A, accessed on March 3, 2012.

3. Japanese Ministry of Internal Affairs and Communications, Statistics Bureau, *The Statistics of Handbook of Japan (2011)*, http://www.stat.go.jp/english/data/handbook/c02cont.htm, accessed August 14, 2012.

4. Japanese Ministry of Internal Affairs and Communications, *Population Estimates*, http://www.stat.go.jp/english/data/jinsui/index.htm, accessed February 12, 2012.

5. Personal communications with Professor Deborah J. Milly at the Virginia Polytechnic Institute and State University and Professor Lonny E. Carlile at the University of Hawaii at Manoa at the Annual Conference of the Association for Asian Studies in Atlanta (April 3–6, 2008). Such concerns have been addressed in various government publications on the problems of an aging society.

6. In Japan, the compulsory retirement age is sixty, but policy makers have been discussing whether to extend it to sixty-five in response to the increase of the pensionable age to sixty-five by the year 2025.

7. For the data on Japan's female labor force participation, see Organisation for Economic Co-operation and Development, Stat Extracts, http://stats.oecd.org/index.aspx?queryid=24861, accessed March 8, 2012.

8. For Korea's female labor force participation rates, see ibid.

9. For youth unemployment rates, see Organisation for Economic Co-operation and Development iLibrary, http://www.oecd-ilibrary.org/employment/youth-unemployment-rate_20752342-table2, accessed August 15, 2012; for average unemployment rates, see Organisation for Economic Co-operation and Development, Stat Extracts, http://stats.oecd.org/Index.aspx?DatasetCode=STLABOUR, accessed August 15, 2012.

10. Organisation for Economic Co-operation and Development, Stat Extracts, the section of "involuntary part-time workers" under the Labor Force Statistics (http://stats.oecd.org/, accessed August 15, 2012); there are no data for Korea.

11. For further details regarding overseas production in these two sectors, see Japan Automobile Manufacturers Association, Inc. (http://www.jama.or.jp/) and Japan Electronics and Information Technology Industries Association (http://www.jeita.or.jp/japanese/).

12. For the data on Japan's outward FDI, see Japanese Ministry of Finance, http://www.mof.go.jp/english/international_policy/reference/itn_transactions_in_securities/fdi/2004b_3.htm, accessed August 13, 2012.

13. Author's interview with a union leader at the Japanese Association of Metal, Machinery, and Manufacturing Workers, November 16, 2005 (Tokyo).

14. For the data on Korea's outward FDI, see Korea EximBank, http://www.koreaexim.go.kr/kr/work/check/oversea/year.jsp, accessed August 13, 2012.

15. For the data on the destination of Korea's outward FDI, see ibid.

16. Regarding the Japanese automobile industry's overseas production strategies, see Noble (2005).

# References

Abe, Yukiko. 2003. "Fringe Benefit Provision for Female Part-Time Workers in Japan." In *Labor Markets and Firm Benefit Policies in Japan and the United States,* edited by Seiritsu Ogura, Toshiaki Tachibanaki, and David A. Wise, 339–370. Chicago: University of Chicago Press.

Ahmadjian, Christina L., and Patricia Robinson. 2001. "Safety in Numbers: Downsizing and the Deinstitutionalization of Permanent Employment in Japan." *Administrative Science Quarterly* 46 (4): 622–654.

Albert, Michel. 1993. *Capitalism vs. Capitalism: How America's Obsession with Individual Achievement and Short-Term Profit Has Led It to the Brink of Collapse.* New York: Basic Books.

Alesina, Alberto, and Allan Drazen. 1991. "Why Are Stabilizations Delayed?" *American Economic Review* 81 (5): 1170–1188.

Amsden, Alice H. 1989. *Asia's Next Giant: South Korea and Late Industrialization.* Oxford: Oxford University Press.

Amyx, Jennifer A. 2004. *Japan's Financial Crisis: Institutional Rigidity and Reluctant Change.* Princeton: Princeton University Press.

———. 2006. "Government Financial Institutions and the Development of a Private Equity Market for Corporate Turnarounds." Paper presented at the conference of the System Restructuring in East Asia, Center for East Asian Studies at Stanford University, June 22–24.

Aoki, Masahiko. 2001. *Toward a Comparative Institutional Analysis.* Cambridge, MA: MIT Press.

Aoki, Masahiko, Gregory Jackson, and Hideaki Miyajima, eds. 2007. *Corporate Governance in Japan: Institutional Change and Organizational Diversity.* Oxford: Oxford University Press.

Araki, Takashi 2004. "Koporeto Gabanansu Kaikaku to Rōdōhō" [Corporate Governance Reforms and the Labor Law]. In *Koporeto Gabanasu to Jūgyōin [Corporate Governance and Employees in the Japanese Political Economy],* edited by Takeshi Inagami and Zyunjiro Mori, 129–172. Tokyo: Tōyō Keizai Shinpōsha.

———. 2005. "Corporate Governance Reforms, Labor Law Developments, and the Future of Japan's Practice-Dependent Stakeholder Model." *Japan Labor Review* 2 (1): 26–57.

Ariga, Kenn, Giorgio Brunello, and Yasuhi Ohkusa. 2000. *Internal Labor Markets in Japan.* Cambridge: Cambridge University Press.

Armstrong, Shiro. 2009. "Japanese FDI in China: Determinants and Performance." *Asia Pacific Economic Paper* no. 378, Australia-Japan Research Centre, Crawford School of Economics and Government, ANU College of Asia and the Pacific.

Barbieri, Paolo, and Stefani Scherer. 2009. "Labour Market Flexibilization and Its Consequences in Italy." *European Sociological Review* 25 (6): 677–692.

Becker, Gary S. 1993. *Human Capital: A Theoretical and Empirical Analysis, with Special Reference to Education.* Chicago: University of Chicago Press.

Becker, Uwe, and Herman Schwartz, eds. 2005. *Employment 'Miracles': A Critical Comparison of the Dutch, Scandinavian, Swiss, Australian and Irish Cases versus Germany and the US.* Amsterdam: Amsterdam University Press.

Berger, Suzanne, and Ronald Dore, eds. 1996. *National Diversity and Global Capitalism.* Ithaca: Cornell University Press.

Berger, Suzanne, and Michael J. Piore. 1980. *Dualism and Discontinuity in Industrial Societies.* Cambridge: Cambridge University Press.

Björklund, Anders. 2000. "Going Different Ways: Labour Market Policy in Denmark and Sweden." In *Why Deregulate Labor Markets?*, edited by Gøsta Esping-Andersen and Marino Regini, 148–180. Oxford: Oxford University Press.

Blanchflower, David G., and Richard B. Freeman. 1993. "Did the Thatcher Reforms Change British Labour Market Performance?" Paper presented at CEP/NIESR Conference: "Is the British Labour Market Different?" London, April 1.

Boix, Carles. 1998. *Political Parties, Growth, and Equality: Conservative and Social Democratic Economic Strategies in the World Economy.* Cambridge: Cambridge University Press.

Botero, Juan C., Simeon Djankov, Rafael La Porta, Florencio Lopez-de-Silanes, and Andrei Shleifer. 2004. "The Regulation of Labor." *Quarterly Journal of Economics* 119 (4): 1339–1382.

Bourguignon, François, and Christian Morrisson. 1998. "Inequality and Development: The Role of Dualism." *Journal of Development Economics* 57 (1): 233–257.

Bradley, David, Evelyne Huber, Stephanie Moller, Francois Nielsen, and John D. Stephens. 2003. "Distribution and Redistribution in Postindustrial Democracies." *World Politics* 55 (4): 193–228.

Brinton, Mary C. 1993. *Women and the Economic Miracle: Gender and Work in Postwar Japan.* Berkeley: University of California Press.

——. 2011. *Lost in Transition: Youth, Work, and Instability in Postindustrial Japan.* Cambridge: Cambridge University Press.

Brown, William, Simon Deakin, and Paul Ryan. 1997. "The Effects of British Industrial Relations Legislation, 1979–1997." *National Institute Economic Review* 161 (2): 69–83.

Cabinet Office, Government of Japan [Naigakufu]. 2004. *Kōjōkaigaku Hyōka Hōgokusho [Report on the Evaluation of the Structural Reform in Japan].* Tokyo: Naigakufu.

Cahuc, Pierre, and Fabien Postel-Vinay. 2001. "Temporary Jobs, Employment Protection and Labor Market Performance." *IZA Discussion Paper* no. 260.

Calder, Kent E. 1988. *Crisis and Compensation: Public Policy and Political Stability in Japan.* Princeton: Princeton University Press.

Caliendo, Marco, and Katharina Wrohlich. 2010. "Evaluating the German 'Mini-Job' Reform Using a Natural Experiment." *Applied Economics* 42 (19): 2475–2489.

Calmfors, Las, and John Driffill. 1988. "Centralization of Wage Bargaining." *Economic Policy* 6 (1): 14–61.

Calmfors, Las, Anders Forslund, and Maria Hemström. 2002. "Does Active Labour Market Policy Work? Lessons from the Swedish Experiences." *Institute for Labour Market Policy Evaluation Working Paper* 2002: 4.

Caraway, Teri L. 2009. "Labor Rights in East Asia: Progress or Regress?" *Journal of East Asian Studies* 9 (2): 153–186.

Carey, John M., and Matthew Soberg Shugart 1995. "Incentives to Cultivate a Personal Vote: A Rank Ordering of Electoral Formulas." *Electoral Studies* 14 (4): 417–439.

Carlile, Lonny E. 1994. "Party Politics and the Japanese Labor Movement: Rengo's New Political Force." *Asian Survey* 34 (7): 606–620.

Cheng, Mariah Mantsun, and Arne L. Kalleberg. 1996. "Labor Market Structures in Japan: An Analysis of Organizational and Occupational Mobility Patterns." *Social Forces* 74 (4): 1235–1260.

Cho, Hyung-je. 2005. *Hangukjŏk Saeng'sanbangsik ŭn Ganŭng'hanga? [A Study on the Possibility of "Hyundaism": Production Systems and Employment Relations in Korea].* Seoul: Hanwul Academy.

Cho, Joonmo, GiSeung Kim, and Taehee Kwon. 2008. "Employment Problems with Irregular Workers in Korea: A Critical Approach to Government Policy." *Pacific Affairs* 81 (3): 407–426.

Cho, Sung-Jae, Byung-Hoon Lee, Jang-Pyo Hong, Sang-Hoon Kim, and Young-Hyung Kim. 2004. *Jadongcha Sanŏp ŭi Dokŭp Gujo wa Goyong Gwangye ŭi Gyechŭng'sŏng [Subcontracting Systems and the Stratification of the Employment Structure in the Korean Automobile Industry].* Seoul: Korea Labor Institute.

Choi, Jang-jip. 1992. "Saero'un Nodong Undong ŭi Bang'hyang Mosaek ŭl Wihayŏ" [Searching for a New Direction of the Korean Labor Movement]. *Sahoe Pyŏngron [Social Critique]* (June): 233–246.

———. 1997. *Hanguk ŭi Nodong Undong gwa Gukga [The Korean Labor Movement and the State].* Seoul: Nanam.

Choi, Young-gi, Kwang-seok Chun, Cheol-su Lee, and Bum-sang You, eds. 2000. *Hanguk ŭi Nodongbŏp Gaejŏng gwa Nosa Gwangye [Labor Law Reforms and Industrial Relations in Korea].* Seoul: Korea Labor Institute.

Chuma, Hiroyuki. 1994. *Kenshō Nihon Kata Koyō Chōsei [The Pattern of Employment Adjustment in the Japanese Labor Market].* Tokyo: Shūeisha.

———. 2002. "Employment Adjustments in Japanese Firms during the Current Crisis." *Industrial Relations* 41 (4): 653–682.

Chung, Erin Aeran. 2010. "Korea and Japan's Multicultural Models for Immigrant Incorporation." *Korea Observer* 41 (4): 649–676.

Clasen, Jochen, and Daniel Clegg. 2003. "Unemployment Protection and Labour Market Reform in France and Great Britain in the 1990s: Solidarity versus Activation?" *Journal of Social Policy* 32 (3): 361–381.

Coe, David T., and Dennis J. Snower. 1997. "Policy Complementarities: The Case for Fundamental Labor Market Reform." *Staff Papers—International Monetary Fund* 44 (1): 1–35.

Corsetti, Giancarlo, Paolo Pesenti, and Nouriel Roubini. 1998. "What Caused the Asian Currency and Financial Crisis? Part II: The Policy Debate." *NBER Working Papers.* Cambridge, MA: National Bureau of Economic Research.

Cox, Gary W. 1990. "Centripetal and Centrifugal Incentives in Electoral Systems." *American Journal of Political Science* 34 (4): 903–935.

Crouch, Colin, and Wolfgang Streeck, eds. 1997. *Political Economy of Modern Capitalism: Mapping Convergence and Diversity.* London: Sage Publications.

Curtis, Gerald L. 1999. *The Logic of Japanese Politics: Leaders, Institutions, and the Limits of Change.* New York: Columbia University Press.

Cusack, Thomas R., Torben Iversen, and David Soskice. 2007. "Economic Interests and the Origins of Electoral Systems." *American Political Science Review* 101 (3): 373–391.

Davis, Christina L., and Yuki Shirato. 2007. "Firms, Governments, and WTO Adjudication: Japan's Selection of WTO Disputes." *World Politics* 59 (2): 274–313.

Deyo, Frederic C. 1987. "State and Labor: Modes of Political Exclusion in East Asian Development." In *The Political Economy of the New Asian Industrialism,* edited by Frederic C. Deyo, 182–202. Ithaca: Cornell University Press.

Dickens, William T., and Kevin Lang. 1985. "A Test of Dual Labor Market Theory." *American Economic Review* 75 (4): 792–805.

Doeringer, Peter B., and Michael J. Piore. 1971. *Internal Labor Markets and Manpower Analysis*. Lexington, MA: Heath.

Dore, Ronald. 1973. *British Factory, Japanese Factory: The Origins of National Diversity in Industrial Relations*. Berkeley: University of California Press.

———. 1986. *Flexible Rigidities: Industrial Policy and Structural Adjustment in Japan, 1970–1980*. London: Athlone Press.

Drazen, Allan, and Vittorio Grilli. 1993. "The Benefit of Crises for Economic Reforms." *American Economic Review* 83 (3): 598–607.

Economic and Social Research Institute [Naigakufu Keizai Shakai Sōgō Kenkyūsho]. 2006. *Nihonkigyō: Jisokuteki Seichō no tame no Senryaku [Japanese Firms: A Strategy for Sustainable Growth]*. Tokyo: Economic and Social Research Institute, Cabinet Office.

Eichengreen, Barry, and Torben Iversen. 1999. "Institutions and Economic Performance: Evidence from the Labor Market." *Oxford Review of Economic Policy* 15 (4): 121–138.

Esping-Andersen, Gøsta. 1990. *The Three Worlds of Welfare Capitalism*. Princeton: Princeton University Press.

———. 2000. "Who is Harmed by Labor Market Deregulations? Quantitative Evidence." In *Why Deregulate Labor Markets?*, edited by Gøsta Esping-Andersen and Marino Regini, 66–98. Oxford: Oxford University Press.

Estévez-Abe, Margarita. 1999. "Welfare and Capitalism in Postwar Japan." PhD diss., Harvard University.

———. 2008. *Welfare and Capitalism in Postwar Japan*. Cambridge: Cambridge University Press.

Estévez-Abe, Margarita, Torben Iversen, and David Soskice. 2001. "Social Protection and the Formation of Skills: A Reinterpretation of the Welfare State." In *Varieties of Capitalism: The Institutional Foundations of Comparative Advantage*, edited by Peter. A. Hall and David Soskice, 145–183. Oxford: Oxford University Press.

Etchemendy, Sebastián. 2004. "Repression, Exclusion, and Inclusion: Government-Union Relations and Patterns of Labor Reform in Liberalizing Economies." *Comparative Politics* 36 (3): 273–290.

Eun, Sumi, Hak-su Oh, and Jin-ho Yoon. 2008. *Bijŏng'gyujik gwa Hankuk Nosa Gwangye System ŭi Byŏnwha [Non-regular Workers and Changes in the Korean Industrial Relations]*. Seoul: Korea Labor Institute.

Evans, Peter. 1995. *Embedded Autonomy: States and Industrial Transformation*. Princeton: Princeton University Press.

Fajertag, Giuseppe, and Philippe Pochet, eds. 2000. *Social Pacts in Europe—New Dynamics*. Brussels: European Trade Union Institute (ETUI).

Finegold, David, and David Soskice. 1988. "The Failure of Training in Britain." *Oxford Review of Economic Policy* 4 (3): 36–61.

Förster, Michael, and Marco Mira d'Ercole 2005. "Income Distribution and Poverty in OECD Countries in the Second Half of the 1990s." *OECD Social, Employment, and Migration Working Papers*. Paris: OECD.

Freeman, Richard, and Jeffry Pelletier. 1989. "The Impact of Industrial Relations Legislation on British Union Density." *NBER Working Paper Series* no. 3167. Cambridge, MA: National Bureau of Economic Research.

Gao, Bai. 2001. *Japan's Economic Dilemma: The Institutional Origins of Prosperity and Stagnation*. Cambridge: Cambridge University Press.

Garon, Sheldon. 1987. *The State and Labor in Modern Japan.* Berkeley: University of California Press.

——. 1997. *Molding Japanese Minds: The State in Everyday Life.* Princeton: Princeton University Press.

Garret, Geoffrey. 1998a. "Global Markets and National Politics: Collision Course or Virtuous Circle?" *International Organization* 52 (4): 787–824.

——. 1998b. *Partisan Politics in the Global Economy.* Cambridge: Cambridge University Press.

Genda, Yuji. 2003. "Who Really Lost Jobs in Japan? Youth Employment in an Aging Japanese Society." In *Labor Markets and Firm Benefit Policies in Japan and the United States,* edited by Seiritsu Ogura, Toshiaki Tachibanaki, and David A. Wise, 103–134. Chicago: University of Chicago Press.

Genda, Yuji, and Marcus Rebick. 2000. "Japanese Labour in the 1990s: Stability and Stagnation." *Oxford Review of Economic Policy* 16 (2): 85–102.

Gerlach, Michael L. 1992. *Alliance Capitalism: The Social Organization of Japanese Business.* Berkeley: University of California Press.

Gerschenkron, Alexander. 1966. *Economic Backwardness in Historical Perspective.* Cambridge, MA: Belknap Press of Harvard University Press.

Gordon, Andrew. 1985. *The Evolution of Labor Relations in Japan: Heavy Industry, 1853–1955.* Cambridge, MA: Harvard University Press.

——. 1998. *The Wages of Affluence: Labor and Management in Postwar Japan.* Cambridge, MA: Harvard University Press.

Gottfried, Heidi. 2008. "Pathways to Economic Security: Gender and Nonstandard Employment in Contemporary Japan." *Social Indicators Research* 88 (1): 179–196.

Gourevitch, Peter. 1986. *Politics in Hard Times: Comparative Responses to International Economic Crises.* Ithaca: Cornell University Press.

Gourevitch, Peter, and James Shinn 2005. *Political Power and Corporate Control: The New Global Politics of Corporate Governance.* Princeton: Princeton University Press.

Griffith, Rachel, Rupert Harrison, and Gareth Macartney. 2007. "Product Market Reforms, Labor Market Institutions and Unemployment." *Economic Journal* 117 (March): 142–166.

Grimes, William W. 2002. *Unmaking the Japanese Miracle: Macroeconomic Politics 1985–2000.* Ithaca: Cornell University Press.

Grofman, Bernand, Sung-Chull Lee, Edwin A. Winckler, and Brian Woodall, eds. 1999. *Elections in Japan, Korea, and Taiwan under the Single Non-transferable Vote: The Comparative Study of an Embedded Institution.* Ann Arbor: University of Michigan Press.

Haggard, Stephan. 1994. "Macroeconomic Policy through the First Oil Shock 1970–1975." In *Macroeconomic Policy and Adjustment in Korea 1980–1990,* edited by Stephan Haggard, 23–47. Cambridge, MA: Harvard Institute for International Development and Korea Development Institute.

——. 2000. *The Political Economy of the Asian Financial Crisis.* Washington, D.C.: Institute for International Economics.

Haggard, Stephan, David Kang, and Chung-In Moon. 1997. "Japanese Colonialism and Korean Development: A Critique." *World Development* 25 (6): 867–881.

Haggard, Stephan, and Robert Kaufman. 2008. *Development, Democracy, and Welfare States: Latin America, East Asia, and Eastern Europe.* Princeton: Princeton University Press.

Hall, Peter A., and Robert J. Franzese, Jr. 1998. "Mixed Signals: Central Bank Independence, Coordinated Wage Bargaining, and European Monetary Union." *International Organization* 52 (3): 505–535.

Hall, Peter A., and Daniel Gingrich. 2004. *Varieties of Capitalism and Institutional Complementarities in the Macroeconomy: An Empirical Analysis.* Cologne: Max Planck Institute for the Study of Societies.

Hall, Peter A., and David Soskice, eds. 2001. *Varieties of Capitalism: The Institutional Foundations of Comparative Advantages.* Oxford: Oxford University Press.

Hall, Peter A., and Kathleen Thelen. 2009. "Institutional Change in Varieties of Capitalism." *Socio-Economic Review* 7 (1): 7–34.

Hamaaki, Junya, Masahiro Hori, Saeko Maeda, and Keiko Murata. 2010. "Is the Japanese Employment System Degenerating? Evidence from the Basic Survey on Wage Structure." *ESRI Discussion Paper Series* no. 232. Tokyo: Economic and Social Research Institute, Cabinet Office.

Hanami, Tadashi. 2004. "The Changing Labor Market, Industrial Relation and Labor Policy." *Japan Labor Review* 1 (1): 4–16.

Hara, Junsuke, and Kazuo Seiyama 2005. *Inequality and Affluence: Social Stratification in Japan.* Translated by Brad Williams. Melbourne: Trans Pacific Press.

Häusermann, Silja. 2010. *The Politics of Welfare Reform in Continental Europe: Modernization in Hard Times.* Cambridge: Cambridge University Press.

Häusermann, Silja, and Hanna Schwander. 2010. "Varieties of Dualization? Labor Market Segmentation and Insider Outsider Divides across Regimes." Paper prepared for the conference of the Dualisation of European Societies, Green Templeton College, University of Oxford, January 14–16.

Hazama, Hiroshi. 1997. *The History of Labor Management in Japan.* New York: St. Martin's Press.

Heckman, James, and Carmen Pagés-Serra. 2000. "The Costs of Job Security Regulation: Evidence for Latin American Labor Markets." *Economia* 1 (1): 109–154.

Henry, S. G. B., and Marika Karanassou. 1996. "The U.K. Labor Market: Analysis of Recent Reforms." In *Economic Policies and Unemployment Dynamics in Europe,* edited by S. G. B. Henry and Dennis J. Snower, 150–174. Washington, D.C.: International Monetary Fund.

Hill, Hal, and Prema-chandra Athukorala. 1998. "Foreign Investment in East Asia: A Survey." *Asia-Pacific Economic Literature* 12 (2): 23–50.

Hiwatari, Nobuhiro. 1999. "Employment Practices and Enterprise Unionism in Japan." In *Employees and Corporate Governance,* edited by M. Blair and Mark J. Roe, 275–313. Washington, D.C.: Brookings Institution Press.

Hiwatari, Nobuhiro, and Mari Miura. 2001. "Export Sector-Led Adjustment in Trouble? Unemployment, Fiscal Reconstruction and Welfare Reform in Germany and Japan." Paper prepared for the annual meeting of the American Political Science Association, San Francisco, August 30–September 2.

Horiuchi, Yusaku, and Jun Saito. 2003. "Reapportionment and Redistribution: Consequences of Electoral Reform in Japan." *American Journal of Political Science* 47 (4): 669–682.

House of Representatives of Japan [Kokkai Shūgiin]. Various years. *Shūgiin no Ugoki [Legislative Activities in the House of Representatives of Japan].* Tokyo: Shūgiin Jimukyoku.

Howard, Christopher. 1993. "The Hidden Side of the American Welfare State." *Political Science Quarterly* 18 (3): 403–436.

Howell, Chris. 2005. *Trade Unions and the State: The Construction of Industrial Relations Institutions in Britain, 1890–2000.* Princeton: Princeton University Press.

Huber, Evelyne, Charles Ragin, and John D. Stephens. 1993. "Social Democracy, Christian Democracy, Constitutional Structure, and the Welfare State." *American Journal of Sociology* 99 (3): 711–749.

Huber, Evelyne, and John D. Stephens. 2001. *Development and Crisis of the Welfare State: Parties and Policies in Global Markets.* Chicago: University of Chicago Press.

Hwang, Soo Kyung. 2006. *Wage Structure and Skill Development in Korea and Japan.* Tokyo: Japan Institute for Labor Policy and Training.

Hyodo, Tsutomu. 1997. *Rōdō no Zengosi Vol. 1 [Labor History in Postwar Japan Vol. 1].* Tokyo: University of Tokyo Press.

Imai, Jun. 2006. "Reform without Labor: The Transformation of Japanese Employment Relations since the 1990s." PhD diss., Stony Book University.

Iversen, Torben 1999. *Contested Economic Institutions: The Politics of Macroeconomics and Wage Bargaining in Advanced Democracies.* Cambridge: Cambridge University Press.

——. 2005. *Capitalism, Democracy, and Welfare.* Cambridge: Cambridge University Press.

Iversen, Torben, and David Soskice. 2006. "Electoral Institutions and the Politics of Coalitions: Why Some Democracies Distribute More than Others." *American Political Science Review* 100 (2): 165–181.

——. 2009. "Dualism and Political Coalitions: Inclusionary versus Exclusionary Reforms in an Age of Rising Inequality." Paper presented at the annual meeting of the American Political Science Association, Toronto, September 3–9.

Iversen, Torben, and John D. Stephens. 2008. "Partisan Politics, the Welfare State, and Three Worlds of Human Capital Formation." *Comparative Political Studies* 41 (4/5): 660–637.

Iversen, Torben, and Anne Wren. 1998. "Equality, Employment, and Budget Restraint: The Trilemma of the Service Economy." *World Politics* 50 (4): 507–546.

Japan Institute for Labor Policy and Training (JILPT). 2010. *Labor Situation in Japan and Analysis: General Overview 2009/2010.* Tokyo: JILPT.

——. 2011. *Labor Situation in Japan and Analysis: Detailed Exposition 2011/2012.* Tokyo: JILPT.

Japan Productivity Center [Seisansei Kenkyūsho]. 1995. *Sairyō Rōdōsei ni Kansuru Chōsa Hōkokusho [Report on the Discretionary Work Hours System].* Tokyo: Japan Productivity Center for Socio-Economic Development.

——. 1996. *Wagakuni Seizōgyō no Sesansei to Kokusai Kyōsōryoku [Productivity and International Competitiveness of the Japanese Manufacturing Industry].* Tokyo: Japan Productivity Center for Socio-Economic Development.

Japanese Business Federation [Nippon Keidanren]. 2002. *Koyō Mondai ni Kansuru Seirōsi Gōi [The Political Agreement for the Employment System among Business, Labor and the Government].* Tokyo: Nippon Keidanren.

——. 2004. *Nihon no Rōdōkeizai Jijō [The Japanese Labor Market].* Tokyo: Nippon Keidanren.

——. 2006. *Nippon Keidanren Chinginsōran 2006 [Nippon Keidanren General Survey on Wage 2006].* Tokyo: Nippon Keidanren.

——. 2007. *Keiei Rōdōseisaku Iinkai Hōkoku Gaiyo [Policy Report on the Management and Labor Policy].* Tokyo: Nippon Keidanren.

Japanese Federation of Employers' Association [Nikkeiren]. 1995. *Sinjidai no Nihontekikeiei [Japanese Management Systems in a New Economic Era].* Tokyo: Nikkeiren.

——. 1997. *Buru-ba-do Puran Purojekuto [Bluebird Plan Project].* Tokyo: Nikkeiren.

——. Various years. *Nikkeiren Times.*

Japanese Ministry of Finance. 2010. *Japanese Public Finance Fact Sheet.* Tokyo: Ministry of Finance.

Japanese Ministry of Health, Labor and Welfare. 2004. *Heisei 16nen Rōdō Keizai Hakusho [Heisei 16 White Paper on Labor Economics].* Tokyo: Ministry of Health, Labor and Welfare.

——. 2005. *Heisei 17nen Rōdō Keizai Hakusho [Heisei 17 White Paper on Labor Economics].* Tokyo: Ministry of Health, Labor and Welfare

——. 2007. *Heisei 19nen Rōdō Keizai Hakusho [Heisei 19 White Paper on Labor Economics].* Tokyo: Ministry of Health, Labor and Welfare.

——. 2009: *Heisei 21nen Rōdō Keizai Hakushō [Heisei 21 White Paper on Labor Economics].* Tokyo: Ministry of Health, Labor and Welfare.

Japanese Ministry of Internal Affairs and Communications. 2008. *Japan Statistics Yearbook 2008.* Tokyo: Ministry of Internal Affairs and Communications.

——. 2011. *The Statistics of Handbook of Japan (2011).* Tokyo: Ministry of Internal Affairs and Communications.

Japanese Ministry of Labor. 1998. *Rōdō Keizai Hakusho [White Paper on Labor Economics].* Tokyo: Ministry of Labor.

——. 1999. *Rōdō Keizai Hakusho [White Paper on Labor Economics].* Tokyo: Ministry of Labor.

Japanese Trade Union Confederation [Rengō]. 2006. *Rengō Hakusho [White Paper on the Japanese Trade Union Confederation].* Tokyo: Japanese Trade Union Confederation [Rengō].

Jeong, Jooyeon 2002. *Sŏnjin'guk gwa Hanguk ŭi Jikŏp Gyoyuk Hun'ryŏn Jedo ŭi Tŭksŏng gwa Hangye [The Characteristics and Limitations of Vocational Training Systems in Korea and Selected Advanced Industrialized Countries].* Seoul: Jipmundang.

Johnson, Chalmers A. 1982. *MITI and the Japanese Miracle: The Growth of Industrial Policy, 1925–1975.* Stanford: Stanford University Press.

——. 1999. "Webs with No Spiders, Spiders with No Webs: The Genealogy of the Developmental State." In *The Developmental State,* edited by Meredith Woo-Cumings, 32–60. Ithaca: Cornell University Press.

Jones, Randall S. 2008. "Reforming the Labour Market in Japan to Cope with Increasing Dualism and Population Ageing." *OECD Economics Department Working Paper.* Paris: OECD.

——. 2009. "Reforming the Tax System in Korea to Promote Economic Growth and Cope with Rapid Population Ageing." *OECD Economics Department Working Papers.* Paris: OECD.

Joo, Moo Hyun. 2002. "Gyŏng'je Wigi Ihu ŭi Giŏp'byŏl Naebu Nodong Sijang ŭi Gujo Byŏnhwa: Hyundai Jadongcha ŭi Sarye" [The Changing Internal Labor Market after the Financial Crisis: A Case Study of Hyundai Motor Company]. *Sanŏp Nodong Yŏngu [Studies on Industry and Labor]* 8 (1): 75–110.

Jung, Eehwan. 1999. *Gyŏng'je Wigi wa Hanguk ŭi Nosa Gwangye [The Asian Financial Crisis and Its Impact on the Korean Industrial Relations System].* Seoul: Korean Labor and Society Institute.

——. 2006. *Hyŏndae Nodong Sijang ŭi Jŏngchi Sahoehak [Political Sociology of the Labor Market].* Seoul: Humanitas.

Jung, Eehwan, and Byung-you Cheon. 2006. "Economic Crisis and Changes in Employment Relations in Japan and Korea." *Asian Survey* 46 (3): 457–476.

Jung, Joo-Youn. 2006. "When Nonliberal Economies Meet Globalization: The Transformation of Interventionist States in East Asia." PhD diss., Stanford University.

Kalleberg, Arne L., Edith Rasell, Naomi Cassirer, Barbara F. Reskin, Ken Hudson, David Webster, and Eileen Appelbaum. 1997. *Nonstandard Work, Substandard Jobs: Flexible Work Arrangements in the US.* Washington, D.C.: Economic Policy Institute.

Kang, Shin-jun, Seong-hee Kim, Min-young Heo, Sang-jo Kim, Duck-ryul Hong, Byeong-gu Kang, and Jae-hee Lee. 2005. *Chaebŏl ŭi Nosa Gwangye wa Sahoejŏk Jaeng'jŏm [Industrial Relations in the Chaebŏl Sector].* Seoul: Nanam.

Kang, Sung Jin, and Hong Sik Lee. 2007. "The Determinants of Location Choice of South Korean FDI in China." *Japan and the World Economy* 19 (4): 441–460.

Kasza, Gregory J. 2006. *One World of Welfare: Japan in Comparative Perspective.* Ithaca: Cornell University Press.

Katzenstein, Peter J. 1985. *Small States in World Markets: Industrial Policy in Europe.* Ithaca: Cornell University Press.

Keizer, Arjan B. 2008. "Non-regular Employment in Japan: Continued and Renewed Dualities." *Work, Employment, and Society* 22 (3): 406–425.

Kim, Byung-Kook. 1994. *Bundan gwa Hyŏkmyŏng ŭi Donghak [The Effect of the War and the Revolution on the Political Dynamics in Korea].* Seoul: Munhakgwa Jisŏngsa.

——. 2000a. "Party Politics in South Korea's Democracy: The Crisis of Success." In *Consolidating Democracy in South Korea,* edited by Larry Diamond and Byung-Kook Kim. 53–86. Boulder: Lynne Rienner.

——. 2000b. "Electoral Politics and Economic Crisis, 1997–1998." In *Consolidating Democracy in South Korea,* edited by Larry Diamond and Byung-Kook Kim, 173–202. Boulder: Lynne Rienner.

——. 2002. "The Park Era: Agent, Structures, and Legacies." Paper presented at the annual meeting of the American Political Science Association, Boston, August 29–September 1.

——. 2003. "The Politics of Chaebŏl Reform." In *Economic Crisis and Corporate Restructuring in Korea,* edited by Wonhyuk Lim, Stephan Haggard, and Euysung Kim, 53–78. Cambridge: Cambridge University Press.

Kim, Byung-Kook, and Hyun-Chin Lim. 2000. "Labor against Itself: Structural Dilemmas of State Monism." In *Consolidating Democracy in South Korea,* edited by Larry Diamond and Byung-Kook Kim, 111–138. Boulder: Lynne Rienner.

Kim, Dae-whan, Young-gi Choi, and Gi-sul Yun. 2010. *Nodong Undong, Sang'saeng inga Gongmyŏl inga? [Labor Movements, Co-prosperity or Collapse?].* Seoul: Wisdom House.

Kim, Dong-bae, Joo-il Kim, Gyu-sik Bae, and Jeong-woo Kim. 2004. *Goyong Yuyŏnhwa wa Injŏk'jawon Gwanri Gwaje [Flexible Employment Systems and Human Resources Management].* Seoul: Korea Labor Institute.

Kim, Dong-One, and Johngseok Bae. 2004. *Employment Relations and HRM in South Korea.* London: Ashgate.

Kim, Eun Mee. 1997. *Big Business, Strong State: Collusion and Conflict in South Korean Development 1960–1990.* Albany: State University of New York Press.

Kim, Eun Mee, and Jai S. Mah. 2006. "Patterns of South Korea's Foreign Direct Investment Flows into China." *Asian Survey* 46 (6): 881–897.

Kim, Ji-hong. 1991. *Korean Industrial Policy in the 1970s: The Heavy and Chemical Industry Drive.* Seoul: Korea Development Institute.

Kim, Pil Ho. 2009. "From Development to Welfare? The State and Welfare Capitalism in Japan and South Korea." PhD diss., University of Wisconsin–Madison.

———. 2010. "The East Asian Welfare State Debate and Surrogate Social Policy: An Exploratory Study on Japan and South Korea." *Socio-Economic Review* 8 (3): 411–435.

Kim, Samuel S., ed. 2000. *Korea's Globalization.* Cambridge: Cambridge University Press.

Kim, Se-gyun. 2002. "1987 Ihu ŭi Hanguk Nodong Undong" [The Korean Labor Movement after 1987]. *Hanguk Jŏngchi Yŏngu [Studies on Korean Politics]* 11 (1): 197–244.

Kim, Sookon. 1983. *Nosa Gwangye Jŏng'chaek Gwaje wa Banghyang [Policy Agendas in the Korean Industrial Relations System].* Seoul: Korea Development Institute.

Kim, Sun-hyuk. 1996. "From Resistance to Representation: Civil Society in South Korean Democratization." PhD diss., Stanford University.

Kim, Sung-jung, and Je-hwan Seong. 2005. *Hanguk ŭi Goyong Jŏng'chaek [Employment Policies in South Korea].* Seoul: Korea Labor Institute.

Kim, Taeseong, and Kyungryung Seong. 2000. *Welfare States [Bokji Gukgaron].* Seoul: Nanam.

Kim, Yong Cheol. 1998. "Industrial Reform and Labor Backlash in South Korea: Genesis, Escalation, and Termination of the 1997 General Strike." *Asian Survey* 38 (12): 1142–1160.

Kim, Yong Cheol, and Chung-In Moon 2000. "Globalization and Workers in South Korea." In *Korea's Globalization,* edited by Samuel S. Kim, 54–75. Cambridge: Cambridge University Press.

King, Desmond, and Stewart Wood. 1999. "The Political Economy of Neoliberalism: Britain and the United States in the 1980s." In *Continuity and Change in Contemporary Capitalism,* edited by Herbert Kitschelt, Peter Lang, Gary Marks, and John D. Stephens, 371–397. Cambridge: Cambridge University Press.

Kitschelt, Herbert. 1991. "Industrial Governance Structures, Innovation Strategies, and the Case of Japan: Sectoral or Cross-National Comparative Analysis?" *International Organization* 45 (4): 453–493.

———. 2000. "Linkages between Citizens and Politicians in Democratic Polities." *Comparative Political Studies* 33 (6/7): 845–879.

Klassen, Thomas R., and Jae-Jin Yang. "Introduction: Population Aging and Income Security." In *Retirement, Work and Pensions in Ageing Korea,* edited by Jae-Jin Yang and Thomas R. Klassen, 1–13. London: Routledge.

Kobayashi, Yoshinobu. 2004. "Koyōsisutemu no Daihenbō to Rōdōkumiai no Mirai" [Changing Employment Systems and the Future of Labor Unions in Japan]. In *Sentaku to Shūchū: Nihon no Denki Jōhōkanren Kigyō ni Okeru Jittai Bunseki [Select and Focus: An Empirical Analysis of the Japanese Electronics and Information Technology Industry],* edited by Tsuyoshi Tsuru, 199–231. Tokyo: Yūhigaku.

Kohli, Atul. 1994. "Where Do High Growth Political Economies Come From: The Japanese Lineage of Korea's Developmental State." *World Development* 22 (9): 1269–1293.

———. 1997. "Japanese Colonialism and Korean Development: A Debate." *World Development* 25 (6): 883–888.

Koike, Kazuo. 1981. *Nihon no Jukuren: Sukureta Jinzai Keisei Sistemu [Skill Formation Systems in Japan].* Tokyo: Yūhigaku.

———. 1988. *Understanding Industrial Relations in Modern Japan.* Translated by Mary Saso. New York: St. Martin's Press.

Kong, Dongsung, Kiwoong Yoon, and Soyung Yu. 2010. "The Social Dimensions of Immigration in Korea." *Journal of Contemporary Asia* 40 (2): 252–274.

Kong, Tat Yan. 2006. "Globalization and Labor Market Reform: Patterns of Response in Northeast Asia." *British Journal of Political Science* 36 (2): 359–383.

Koo, Hagen. 2000. "The Dilemmas of Empowered Labor in Korea: Korean Workers in the Face of Global Capitalism." *Asian Survey* 40 (2): 227–250.

———. 2001. *Korean Workers.* Ithaca: Cornell University Press.

Korea Development Institute. 2006. *Yang'gŭk'hwa Gŭk'bok gwa Sahoe Tonghap ŭl Wihan Sahoe Gyŏngje Jŏngchaek Je'an [Policy Proposals for Solving Inequality and Promoting Social Integration].* Seoul: Korea Development Institute.

Korea Immigration Service, Ministry of Justice. 2010. *Chul'ip'guk Oe'gukin Jŏngchak Tonggye Yŏnbo [KIS Statics 2010].* Seoul: Korea Immigration Service.

Korea Labor Institute. 2002. *KLI Nodong'tonggye [KLI Labor Statistics].* Seoul: Korea Labor Institute.

———. 2005. *KLI Nodong'tonggye [KLI Labor Statistics].* Seoul: Korea Labor Institute.

———. 2008. *KLI Nodong'tonggye [KLI Labor Statistics].* Seoul: Korea Labor Institute.

———. 2009. *KLI Nodong'tonggye [KLI Labor Statistics].* Seoul: Korea Labor Institute.

Korea Participatory Government PR Team [Chamyŏ Jŏngbu Guk'jŏng Briefing Team]. 2009. *Rho Moo-hyun gwa Chamyŏjŏngbu Gyŏng'je 5 nyŏn [Korea's Economic Policies during the Roh Moo-hyun Government].* Seoul: Hansmedia.

Korea Presidential Commission on Industrial Relations Reform (PCIRR) [Nosajŏng Gaehyŏk Wiwŏnhoe]. 1996. *Nodong Gwangye'bŏp Jaengjŏm Jaryojip [Report on the Labor Relations Law].* Seoul: PCIRR.

Korean Administration of Labor Affairs [current Korean Ministry of Labor]. Various years. *Maewŏl Nodong Tonggye Josa Bogosŏ [Report on Monthly Labor Statistics].* Seoul: Administration of Labor Affairs.

Korean Employers' Federation. 2000. *Industrial Relations and the Labor Market in Korea.* Seoul: Korean Employers' Federation.

———. 2006. *Industrial Relations and Labor Market of Korea.* Seoul: Korean Employers' Federation.

———. Various years. *Gyŏngchong Saŏp Bogosŏ [Annual Report of the Korean Employers Federation].* Seoul: Korean Employers' Federation.

Korean Ministry of Labor. 2005. *Nodong Baeksŏ 2005 [White Paper on Labor 2005].* Seoul: Ministry of Labor.

———. 2008a. *Goyong Bohŏm Baeksŏ 2008 [White Paper on the Employment Insurance Program 2008].* Seoul: Ministry of Labor.

———. 2008b. *Nodong Baeksŏ 2008 [White Paper on Labor 2008].* Seoul: Ministry of Labor.

———. Various years. *Nondong Tonggye Yŏngam [Yearbook of Labor Statistics].* Seoul: Ministry of Labor.

Korean National Assembly Secretariat [Gukhoe Samuchŏ]. Various years. *Gukhoe Hoe'ŭi'rok [Parliamentary Debates].* Seoul: Korean National Assembly Secretariat [Gukhoe Samuchŏ].

Korean Tripartite Commission. 2003. *Nosajŏng Wiwŏnhoe 5 nyŏn Baeksŏ [White Paper on the Korean Tripartite Commission].* Seoul: Korean Tripartite Commission.

———. 2005. *Major Agreements at the Tripartite Commission between 1998–2005.* Seoul: Korean Tripartite Commission.

Korpi, Walter. 2006. "Power Resources and Employer-Centered Approaches in Explanations of Welfare States and Varieties of Capitalism." *World Politics* 58 (2): 167–206.

Kruger, Anne O. 1993. *Political Economy of Policy Reform in Developing Countries.* Cambridge, MA: MIT Press.

Kume, Ikuo. 1998. *Disparaged Success: Labor Politics in Postwar Japan.* Ithaca: Cornell University Press.

———. 2000. "Rōdō Seisaku Katei no Seijuku to Henyō" [Japanese Labor Policymaking in Transition]. *Nihon Rōdō Kenkyū Zassi [Research Journal on Japan's Labor Politics]* 475 (January): 2–13.

———. 2005. *Rōdō Seiji [Labor Politics in Japan].* Tokyo: Chūōkōron-Shinsha.

Kwon, Huck-Ju. 1999. *The Welfare State in Korea: The Politics of Legitimation.* London: Macmillan.

Lansbury, Russell D., Chung-Sok Suh, and Seung-Ho Kwon. 2007. *The Global Korean Motor Industry: The Hyundai Motor Company's Global Strategy.* London: Routledge.

Lee, Byung-hee. 2005. "Nodong I'dong gwa In'ryŏk Gaebal" [Labor Mobility and Human Capital Investment]. *Nodong Gyŏngje Nonjip [Labor Economics Review]* 28 (4): 1–28.

Lee, Byung-hoon, and Bum-sang You. 2001. "Nodongbŏp ŭi Hyŏng'sŏng gwa Jip'haeng e Gwanhan Nodong Jŏngchi Yŏngu" [Labor Law Reforms in Korea]. *Hanguk Sahoehak [Korean Journal of Sociology]* 35 (2): 177–204.

Lee, Cheolsu, and Bum-sang You. 2000. "1987 Nyŏn ŭi Nodongbŏp Gaejŏng gwa Nosa Gwangye Jil'sŏ ŭi Mosaek" [The 1987 Labor Law Reform and the New Industrial Relations System in Korea]. In *Hanguk ŭi Nodongbŏp Gaejŏng gwa Nosa Gwangye [Labor Law Reforms and Industrial Relations Systems in Korea],* edited by Young-gi Choi, Gwang-seok Chun, Cheolsu Lee, and Bum-sang You, 23–60. Seoul: Korea Labor Institute.

Lee, Cheol-Sung. 2007. "Labor Unions and Good Governance: A Cross-National, Comparative Analysis." *American Sociological Review* 72 (4): 585–609.

Lee, Chol, and Paul W. Beamish. 1995. "The Characteristics and Performance of Korean Joint Ventures in LDCs." *Journal of International Business Studies* 26 (3): 637–654.

Lee, Hong-Kyu, Seong-Ho Lim, Jin-Young Chung, Won-Taek Kang, and Byung-Kook Kim. 2007. *Dae'tong'ryŏng'jik Insu ŭi Sŏng'gong Jogŏn [Presidential Transitions in Korea].* Seoul: EAI.

Lee, Wonduck. 1997. *Nosa Gwangye Gaehyŏk: Mirae'rŭl wihan Sŏn'taek [Reforming Industrial Relations Systems].* Seoul: Korea Labor Institute.

Lee, Wonduck, and Joohee Lee. 2004. "Will the Model of Uncoordinated Decentralization Persist?" In *The New Structure of Labor Relations: Tripartism and Decentralization,* edited by Wonduck Lee, Harry C. Katz, and Joohee Lee, 143–165. Ithaca: Cornell University Press.

Lee, Yoonkyung. 2009. "Diverging Outcomes of Labor Reform Politics in Democratized Korea and Taiwan." *Studies in Comparative and International Development* 44 (1): 47–70.

Leschke, Janine, Günther Schmid, and Dorit Griga. 2006. "On the Marriage of Flexibility and Security: Lessons from the Hartz-Reforms in Germany." *Wissenschaftszentrum Berlin für Sozialforschung (WZB) Discussion Paper.*

Levy, Jonah D. 1999. "Vice into Virtue? Progressive Politics and Welfare Reform in Continental Europe." *Politics & Society* 27 (2): 239–273.

———. 2005. "Redeploying the State: Liberalization and Social Policy in France."  · In *Beyond Continuity: Institutional Change in Advanced Political Economies,* edited by Wolfgang Streeck and Kathleen Thelen, 103–126. Oxford: Oxford University Press.

Levy, Jonah D., Mari Miura, and Gene Park 2006. "Exiting Statism? New Directions in State Policy in France and Japan." In *The State after Statism,* edited by Jonah D. Levy, 93–136. Cambridge, MA: Harvard University Press.

Liberal Democratic Party of Japan [Jiyūminshutō]. 2006. *Jiyūminshutō Gojūnenshi [The Fifty Year History of the Liberal Democratic Party]*. Tokyo: Jiyūminshutō.

Lim, Wonhyuk. 2003. "The Emergence of the Chaebŏl and the Origins of the Chaebŏl Problem." In *Economic Crisis and Corporate Restructuring in Korea*, edited by Stephan Haggard, Wonhyuk Lim, and Euysung Kim, 35–52. Cambridge: Cambridge University Press.

Liu, Hwa-Jen. 2006. "Red and Green: Labor and Environmental Movements in Taiwan and South Korea." PhD diss., University of California, Berkeley.

Mahoney, James, and Kathleen Thelen. 2010. "A Theory of Gradual Institutional Change." In *Explaining Institutional Change: Ambiguity, Agency, and Power*, edited by James Mahoney and Kathleen Thelen, 1–37. Cambridge: Cambridge University Press.

Mares, Isabela. 2003. *The Politics of Social Risk: Business and Welfare State Development*. Cambridge: Cambridge University Press.

———. 2006. *Taxation, Wage Bargaining, and Unemployment*. Cambridge: Cambridge University Press.

Martin, Cathie Jo, and Duane Swank. 2004. "Does the Organization of Capital Matter?" *American Political Science Review* 98 (4): 593–611.

———. 2008. "The Political Origins of Coordinated Capitalism: Business Organization, Party Systems, and State Structure in the Age of Innocence." *American Political Science Review* 102 (2): 181–198.

Martin, Cathie Jo, and Kathleen Thelen. 2007. "The State and Coordinated Capitalism: Contributions of the Public Sector to Social Solidarity in Postindustrial Societies." *World Politics* 60 (1): 1–36.

Masujima, Toshiyuki. 1999. "Evaluating Administrative Reform: An Insider's Report." *Social Science Japan Journal* 2 (2): 215–228.

Matsubuchi, Atsuki. 2005. *Sengo Koyōseisaku no Gaikan to 1990 nendai igo no Seisaku no Tenkan [Employment Policies in Postwar Japan and Their Changes since the 1990s]*. Tokyo: Japan Institute for Labor Policy and Training.

Mayhew, Ken. 1991. "The Assessment: The UK Labour Market in the 1980s." *Oxford Review of Economic Policy* 7 (1): 1–17.

Milly, Deborah J. 1999. *Poverty, Equality, and Growth: The Politics of Economic Need in Postwar Japan*. Cambridge, MA: Harvard University Press.

Michie, Jonathan, and Maura Sheehan. 2003. "Labour Market Deregulation, 'Flexibility' and Innovation." *Cambridge Journal of Economics* 27 (1): 123–143.

Miura, Mari. 2002a. "Rōdōkisei" [Labor Regulations: Labor Politics and Political Veto Power]. In *Ryūdōki no Nihon Seiji [Japanese Politics in the Period of Change]*, edited by Nobuhiro Hiwatari and Mari Miura, 259–277. Tokyo: University of Tokyo Press.

———. 2002b. "From Welfare through Work to Lean Work: The Politics of Labor Market Reform in Japan." PhD diss., University of California, Berkeley.

———. 2005. "Rengō no Seisakusanka" [Rengō's Participation in Policymaking]. In *Suitaika Saiseika: Rōdōkumiai Kasseika eno Michi [Decline or Revival? Reviving Labor Unions]*, edited by Keisuke Nakamura, 169–192. Tokyo: Keishoshobo.

Miyuki, Mitsuyoshi. 2001. *Gendai Kigyōrōdō no Kenkyū [Study on the Labor Management System in Japan]*. Kyoto: Hōritsubunkasha.

Mo, Jongryn. 1999. "Democratization, Labor Policy, and Economic Performance." In *Democracy and the Korea Economy*, edited by Jongryn Mo and Chung-In Moon, 97–134. Stanford: Hoover Institution Press.

———. 2001. "Political Culture and Legislative Gridlock: Politics of Economic Reform in Precrisis Korea." *Comparative Political Studies* 34 (5): 467–492.

Mochida, Nobuki. 2008. *Fiscal Decentralization and Local Public Finance in Japan.* London: Routledge.

Mochizuki, Mike. 1993. "Public Sector Labor and the Privatization Challenge: The Railway and Telecommunications Unions." In *Political Dynamics in Contemporary Japan,* edited by Gary D. Allison and Yasunori Sone, 181–199. Ithaca: Cornell University Press.

Moriguchi, Chiaki. 1998. "The Evolution of Employment Systems in the United States and Japan, 1900–1960: A Comparative Historical and Institutional Analysis." PhD diss., Stanford University.

Moriguchi, Chiaki, and Hiroshi Ono. 2006. "Japanese Lifetime Employment: A Century's Perspective." In *Institutional Change in Japan,* edited by Magnus Blomstrom and Sumner La Croix, 152–176. London: Routledge.

Mulgan, Aurelia George. 2003. "Japan's 'Un-Westminster' System: Impediments to Reform in a Crisis Economy." *Government and Opposition* 38 (1): 73–91.

Murillo, M. Victoria, and Andrew Schrank. 2005. "With a Little Help from My Friends: Partisan Politics, Transnational Alliances, and Labor Rights in Latin America." *Comparative Political Studies* 38 (8): 971–999.

Murasugi, Yasuo. 2010. "Current Situation and Issues of Healthcare for Employees: Based on Analysis of Recent Trend and Cases." *Japan Labor Review* 7 (1): 47–65.

Nakagubo, Hiroya. 2004. "The 2003 Revision of the Labor Standards Law: Fixed-Term Contracts, Dismissal, Discretionary-Work Scheme." *Japan Labor Review* 1(2): 4–25.

Nakamura, Keisuke. 2005a. "Kaikaku no Naka no Itsudatsu" [Deviation from the Previous Labor Reform Pathway]. In *Usinawareta 10 nen o Koete II: Koizumi Kaikaku no Jidai [Beyond the 'Lost Decade' Volume 2: The Koizumi Reforms],* edited by the Institute of Social Science, 251–278. Tokyo: University of Tokyo Press.

——. 2005b. "Sōron: Suitaika Saiseika?" [Overview: Decline or Revival?] In *Suitaika Saiseika? [Decline or Revival?],* edited by Keisuke Nakamura, 3–26. Tokyo: Keishoshobo.

Nihon Seikei Shimbun Shūppanbu. Various years. *Kokkai Binran [A Handbook of the Japanese Diet].* Tokyo: Nihon Seikei Shimbun Shūppanbu.

Nishikubo, Koji. 2010. "Current Situation and Future Direction of Employee Benefits." *Japan Labor Review* 7 (1): 4–27.

Noble, Gregory W. 1998. *Collective Action in East Asia: How Ruling Parties Shape Industrial Policy.* Ithaca: Cornell University Press.

——. 2003. "Reform and Continuity in Japan's *Shingikai* Deliberation Councils." In *Japanese Governance: Beyond Japan Inc.,* edited by Jennifer Amyx and Peter Draslade, 113–133. London: Routledge.

——. 2005. "Globalization Meets Coordinated Capitalism in the Japanese and Korean Auto Industries." Paper presented at the annual meeting of the American Political Science Association, Washington, D.C., August 31–September 3.

——. 2006. "Koizumi's Complementary Coalition for (Mostly) Neo-liberal Reform in Japan." Paper presented at the conference of the System Restructuring in East Asia, Center for East Asian Studies, Stanford University, June 22–24.

——. 2011. "Changing Politics of Japanese Corporate Governance: Party Dynamics and the Myth of the Myth of Permanent Employment." Paper presented at the Joint Conference of the Association for Asian Studies and International Convention of Asia Scholars, Honolulu, March 31–April 3.

OECD [Organisation for Economic Co-operation and Development]. 1994. *The OECD Job Study: Evidence and Explanations.* Paris: OECD.

——. 1997. *OECD Employment Outlook.* Paris: OECD.

——. 1999a. *OECD Employment Outlook*. Paris: OECD.

——. 1999b. *Regulatory Reform in Japan*. Paris: OECD.

——. 2000. *Pushing Ahead with Reform in Korea*. Paris: OECD.

——. 2004. *OECD Employment Outlook*. Paris: OECD.

——. 2006a. *OECD Employment Outlook*. Paris: OECD.

——. 2006b. *OECD Factbook*. Paris: OECD.

——. 2007a. *OECD Employment Outlook*. Paris: OECD.

——. 2007b. *OECD Indicators*. Paris: OECD.

——. 2007c. *Jobs for Youth: Korea*. Paris: OECD.

——. 2008. *OECD Employment Outlook*. Paris: OECD.

Ohtake, Fumio. 2008. "Inequality in Japan." *Asian Economic Policy Review* 3 (1): 87–109.

Olson, Mancur. 1965. *The Logic of Collective Action: Public Goods and the Theory of Groups*. Cambridge, MA: Harvard University Press.

——. 1982. *The Rise and Decline of Nations: Economic Growth, Stagflation, and Social Rigidities*. New Haven: Yale University Press.

Osawa, Mari. 2002. "Twelve Million Full-Time Housewives: The Gender Consequences of Japan's Postwar Social Contract." In *Social Contracts under Stress: The Middle Classes of America, Europe, and Japan at the Turn of the Century*, edited by Oliver Zunz, Leonard Schoppa, and Nobuhiro Hiwatari, 255–280. New York: Russell Sage Foundation.

——. 2007. "Comparative Livelihood Security Systems from a Gender Perspective, with a Focus on Japan." In *Gendering the Knowledge Economy: Comparative Perspective*, edited by Sylvia Walby, Heidi Gottfried, Karin Gottschall, and Mari Osawa, 81–108. Palgrave Macmillan.

Palier, Bruno. 2005. "Ambiguous Agreement, Cumulative Change: French Social Policy in the 1990s." In *Beyond Continuity: Institutional Change in Advanced Political Economies*, edited by Wolfgang Streeck and Kathleen Thelen, 127–144. Oxford: Oxford University Press.

Palier, Bruno, and Kathleen Thelen. 2010. "Institutionalizing Dualism: Complementarities and Change in France and Germany." *Politics & Society* 38 (1): 119–148.

Park, Dong. 2001. "Hangukesŏ Sahoehyŏp'yak Jŏngchi ŭi Chulbal gwa Kŭ Bul'anjŏngsŏng Yoinbunsŏk" [The Emergence of the Social Pact and Its Instability in Korea]. *Hanguk Jŏngchi Hakhoebo [Korean Political Science Review]* 34 (4): 161–177.

Park, Gene. 2011. *Spending without Taxation: FILP and the Politics of Public Finance in Japan*. Stanford: Stanford University Press.

Park, Se-il. 2000. *Reforming Labor Management Relations: Lessons from the Korean Experience 1996–97*. Seoul: Korea Development Institute.

Park, Seung-jun, and Seung-gil Lee. 2004. *Chamyŏ Jŏngbu Nosa Gwangyebŏp Jedo ŭi Sŏn'jin'hwa Bangan e Daehan Mosaek [Searching for a New Industrial Relations System during the Roh Moo-hyun Government]*. Seoul: Korea Economic Research Institute.

Pempel, T. J. 1982. *Policy and Politics in Japan: Creative Conservatism*. Philadelphia: Temple University Press.

——. 1998. *Regime Shift: Comparative Dynamics of the Japanese Political Economy*. Ithaca: Cornell University Press.

——. 1999. "Structural Gaiatsu: International Finance and Political Change in Japan." *Comparative Political Studies* 32 (8): 907–937.

——. 2006. "A Decade of Political Torpor: When Political Logic Trumps Economic Rationality." In *Beyond Japan: The Dynamics of East Asian Regionalism*, edited by Peter. J. Katzenstein and Takashi Shiraishi, 37–62. Ithaca: Cornell University Press.

Pempel, T. J., and Keiichi Tsunekawa 1979. "Corporatism without Labor? The Japanese Anomaly." In *Trends toward Corporatist Intermediation*, edited by Philippe C. Schmitter and Gerhard Lehmbruch, 231–270. London: Sage Publications.

Pérez, Sofia A. 2000. "From Decentralization to Reorganization: Explaining the Return to National Bargaining in Italy and Spain." *Comparative Politics* 32 (4): 437–458.

Pérez-Díaz, Victor. 1987. "Neo-Corporatist Experiments in a New and Precariously Stable State." In *Political Stability and Neo-Corporatism*, edited by Ilja Scholten, 216–246. London: Sage Publications.

Pierson, Paul. 1996. "The New Politics of the Welfare State." *World Politics* 48 (2): 143–179.

———. 2001. "Post-Industrial Pressures on the Mature Welfare States." In *The New Politics of the Welfare State*, edited by Paul Pierson, 80–104. Oxford: Oxford University Press.

———. 2004. *Politics in Time: History, Institutions, and Social Analysis*. Princeton: Princeton University Press.

Polavieja, Javier G. 2003. "Temporary Contracts and Labour Market Segmentation in Spain: An Employment-Rent Approach." *European Sociological Review* 19 (5): 501–517.

Pontusson, Jonas, and Peter Swenson. 1996. "Labor Markets, Production Strategies, and Wage Bargaining Institutions: The Swedish Employer Offensive in Comparative Perspective." *Comparative Political Studies* 29 (2): 223–250.

Przeworski, Adam. 1991. *Democracy and the Market: Political and Economic Reforms in Eastern Europe and Latin America*. Cambridge: Cambridge University Press.

Przeworski, Adam, and Henry Teune. 1982. *The Logic of Comparative Social Inquiry*. Malabar, Fla.: Krieger.

Putnam, Robert D. 1988. "Diplomacy and Domestic Politics: The Logic of Two-Level Games." *International Organization* 42 (3): 427–460.

Radelet, Steven, and Jeffrey Sachs 1998. "The East Asian Financial Crisis: Diagnosis, Remedies, Prospects." *Brookings Papers on Economic Activity* 1: 1–74.

Ramseyer, J. Mark, and Frances McCall Rosenbluth. 1997. *Japan's Political Marketplace*. Cambridge, MA: Harvard University Press.

Rebick, Marcus. 2005. *The Japanese Employment System: Adapting to a New Economic Environment*. Oxford: Oxford University Press.

Reed, Steven R. 1993. *Making Common Sense of Japan*. Pittsburgh: University of Pittsburgh Press.

———, ed. 2003. *Japanese Electoral Politics: Creating a New Party System*. London: Routledge.

Rhodes, Martin, and Yves Mény. 1998. *The Future of European Welfare: A New Social Contract?* New York: St. Martin's Press.

Rhodes, Martin, and Oscar Molina. 2005. "Conflict, Complementarities & Institutional Change: Reforming Production & Protection Systems in Mixed Market Economies." Paper presented at the annual meeting of the American Political Science Association, Washington, D.C., August 31–September 3.

Roh, Joong-gi. 1999. "Nosajŏng Wiwŏnhoe" [Korean Tripartite Commission]. In *Hanguk ŭi Nosa Gwagye wa Nodong Jŏngchi 1 [Industrial Relations and Labor Politics in Korea 1]*, edited by Young-gi Choi, Jun Kim, Joong-gi Rho, and Bumsang You, 202–276. Seoul: Korea Labor Institute.

———. 2006. "Rho Moo-hyun Jŏngbu ŭi Nodong Jŏng'chaek" [Labor Policies During the Roh Moo-hyun Administration]. *Sanŏp Nodong Yŏngu [Studies on Industry and Labor]* 12 (2): 1–28.

Rueda, David. 2007. *Social Democracy Inside Out: Government Partisanship, Insiders, and Outsiders in Industrialized Democracies*. Oxford: Oxford University Press.

Rueda, David, and Jonas Pontusson. 2000. "Wage Inequality and Varieties of Capitalism." *World Politics* 52 (3): 350–383.

Sakamoto, Junichi. 2005. "Japan's Pension Reform." *SP Discussion Paper* no. 0541. World Bank.

Sako, Mari, and Hiroki Sato, eds. 1997. *Japanese Labor and Management in Transition: Diversity, Flexibility, and Participation.* London: Routledge.

Schaede, Ulrike. 2006. "The Strategic Logic of Japanese Keiretsu, Main Banks and Cross-Shareholdings, Revisited." Paper presented at the conference of the System Restructuring in East Asia, Center for East Asian Studies, Stanford University, June 22–24.

———. 2008. *Choose and Focus: Japanese Business Strategies for the 21st Century.* Ithaca: Cornell University Press.

Scheiner, Ethan. 2006. *Democracy without Competition in Japan: Opposition Failure in a One-Party Dominant State.* Cambridge: Cambridge University Press.

Schmitter, Philippe C., and Gerhard Lehmbruch, eds. 1979. *Trends toward Corporatist Intermediation.* London: Sage Publications.

Schoppa, Leonard J. 1997. *Bargaining with Japan: What American Pressure Can Do and Cannot Do.* New York: Columbia University Press.

———. 2006. *Race for the Exits: The Unraveling of Japan's System of Social Protection.* Ithaca: Cornell University Press.

Schwartz, Frank J. 1998. *Advice and Consent: The Politics of Consultation in Japan.* Cambridge: Cambridge University Press.

Shimada, Haruo. 1983. "Wage Determination and Information Sharing: An Alternative Approach to Incomes Policy?" *Journal of Industrial Relations* 25 (2): 177–200.

Shinkawa, Toshimitsu. 2003. "The Politics of Pension Retrenchment in Japan." *Japanese Journal of Social Security Policy* 2 (2): 25–33.

Shinoda, Toru. 2008. "The Return of Japanese Labor? The Mainstreaming of the Labor Question in Japanese Politics." *Labor History* 49 (2): 145–159.

Shinotsuka, Eiko. 1989. *Nihon no Koyōchōsei [The Pattern of Employment Adjustment in Japan].* Tokyo: Tōyō Keizai Shinpōsha.

Shire, Karen, and Danielle van Jaarsveld. 2008. "The Temporary Staffing Industry in Protected Employment Economies: Germany, Japan and the Netherlands." Paper presented at the annual conference of the Alfred P. Sloan Foundation Industry Studies program, May 1–2.

Shugart, Matthew Soberg, and Martin P. Wattenberg, eds. 2001. *Mixed-Member Electoral Systems: The Best of Both Worlds?* Oxford: Oxford University Press.

Siebert, Horst. 1997. "Labor Market Rigidities: At the Root of Unemployment in Europe." *Journal of Economic Perspectives* 11(3): 37–54.

Simmons, Beth A., Frank Dobbin, and Geoffrey Garret, eds. 2008. *The Global Diffusion of Markets and Democracy.* Cambridge: Cambridge University Press.

Simmons, Beth A., and Zachary Elkins. 2004. "The Globalization of Liberalization: Policy Diffusion in the International Political Economy." *American Political Science Review* 98 (1): 171–189.

Sommer, Martin. 2009. "Why Are Japanese Wages so Sluggish?" *IMF Working Paper* SP/09-97. Washington, D.C.: International Monetary Fund.

Song, Ho-Keun 1991. *Hanguk ŭi Nodong Jŏng'chi wa Sijang [Labor Politics and Market in Korea].* Seoul: Nanam.

———. 1993. "Kwonwiju'ŭi Hanguk ŭi Gukga wa Imkŭm Jŏngchak (II)" [The Authoritarian Government and the Wage Policy in Korea (II)]. *Hanguk Jŏng'chi Hakhoebo [Korean Political Science Review]* 27 (1): 65–97.

——. 2003. "The Birth of a Welfare State in Korea: The Unfinished Symphony of Democratization and Globalization." *Journal of East Asian Studies* 3 (3): 405–432.

Song, Ho-Keun, and Kyung-Zoon Hong. 2006. *Bokji Gukga ŭi Taedong [The Birth of Welfare State: Globalization, Democratization, and the New Politics of Welfare in South Korea].* Seoul: Nanam.

Song, Jiyeoun. 2010. "Japan's Labor Market Reform after the Collapse of the Bubble Economy: Political Determinants of Regulatory Changes." *Asian Survey* 50 (6): 1011–1031.

——. 2012a. "The Diverging Political Pathways of Labor Market Reform in Japan and Korea." *Journal of East Asian Studies* 12 (2): 161–192.

——. 2012b. "Economic Distress, Labor Market Reforms, and Dualism in Japan and Korea." *Governance: An International Journal of Policy, Administration, and Institutions* 25 (3): 415–438.

——. 2012c. "Enterprise Unions and the Segmentation of the Labor Market: Labor, Unions, and Corporate Restructuring in Korea." In *Adapt, Fragment, Transform: Corporate Restructuring and System Reform in South Korea,* edited by Byung-Kook Kim, Eun Mee Kim, and Jean C. Oi, 235–278. Washington, D.C.: Brookings Institution Press.

Song, Won-keun, and Sang-ho Lee 2005. *Chaebŏl ŭi Saŏp Gujo wa Gyŏngje'ryŏk Jipjung [The Business Structure of Chaebŏl].* Seoul: Nanam.

Soskice, David. 1990. "Wage Determination: The Changing Role of Institutions in Advanced Industrialized Countries." *Oxford Review of Economic Policy* 6 (4): 36–61.

——. 1999. "Divergent Production Regimes: Coordinated and Uncoordinated Market Economies in the 1980s and 1990s." In *Continuity and Change in Contemporary Capitalism,* edited by Herbert Kitschelt, Peter Lange, Gary Marks, and John D. Stephens, 101–134. Cambridge: Cambridge University Press.

Steiner, Viktor, and Katharina Wrohlich. 2005. "Work Incentives and Labor Supply Effects of the 'Mini-Jobs Reform' in Germany." *Empirica* 32 (1): 91–116.

Streeck, Wolfgang, and Anke Hassel. 2003. "The Crumbling Pillars of Social Partnership." *Western European Politics* 26 (4): 101–124.

Streeck, Wolfgang, and Kozo Yamamura, eds. 2001. *The Origins of Neoliberalism: Germany and Japan in Comparison.* Ithaca: Cornell University Press.

Suzuki, Akira. 2004. "The Rise and Fall of Interunion Wage Coordination and Tripartite Dialogue in Japan." In *The New Structure of Labor Relations: Tripartism and Decentralization,* edited by Wonduck Lee, Harry C. Katz, and Joohee Lee, 119–142. Ithaca: Cornell University Press.

Suzuki, Hiromasa. 2010. "Employment Relations in Japan: Recent Changes under Global Competition and Recession." *Journal of Industrial Relations* 52 (3): 387–401.

Swenson, Peter A. 2002. *Capitalists against Markets: The Making of Labor Markets and Welfare States in the United States and Sweden.* Oxford: Oxford University Press.

Tachibanaki, Toshiaki. 2005. *Confronting Income Inequality in Japan.* Cambridge, MA: MIT Press.

Tak, Hee-jun. 1974. "Hanguk Imkŭm Jŏngchak ŭi Sŏng'gyŏk" [The Characteristics of the Korean Wage Policy]. *Hanguk Gyŏngje [Korean Economics]* 2: 101–118.

Takanashi, Akira, ed. 1999. *Japanese Employment Practices, Japanese Economy & Labor Series.* Tokyo: Japan Institute of Labor.

——. 2005. *Nihon no Koyōsenryaku [Employment Strategies in the Japanese Labor Market].* Tokyo: Eideru Kenkyūjyo.

Thelen, Kathleen 1999. "Historical Institutionalism in Comparative Politics." *Annual Review of Political Science* 2: 369–404.

——. 2001. "Varieties of Labor Politics in the Developed Democracies." In *Varieties of Capitalism: The Institutional Foundations of Comparative Advantage,* edited by Peter A. Hall and David Soskice, 71–103. Oxford: Oxford University Press.

——. 2004. *How Institutions Evolve: The Political Economy of Skills in Germany, Britain, the United States, and Japan.* Cambridge: Cambridge University Press.

——. 2012. "Varieties of Capitalism: Trajectories of Liberalization and the New Politics of Social Solidarity." *Annual Review of Political Science* 15: 137–159.

Thelen, Kathleen, and Marius R. Busemeyer. 2008. "From Collectivism toward Segmentalism: Institutional Change in German Vocational Training." *MPIfG Discussion Paper* 08/13. Cologne: Max Planck Institute for the Study of Societies.

Thelen, Kathleen, and Ikuo Kume. 1999. "The Rise of Non-Market Training Regimes: Germany and Japan Compared." *Journal of Japanese Studies* 25 (1): 33–64.

——. 2001. "The Rise of Nonliberal Training Regimes: Germany and Japan Compared." In *The Origins of Nonliberal Capitalism,* edited by Wolfgang Streeck and Kozo Yamamura, 200–228. Ithaca: Cornell University Press.

——. 2003. "The Future of Nationally Embedded Capitalism: Industrial Relations in Germany and Japan." In *The End of Diversity? Prospects for German and Japanese Capitalism,* edited by Kozo Yamamura and Wolfgang Streeck, 183–211. Ithaca: Cornell University Press.

Tiberghien, Yves. 2007. *Entrepreneurial States: Reforming Corporate Governance in France, Japan, and Korea.* Ithaca: Cornell University Press.

——. 2011. "The Political Consequences of Inequality in Japan." *Shakai Kagaku Kenkyu [Social Science Research]* 62 (1): 77–99.

Tsujinaka, Yutaka. 1993. "Rengō and Its Osmotic Networks." In *Political Dynamics in Contemporary Japan,* edited by Gary D. Allison and Yasunori Sone, 200–213. Ithaca: Cornell University Press.

Tsuru, Kotaro. 2008. "Non-Regular Employment and Inequality among Workers: Institutional Reform toward Equitable Treatment." Research Institute of Economy, Trade and Industry (RIETI), http://www.rieti.go.jp/jp/papers/contribution/tsuru/13.html.

Urata, Shujiro. 2002. "Japanese Foreign Direct Investment in East Asia with Particular Focus on ASEAN 4." Paper presented at the conference on the Foreign Direct Investment: Opportunities and Challenges for Cambodia, Laos, and Vietnam, Hanoi, Vietnam, August 16–17.

Uriu, Robert M. 1996. *Troubled Industries: Confronting Economic Change in Japan.* Ithaca: Cornell University Press.

Visser, Jelle, and Anton Hemerijck. 1997. *A Dutch Miracle: Job Growth, Welfare Reform and Corporatism in the Netherlands.* Amsterdam: Amsterdam University Press.

Vogel, Steven K. 1996. *Freer Markets, More Rules: Regulatory Reform in Advanced Industrial Countries.* Ithaca: Cornell University Press.

——. 1999. "Can Japan Disengage? Winners and Losers in Japan's Political Economy, and the Ties that Bind Them." *Social Science Japan Journal* 2 (1): 3–21.

——. 2006. *Japan Remodeled: How Government and Industry Are Reforming Japanese Capitalism.* Ithaca: Cornell University Press.

Wade, Robert. 1990. *Governing the Market: Economic Theory and the Role of Government in East Asian Industrialization.* Princeton: Princeton University Press.

Weathers, Charles. 1999. "The 1999 Shunto and the Restructuring of Japan's Wage System." *Asian Survey* 39 (6): 960–985.

——, ed. 2000. *A Fifty Year History of Industry and Labor in Postwar Japan.* Tokyo: Japan Institute of Labor.

——. 2001. "Globalization and the Paradigm Shift in Japanese Industrial Relations." In *The Politics for Labor in a Global Age: Continuity and Change in Late-Industrializing and Post-Socialist Economies,* edited by Christopher Chandland and Rudra Sil, 156–180. Oxford: Oxford University Press.

——. 2003. "Decentralization of Japan's Wage Setting System in Comparative Perspective." *International Relations Journal* 34 (2): 119–134.

——. 2008. "Shuntō and the Shackles of Competitiveness." *Labor History* 49 (2): 177–197.

Weathers, Charles, and Scott North. 2009. "Overtime Activists Take on Corporate Titans: Toyota, McDonald's, and Japan's Work Hour Controversy." *Pacific Affairs* 82 (4): 615–636.

Williamson, John, and Stephan Haggard. 1994. "The Political Conditions for Economic Reform." In *The Political Economy of Policy Reform,* edited by John Williamson, 525–596. Washington, D.C.: Institute for International Economics.

Wong, Joseph. 2004. *Health Democracies: Welfare Politics in Taiwan and South Korea.* Ithaca: Cornell University Press.

Woo, Jung-en. 1991. *Race to the Swift: State and Finance in Korean Industrialization.* New York: Columbia University Press.

Woo-Cumings, Meredith, ed. 1999. *The Developmental State.* Ithaca: Cornell University Press.

Wood, Stewart. 2001. "Business, Government, and Patterns of Labor Market Policy in Britain and the Federal Republic of Germany." In *Varieties of Capitalism: The Institutional Foundations of Comparative Advantage,* edited by Peter A. Hall and David Soskice, 247–274. Oxford: Oxford University Press.

Woodall, Brian. 1996. *Japan under Construction: Corruption, Politics, and Public Works.* Berkeley: University of California Press.

World Bank. 1993. *The East Asian Miracle: Economic Growth and Public Policy.* Oxford: Oxford University.

Yamamura, Kozo, and Wolfgang Streeck, eds. 2003. *The End of Diversity? Prospects for German and Japanese Capitalism.* Ithaca: Cornell University Press.

Yamanaka, Keiko, and Nicola Piper. 2005. "Feminized Migration in East and Southeast Asia: Policies, Actions, and Empowerment." *United Nations Research Institute for Social Development Occasional Paper* no. 11.

Yang, Jae-jin. 2004. "Hanguk ŭi San'ŏphwa'sigi Sukryŏn gwa Bokji Jedo ŭi Giwon" [Skill Formation Systems and the Origin of the Korean Welfare System]. *Hanguk Jŏngchi Hakhoebo [Korean Political Science Review]* 38 (5): 85–103.

——. 2006. "Corporate Unionism and Labor Market Flexibility in South Korea." *Journal of East Asian Studies* 6 (2): 205–231.

Yang, Jae-jin, and Thomas R. Klassen eds. 2010. *Retirement, Work, and Pensions in Ageing Korea.* London: Routledge.

Yashiro, Naohiro. 2007. *Kenzen na Sijō Shakai eno Senryaku [A Strategy toward a Strong Market Economy].* Tokyo: Tōyō Keizai Shinpōsha.

You, Bum-sang. 1999. "Nosa Gwangye Gaehyŏk Wiwŏnhoe" [Presidential Commission on Industrial Relations Reform]. In *Hanguk ŭi Nosa Gwangye wa Nodong Jŏngchi 1 [Industrial Relations and Labor Politics in Korea 1],* edited by Young-gi Choi, Jun Kim, Joonggi Rho, and Bum-sang You, 113–201. Seoul: Korea Labor Institute.

——. 2000. "Nosajŏng Wiwŏnhoe wa Nodongbŏp ŭi Jaejŏng'bi" [The Korean Tripartite Commission and Labor Law Reforms]. In *Hanguk ŭi Nodongbŏp Gaejŏng gwa Nosa Gwangye [Labor Law Reforms in Korea],* edited by Young-gi Choi,

Gwang-seok Chun, Cheolsu Lee, and Bum-sang You, 351–431. Seoul: Korea Labor Institute.

———. 2005. *Hanguk ŭi Nodong Undong Inyŏm [An Ideology of the Korean Labor Movement]*. Seoul: Korea Labor Institute.

You, Jong-Il. 1998. "Income Distribution and Growth in East Asia." *Journal of Developmental Studies* 34 (6): 37–65.

Yun, Ji-whan. 2009. "Regulatory Contradictions: The Political Determinants of Labor Market Inequality in Korea and Japan." *Governance: An International Journal of Policy, Administration and Institutions* 22 (1): 1–25.

Zhou, Changhui, Andrew Delios, and Jing Yu Yang. 2002. "Location Determinants of Japanese Foreign Direct Investment in China." *Asia Pacific Journal of Management* 19 (1): 63–86.

Zunz, Oliver, Leonard J. Schoppa, and Nobuhiro Hiwatari. 2002. *Social Contracts under Stress: The Middle Classes of America, Europe, and Japan at the Turn of the Century*. New York: Russell Sage Foundation.

# Index

Note: Pages number followed by *f, t,* or *n* indicate figures, tables, and notes.

Aging workforce
  prospects for politics of future
    reforms, 170–73
  seniority-based wages and, 27–28, 39*f,*
    183n24
  *see also* Pension programs
Asian financial crisis, Korea and, 2, 13–14,
  31–34, 36, 43, 83, 119, 121–22, 184n27
  details of reforms after, 144–61, 196n42
Asset bubble, collapse of in Japan, 1, 13, 30, 34,
  52, 53, 83–84. *See also* Protracted
  recession, in Japan
Automotive industry, in Japan, 71, 91,
  92–93, 175

"Back-door" ("side-door") policy, foreign
  workers and, 16, 181n19
Banking sector, in Japan, 86
Basic Pension, in Japan, 113
Birth rate, in Japan, 115
Business community, positions on labor
  reform
  in Japan, 89–92
  in Korea, 122, 123–26, 124*f,* 125*f*

Centralized industrial relations, dualism and
  politics of labor reform and, 53–56, 54*t*
Chaebŏl, 14, 180n14
  dualism and SMEs, 77
  employment protection and, 28–29, 61,
    185n16
  origins of, 74, 187n18
  skills training and, 78–79
  transition to democracy and, 120–22
  *see also* Korea, liberalization except for
    chaebŏl workers
Christian democratic governments, politics of
  labor reform and, 48
Christian Democratic Party (CDU), in
  Germany, 167
Chuma, Hiroyuki, 182n15

Chun Doo-hwan regime, 76–77, 120, 134,
  187n25
Chūritsu Rōren (Federation of Independent
  Labor Unions), in Japan, 96
Comprehensive labor market reform
  centralized and decentralized industrial
    relations and, 53–56, 54*t*
  generally, 4–8, 5*t,* 10
  in Korea, generally, 13–15, 28–29, 33, 52, 65
  in United Kingdom, 167–69
  *see also* Korea, liberalization except for
    chaebŏl workers
Construction industry, in Japan, 73, 190n35
Coordinated market economies (CMEs)
  employment protection and, 21, 22*f,*
    23–24, 23*f*
  Japan as, 85–86, 89
  Korea as, 120
  politics of labor reform and, 50–52
  wage-bargaining and, 35
Council on Economic and Fiscal Policy, in
  Japan, 115, 192n65
Creative conservatism, in Japan, 49

Davis, Christina L., 189n19
Decentralized industrial relations, dualism and
  politics of labor reform and, 53–56, 54*t*
Deliberative councils, in Japan, 101–2,
  191n38
Democratic Justice Party (DJP), in Korea,
  130, 133–35
Democratic Labor Party, in Korea, 155, 157,
  194n15, 197n61
Democratic Liberal Party (DLP), in Korea,
  135–36, 138, 139, 195n35
Democratic Party of Japan (DPJ), 48, 104,
  116–17, 184n4
Denki Rengō (Japanese Electrical Electronic
  and Information Union), 93, 96–97,
  190n22
Denmark, 21, 22*f,* 24

Depressed Industry Subsidy Program, in Japan, 73
Deregulation
in Japan, 100–102, 106–7, 110
use of term, 179n3
Deregulation Subcommittee, in Japan, 100–102, 104, 106, 110
Discretionary Work Hours Rule, in Japan, 103–5
Dispatched workers. *See* Employment protection; Worker Dispatch Law
Dōmei (Japanese Confederation of Labor), 70, 95–96

Early-retirement program, in Japan, 94–95, 94*t*
Economic and Social Development Commission, in Korea, 159
Economic crises
politics of labor reform and, 52–53, 185nn9, 10, 11
shaping of patterns of reform and, 10
*see also* Asian financial crisis; Asset bubble; Global economic crisis; Oil crisis; Protracted recession
Economic Planning Board (EPB), in Korea, 74, 77
Elderly Employment Stabilization Law, in Japan, 111
Electoral system approach, shaping of patterns of reform and, 10
Electronics industry
in Japan, 93, 95, 175, 189n21
in Korea, 176
Emergency Decree for Economic Stability, in Korea, 187n21
Employees' Pension Fund, in Japan, 72
Employees' Pension Insurance, in Japan, 72, 113–14
Employment Insurance Program
in Japan, 43, 72–73, 112, 113–14, 117, 192nn60, 61
in Korea, 79, 152, 184n27
Employment protection
comparative perspective, 20–24, 22*f*, 23*f*
content and scope of reforms, 22*f*, 24–29, 25*t*, 27*t*
definitions and measurement methods, 181n2
inequality and dualism, 29–34, 30*f*, 32*f*, 33*f*
institutional origins of, 67–83, 76*f*, 186nn2, 3, 8, 9, 10
politics of labor reform and, 53–56, 54*t*
politics of labor reform and effects of, 57–63, 58*f*, 59*f*, 60*f*, 62*f*

shaping of patterns of reform and, 6–7, 10–11
Employment protection legislation (EPL), OECD Index of, 23–24, 23*f*, 57–59, 59*f*, 62, 181n2
Employment Stability Fund, in Japan, 73
Enterprise tenure years, employment protection and, 57–62, 60*f*, 62*f*, 185n14
Enterprise unions
in Japan, 68, 69–70
in Korea, 77
Estévez-Abe, Margarita, 184n8

Federation of Korean Industries (FKI), 123, 140–41, 149, 154, 195n31
Federation of Korean Trade Unions (FKTU), 75, 78, 126–28, 134, 140, 141, 143, 147–49, 153–57, 159–60, 187n23, 188n31, 194n13, 195n29, 196nn40, 42, 45, 48
"First year of welfare," in Japan, 72
Flexicurity, 24, 155, 156, 174–75
Foreign direct investment (FDI), 175–77
Foreign workers, 16–17, 181n19
Fukuda cabinet, in Japan, 116

Garret, Geoffrey, 177
Gender. *See* Women in workforce
Germany, 3, 165–69
Gerschenkron, Alexander, 186n6
Gini coefficients, 13, 180n8
Global economic crisis (2008), Japan and, 43, 109, 193n66
Globalization, as Kim Young-sam agenda, 139
Globalization and outsourcing, and prospects for politics of future reforms, 175–77
Gottfried, Heidi, 192n52
Grand National Party (GNP), in Korea, 146–49, 156, 159, 195n35
Greece, 10
Green Social Democratic Party, in Korea, 155

Haggard, Stephan, 180n8
*Haken no Hinkaku* (*Haken's Dignity*) television program, 1
Hanbo Steel, 143
Hangyŏre Democratic Party, in Korea, 133
Hanjin Heavy Industries, 176–77
Han Kwang-ok, 146
Hashimoto cabinet, 102, 104
Häusermann, Silja, 184n2
Health insurance programs. *See Social protection entries*
Heavy and Chemical Industrialization (HCI), in Korea, 75, 77–78, 79, 187n22

Hiraiwa Gaishi, 100
Hitachi, 71
Hiwatari, Nobuhiro, 190n35
Hosokawa cabinet, 100
Hyundai Group, 139
Hyundai Motor Company, 150–51, 196nn50, 51, 197n52

IMF-JC (Japan Council of the International Metalworkers Federation), 70
Industrial relations
    politics of labor reform and, 53–56, 54t, 63–64
    shaping of patterns of reform and, 7–8, 10–11
Industrial Relations Law, in Korea, 134, 135
Inequality and dualism
    dualism, use of term, 179nn1, 2
    employment protection and rise in, 2, 5, 5t, 13, 29–34, 30f, 32f, 33f
Insiders
    dualism and politics of labor reform and, 53–56, 54t
    employment protection and, 22f, 23–24, 23f, 26–29, 27t
    use of term, 179n2
    see also Japan, liberalization for outsiders, protection for insiders
"Institutional complementarities," 181n1
Institutional origins, of labor markets and social protections, 67–83
    in Japan, 68–73, 71f
    Japan and Korea compared, 80–82
    in Korea, 73–80, 76f
    recent challenges to institutions, 82–83
International Monetary Fund (IMF), Korea and, 145
Intra-firm labor market flexibility, in Japan, 68, 69, 70
Ishikawajima-Harima, 71
Italy, 10
Iversen, Torben, 49, 189n15

Japan
    economic growth in, 11–13, 12t
    employment protection, comparative perspective, 20–34, 22f, 23f
    employment protection, institutional origins, 68–70, 80–81, 186nn2, 3, 8, 9, 10
    foreign workers in, 16–17
    labor disputes in, 71–72, 71f
    labor market reforms and consequences, generally, 1–2, 8–9, 10, 13–16

organized labor in, 182n8
    politics of labor reform and, 48–53, 184nn4, 7, 185nn10, 11, 17, 186n18
    politics of labor reform and effects of employment protection, 57–63, 58f, 59f, 60f, 62f
    prospects for politics of future reforms, 170–77, 198n6
    social protection, comparative perspective, 39–44, 40t, 42t, 43t
    social protection, institutional origins, 72–73, 81–82, 88, 107–8
    wage-bargaining, comparative perspective, 34–39, 35f, 37f, 38t, 39f, 183nn22, 23
    wage coordination, institutional origins, 70–72, 71f, 81
Japan, liberalization for outsiders, protection for insiders, 84–118, 163–65
    business community's positions, 88–95, 189nn12, 14
    changes through political eras, 98–117, 99–100t
    institutional changes and continuities, 85–88, 86f, 189nn6, 8, 10, 11
    labor unions' positions, 88–89, 95–97, 190n26, 29, 30
Japan National Railway, 72
Japan Productivity Center, 186n5
Japan Socialist Party (JSP), 48, 100, 102, 106, 184n4. See also Social Democratic Party of Japan
Jidōsha Sōren (Confederation of Japan Automobile Workers' Unions), 96–97
Job security. See Employment protection
Johnson, Chalmers, 11

Kakuei, Tanaka, 72
Kang, David, 180n8
Kasza, Gregory J., 73
Kawasaki Steel Corporation, 93–94
Keidanren (Japanese Federation of Economic Organizations), 188n31, 189n14
Keiretsu, 14, 86, 180n14
Keizai Dōyūkai (Japanese Association of Economic Executives), 91, 189n17
Kim Dae-jung regime, 133–34, 145–53, 158, 185n9, 195nn37, 39, 196nn40, 42, 49
Kim Jong-pil, 133–34, 135, 195n37
Kim Kwang-il, 195n34
Kim Young-Sam regime, 133, 135, 139–44, 146, 195n26, 196n41
Kobe Steel, 93–94
Kohl, Helmut, 167

Kohli, Atul, 180n8
Koizumi cabinet, labor market reforms under, 107, 108–14
Korea
  economic growth in, 11–13, 12t
  employment protection, comparative perspective, 20–34, 22f, 23f
  employment protection, institutional origins, 73–77, 76f, 80–81
  foreign workers in, 16–17, 181n19
  labor market reforms and consequences, generally, 2, 8–9, 13–16, 180n12
  labor ministers in, 75–76, 76f
  organized labor in, 182n8
  politics of labor reform and, 48–53, 184nn4, 5, 185n9
  politics of labor reform and effects of employment protection, 57–63, 58f, 59f, 60f, 62f, 185n16
  prospects for politics of future reforms, 170–77
  skills formation system, institutional origins, 78–79
  social protection, comparative perspective, 39–44, 40t, 42t, 43t
  social protection, institutional origins, 79–81, 188n32, 33, 34, 35
  wage-bargaining, comparative perspective, 34–39, 35f, 37f, 38t, 39f, 183nn22, 23
  wage coordination, institutional origins, 77–78, 81, 188n28
Korea, liberalization except for chaeböl workers, 119–61, 163–65
  business community's positions, 122, 123–26, 124f, 125f
  changes through political eras, 129–60, 131–33t
  labor unions' positions, 122, 126–29
  political and economic challenges and, 120–22, 193nn3, 4
Korean Central Intelligence Agency (KCIA), 75, 139
Korean Chamber of Commerce and Industry, 154
Korean Confederation of Trade Unions (KCTU), 127–28, 140, 141, 143, 147–49, 153–57, 194nn13, 14, 195nn28, 29, 196nn42, 45, 46, 48
Korean Employers' Federation (KEF), 78, 123, 140–42, 154, 155, 160, 188n31, 195n31, 195n39
Korean Supreme Court, 136
Kume, Ikuo, 184n7
Kwon Gi-hong, 197n55

Labor Contract Law, in Japan, 111
Labor Contract Succession Law, in Japan, 109, 192n54
Labor market reforms
  approaches to, 9–11
  generally, 1–4
  implications for politics of, 169–70
  outside Korea and Japan, 3, 21, 22f, 24, 165–69, 198n1
  prospects for future, 170–77
  types of, 4–5, 5t
  see also Employment protection; Politics, of labor market reforms; Social protection entries; Wage-bargaining
Labor Standards Law
  in Japan, 101, 103–5, 108–10, 111, 115
  in Korea, 25, 28, 74, 134, 135, 156
Labor Union Law
  in Japan, 186n3
  in Korea, 134, 135
Lee Hong-gu, 195n34
Lee Joung-woo, 153–54, 197n57
Lee Myung-bak regime, 159–60
Legal theory approach, to study of employment protection, 21, 22
Liberal Democratic Party (LDP), in Japan, 84, 100, 102, 104, 106, 114–16
Liberal market economies (LMEs)
  employment protection and, 21, 22f, 23–24, 23f
  politics of labor reform and, 50–52
  wage-bargaining and, 35

Mini-Job Reform, in Germany, 3
Ministry of Economy, Trade and Industry (METI), in Japan, 191n37
Ministry of Health, Labor and Welfare (MOHLW), in Japan, 95, 109, 111
Ministry of Labor (MOL)
  in Japan, 101–6
  in Korea, 75, 77, 130, 136–38, 142, 148, 155–56, 159, 187n25, 195n33
Ministry of Trade and Industry (MTI), in Korea, 136–38
*MITI and the Japanese Miracle* (Johnson), 11
Mitsubishi Heavy Industries, 71
Mitsui Kinzoku, 93–94
Miura, Mari, 190n35
Miyauchi Yoshihiko, 91, 101–2
Moon, Chung-In, 180n8
Murayama Tomiichi, 100, 102
Mutual Aid Association Scheme, in Japan, 113

Nagase Jinen, 111
Nakamura Keisuke, 87
National Congress for New Politics (NCNP),
  in Korea, 143, 146, 148, 153, 197n54
National Congress of Trade Unions (NCTU),
  in Korea, 127
National Pension Program, in Korea, 152,
  157–58
National People's Pension, in Japan, 113
"Negative system," in Japan, 106–7
Neo-corporatist institutions, shaping of
  patterns of reform and, 9–10
Netherlands, 22f, 24, 153–54
New Democratic Republican Party (NDRP),
  in Korea, 133–35
New Kōmeitō, in Japan, 115–16
New Korea Party, 143, 195n35
Nihon Shōkō Kaigisho (Japanese Chamber of
  Commerce and Industry), 90–91
Nikkeiren (Japanese Federation of
  Employers' Association), 71, 87, 90, 91,
  102, 106, 188n31, 189n14
Nippon-Keidanren (Japanese Business
  Federation), 89–90, 189nn12, 14
Nippon Steel Corporation, 71, 93–94, 190n24
Nippon Telegraph and Telephone, 72
Nissan, 71, 93
NKK, 71, 93–94
Noble, Gregory W., 189n6
Non-Regular Worker Protection Law, in Korea,
  156, 159, 174–75, 197n62
Non-Regular workers. *See* Outsiders

Obuchi Keijo, 102, 103–8
OECD EPL Index. *See* Employment protection
  legislation (EPL), OECD Index of
Oil crisis, Japan and, 69–72, 75, 110, 112,
  116, 173, 182n15, 187n22, 192n60,
  197n53
Okuda Hiroshi, 92
Organized labor
  positions on labor reform in Japan, 88–89,
    95–97, 190nn26, 29, 30
  positions on labor reform in Korea,
    122, 126–29
  strength of, 182n8
  wage-bargaining and, 36–37, 38t
Outsiders
  dualism and politics of labor reform and,
    53–56, 54t
  employment protection and, 22f, 23–24, 23f,
    26–29, 27t
  use of term, 179n2
  *see also* Inequality and dualism

Park Chung Hee regime, 73–79, 120, 127, 134,
  180n8, 197n26
Park Se-il, 140, 195nn27, 34
Park Tae-jun, 195n37
Peace Democratic Party (PDP), in Korea,
  133, 134
Pempel, T. J., 89–90, 184n7
Pension programs
  in Japan, 72, 113–14
  in Korea, 79, 152, 157–58, 188n32
  *see also* Aging workforce
People's Party, in Korea, 133
Performance-based wages, in Japan, 88
"Pioneer Shock," 185n17
Politics, of labor market reforms, 46–66
  economic crisis and, 52–53, 185nn9, 10, 11
  employment protection, effects of, 57–63,
    58f, 59f, 60f, 62f
  employment protection and industrial
    relations, 53–56, 54t, 64–65
  political institutions and, 50–52, 184n7
  political partisanship and, 47–49,
    184nn2, 3
  shaping of patterns of reform and, 9, 10
  *see also* Japan; Korea
Power resource theory, study of employment
  protection and, 21, 22, 28
Presidential Commission on Industrial
  Relations Reform (PCIRR), in Korea,
  140–44
Proportional representation (PR) systems, 10,
  50–51, 155, 184–85n8, 194n16
Protracted recession, in Japan, 1, 36, 52, 53,
  83–84, 100–101, 110, 163, 182n15
Public works projects, in Japan, 73, 112

Quality Control (QC) circles, in Japan,
  186n5

Railway industry, in Japan, 87
Recession. *See* Protracted recession, in Japan
"Red Purge," in Japan, 186n3
Regular workers. *See* Insiders
Regulatory Reform Committee, in Japan, 110
Rengō (Japanese Trade Union
  Confederation), 87, 95–97, 102, 104, 106,
  108, 110, 190nn26, 30, 191n48
Research Committee on the Revision of the
  Labor Law (RCRLL), in Korea, 138,
  195n25
Retirement age, in Japan, 111
Retirement allowance program, in Korea, 80,
  188n35
Rhee In-je, 139

Roh Moo-hyun government, 153–59, 181n19, 198n65
Roh Tae-woo government, 79, 126, 130, 133–38, 139, 196n41
Rueda, David, 47, 48, 158, 184n3

Sakigake Party, 100, 102, 106
*Samje* (three systems) and *samkŭm* (three prohibitions), 77, 140–42, 195n33
Sanrōkon (Roundtable Conference on Industry and Labor), in Japan, 71
Scandinavian countries, social protection and, 39, 40*t*, 41. *See also* Denmark
Schaede, Ulrike, 189n6
Schoppa, Leonard J., 176
Segmentalist approach, to labor reform, 15, 179n1
Selective labor market reform
    centralized and decentralized industrial relations and, 53–56, 54*t*
    generally, 4–8, 5*t*
    in Germany, 165–69
    in Japan, generally. 64–65, 89, 111
    *see also* Japan, liberalization for outsiders, protection for insiders
Seniority-based wages, 37–38, 39*f*, 68, 83, 88, 91, 101, 103, 113, 121, 124, 172
Shiina Takeo, 91, 101
Shin Sanbetsu (National Federation of Industrial Organizations), 190n26
Shipbuilding industry, in Japan, 70, 71
Shirato, Yuki, 189n19
*Shukkō* (temporary work transfer to affiliate firms), in Japan, 69
*Shuntō* (spring offensive), 36, 70–71, 81, 82, 87, 92, 123
Single-member district (SMD) systems, 10, 155, 184–85n8, 194n16
Skills training systems
    in Japan, 68–69
    in Korea, 78–79
Small- and medium-sized enterprises (SMEs)
    dualism and chaebŏls, 77
    employment protection and, 26, 68–69
    Japan and, 90–91
    skills training and, 78
Social democratic governments, politics of labor reform and, 47–49
Social Democratic Party of Japan, 48, 184n4
Social protection
    comparative perspective, 39–44, 40*t*, 42*t*, 43*t*
    in Japan, 72–73, 81–82, 88, 107–8
    in Korea, 79–81, 188n32, 33, 34, 35

Sōhyō (General Council of Trade Unions of Japan), 70, 96, 102, 190n26
"Solidarist" approaches, to labor market reforms, 8, 55, 56, 63, 157, 168
Soskice, David, 49, 89
Spain, 10
Special Emergency Law for the Coal Mining Industry, in Japan, 73
Special Emergency Law for Workers in the Depressed Industrial Sector, in Japan, 73
Special Emergency Measure for Promoting Employment for Old-Aged Workers, in Japan, 73
State-led developmental models (*dirigiste* states), 11–16, 74, 180n8
Steel industry, in Japan, 70, 71, 87, 93–94, 190n24
Stephens, John D., 49
Suzuki, A., 187n14
Sweden, 3, 198n1
Switzerland, 21, 22*f*

Takanashi Akira, 105, 181n19
*Tenseki* (permanent work transfer), in Japan, 69
Tenure years. *See* Enterprise tenure years, employment protection and
"Time-off system," in Korea, 160
Toshiba, 71
Toyota, 71
Transportation industry, in Korea, 176
Tripartite Commission (Korea), 50, 146–49, 154–55, 159
Tsunekawa, Keiichi, 184n7

Unemployment Insurance Program, in Japan, 72–73, 187n16
Unified Democratic Party (UDP), in Korea, 133–35
United Kingdom
    Gini coefficients in, 180n10
    labor market reforms and consequences, 2–3, 4, 10, 165–69
    as liberal market economy, 21
United Liberal Democrats (ULD), in Korea, 143, 146, 148, 149
United States
    Gini coefficients in, 180n10
    Korea and, 145
    labor market reforms in, 4
    as liberal market economy, 21
    welfare capitalism in, 182n9
Uri Party, in Korea, 156

Varieties of capitalism (VOC) framework, in study of employment protection, 20–22, 51–52, 179n4

Vogel, Steven K., 89–90, 179n3

Wage-bargaining
  comparative perspective, 34–39, 35*f*, 37*f*, 38*t*, 39*f*, 183nn22, 23
  in Japan, 70–72, 71*f*, 81, 87–88
  in Korea, 77–78, 81, 188n28
"Wage peak system," in Japan, 113
Welfare capitalism, in United States, 182n9
"White-collar exemption," in Japan, 115
Women in workforce
  in Japan, 97

and prospects for politics of future reforms, 173–75
Worker Dispatch Law
  in Japan, 15, 27–28, 101, 105–10, 116–17, 174–75
  in Korea, 15, 147, 195n39
Workforce, changing composition of, 173–75

Y. H. Industry Company, 76
Young workers, and prospects for politics of future reforms, 173–75

*Zaibatsu*, 87
Zenrōkyō, 96
Zenrōren, 96